Cleaning and Stain Removal F...

C000113589

Cleaning Tips

It's not rocket science, but certain techniques enable you to clean faster and more efficiently:

- Start at the far side of the room when you do the floors so that you don't walk back into the clean or wet area.

- Use a handled tray to off-load a shelf's contents whilst you clean the shelf.

- Wash walls from top to bottom so that you can wipe away drips as you go.

- Resist the urge to rub quickly back and forth, which can rub dirt back in.

- Make your dust cloth into a small pad and keep turning it over so that you always present a clean section to the furniture.

before the wet cloth. Never add water to dry powders. This is especially true for things dropped onto the carpet.

- Keep it **calm.** There is more time than you think before a wet spill turns into a set stain.

- Keep it **white.** Blot up spills using white cloths only.

- Keep it **cool.** When you decide to try washing your wet stain away, always go to the cold tap unless you specifically know otherwise.

- Keep it **simple.** Modern biological detergents are great. So don't let what's bound to be a temporary stain ruin your fun.

Stain Kit Shopping Lists

Use these shopping lists to get yourself properly equipped:

From the chemist (drugstore):

- Acetone (nail polish remover contains it)
- Denture tablets
- Glycerine
- Hydrogen peroxide

From the DIY (hardware) store:

- Lubricant spray such as WD-40
- Methylated spirit (rubbing alcohol)
- White spirit (turpentine)

From the supermarket:

- Biological clothes detergent (detergent with enzymes)
- Fizzy bottled water (club soda)
- Household soap
- Spot stain remover
- Washing-up (dishwashing) liquid
- White vinegar

Opening Champagne without Spills

Keep the carpet clean and enjoy every drop of pricey champagnes and sparkling wines by opening them correctly. First, grab a tea towel. If you feel opening up wine under a cloth doesn't look cool, retire to the kitchen with your bottle.

Take off the foil seal, and with the bottle pointing away from you, unwrap the wire. Next, slide the towel over the cork and pop your left thumb on top of the towel and cork (these instructions are for right-handed people, so reverse the directions if you're a lefty). Hold the base of the bottle firmly in your right hand. You're all set to open. The secret is to turn the bottle – not the cork. You'll be rewarded with a soft whimper, not a pop, and with all the lovely champagne still in the bottle, ready to be poured and enjoyed.

For Dummies: Bestselling Book Series for Beginners

Cleaning and Stain Removal For Dummies®

Cheat Sheet

Cleaning Benefits

A clean home not only looks great, it also grants you additional benefits:

- Fewer home accidents: In the UK, almost three million home-accident injuries need hospital attention. Falls, the number one home accident, frequently happen as people trip over clutter or spills that weren't immediately cleared up.

- Fresher air: You eliminate unpleasant odours and promote easier breathing for anyone who has allergies or asthma.

- A greater profit when you go to sell your home: It's a fact that clean homes sell faster and for more money than dirty ones.

- Lower furnishing bills: With proper care, carpets, upholstery, and curtains may last up to twice as long as those that aren't tended to.

- Lower restaurant bills: If the kitchen's under control, you're more likely to enjoy cooking and eating at home.

- More spontaneity: Whether it's inviting friends back to your place or getting romantic exactly where the mood strikes, you can go with the moment if you're confident of a clean, welcoming environment.

- A daily dollop of smugness! Yes, anyone *can* keep a clean home, but you actually do it. So you can now consider yourself to be one step ahead of all those others who are too lazy, disorganised, or time-pressed to make the effort.

Six Steps for Treating Fresh Stains

If you can react right away to an accident, you increase the odds of being able to remove all traces of the potential stain. Follow these steps in dealing with any fresh stain:

1. **Limit the damage.**

   Blot up as much as you can with a plain white – not coloured – paper or cloth towel. Use a clean make-up brush to shift powders.

2. **Use a spoon and/or knife to lift off solids.**

3. **Stop and think! Identify the stain and its stain group – water-based, grease-based, and so on.**

   Read the care label, if there is one, so that you know what this fabric can happily withstand.

4. **Unlock the stain by turning it into a liquid.**

   Cold water, the simplest solvent, works in many situations. Look up the individual stain in the Appendix at the back of the book.

5. **Work from the inside out if you can.**

   It's far simpler to push the liquid back out the way it came, and doing so stops the stain from going right through the fabric on it's journey out. (Clearly you can't do this with fitted carpets).

6. **Be ready to repeat everything, perhaps several times.**

For Dummies: Bestselling Book Series for Beginners

Cleaning & Stain Removal

FOR DUMMIES®

by Gill Chilton

JOHN WILEY & SONS, LTD

Cleaning & Stain Removal For Dummies®

Published by
John Wiley & Sons, Ltd
The Atrium
Southern Gate
Chichester
West Sussex
PO19 8SQ
England

E-mail (for orders and customer service enquires): cs-books@wiley.co.uk

Visit our Home Page on www.wileyeurope.com

Wiley also publishes its books in a variety of electronic formats. Some content that appears in print may not be available in electronic books.

Library of Congress Control Number: 2004008490

British Library Cataloguing in Publication Data: A catalogue record for this book is available from the British Library

ISBN: 0-7645-7029-3

Printed and bound in Great Britain by TJ International Ltd, Padstow, Cornwall

10 9 8 7 6 5 4 3 2 1

WILEY

About the Author

Gill Chilton is a consumer journalist with 20 years experience in writing on practical subjects. She writes for, among others, *Family Circle, Woman,* and *Good Housekeeping* magazines, and answers questions on a regular consumer advice page for *Family Circle.* Cleaning is forever a hot topic: Readers may love or loathe it, but, as they tell Gill, they can't ignore it.

Gill is also the author of *Home Basics: The Complete Guide to Running Today's Home* published by *Reader's Digest* and she has appeared on radio and TV demonstating practical household tips.

Gill lives in a beautiful Cotswolds village where, despite her best endeavours, the three children and two cats with whom she so happily shares her home present a constant cleaning challenge.

Dedication

This book is dedicated to Holly, to Alice, and to Robin. I can't wait until you all get old enough to put its advice into regular practise. Also to my beloved parents and to Sue and Tim for your love and continual support through changing times.

Author's Acknowledgments

I'd like to thank my editors, Jason Dunne, Amie Tibble, and Kathleen Dobie for introducing me to the good-sense, clear-read concept that is Dummies. Your skill and enthusiasm made the months I spent writing this book a real pleasure. Thanks also to Sam Clapp at Wiley for beautifully smooth admin support.

A subject as wide-ranging as cleaning calls for a multitude of research. So I'd like to acknowledge the PR teams for Addis, Armitage Shanks, Bissell, Brabantia, Cif, Domestos, Dri-Pak, Electrolux, the Home Laundering Consultative Council, Jeyes, JVC, and WD-40. Thanks also to Dale Courtman, Institute of Plumbing; Bob Moore, Jessops School of Photography; and David Rogers at Autoglym.

Finally, to get back to the very start: Many thanks indeed to Aggie MacKenzie for recommending me for the project.

Publisher's Acknowledgments

We're proud of this book; please send us your comments through our Dummies online registration form located at www.dummies.com/register/.

Some of the people who helped bring this book to market include the following:

Acquisitions, Editorial, and Media Development

Executive Editor: Jason Dunne

Project Editors: Amie Jackowski Tibble, Daniel Mersey

Development Editor: Kathleen A. Dobie

Copy Editor: Martin Key

Technical Editor: George Hughes, TipKing.com

Editorial Assistant: Samantha Clapp

Cover Photos: © Peter Samuels/Getty Images

Cartoons: Rich Tennant, www.the5thwave.com

Production

Project Coordinator: Erin Smith

Layout and Graphics: Amanda Carter, Denny Hager, Stephanie D. Jumper, Michael Kruzil, Heather Ryan, Jacque Schneider, Julie Trippetti, Mary Gillot Virgin

Proofreaders: Andy Hollandbeck, Carl Pierce, Brian H. Walls

Indexer: TECHBOOKS Production Services

Publishing and Editorial for Consumer Dummies

    Diane Graves Steele, Vice President and Publisher, Consumer Dummies

    Joyce Pepple, Acquisitions Director, Consumer Dummies

    Kristin A Cocks, Product Development Director, Consumer Dummies

    Michael Spring, Vice President and Publisher, Travel

    Brice Gosnell, Associate Publisher, Travel

    Kelly Regan, Editorial Director, Travel

Publishing for Technology Dummies

    Andy Cummings, Vice President and Publisher, Dummies Technology/General User

Composition Services

    Gerry Fahey, Vice President of Production Services

    Debbie Stailey, Director of Composition Services

Contents at a Glance

Table of Contents

Introduction

o you see yourself in any of these scenarios?

- ✔ Your home circumstances have changed, and you need a fast, effective cleaning system that won't take up too much of your time.
- ✔ You're excited about moving into a new home until you discover that it's filthy.
- ✔ You want to stop the stress that comes with living in a chaotic home.
- ✔ You and your partner are arguing over dirty socks in the bathroom and grunge on the cooker, and you're seeking a way to help stop the rows and get you both onto the same cleaner and more organised level.
- ✔ You currently have a problem with a particular stain and are looking to find some way to shift it.

If you fit any of these situations, or if you're just looking for a reference book that tells you how to clean correctly, *Cleaning & Stain Removal For Dummies* is the book for you. Reading it won't turn you into an obsessive housekeeper, but it can help you smarten up your place at your own pace and maybe improve your love life, too.

I wrote this book because the best ways to clean today are different from what they were twenty – or even ten – years ago. It's not just that you have to know how to use new products and new equipment. The surfaces in your home and the fibres used to make your clothes have moved onwards. And the time you have to clean has shrunk.

I am a consumer journalist and have spent twenty years looking at practical ways to make everyday life run smoothly. My approach is results-based: A stain, after all, is either history or still visible – there's no margin for maybe. I believe that success comes from identifying the smartest, quickest way to tackle a task and in this book it is my pleasure to share my research and experience with you.

About This Book

Cleaning & Stain Removal For Dummies is a ready reference for people wanting to make their home life run smoothly. This book is designed to help you to maintain a clean home and to do so cheerfully and without undue effort. The sections on stain removal provide easy-to-follow solutions when accidents happen.

The tips and advice work for you if you have just moved into your first home and so are new to cleaning. Maybe changed domestic circumstances such as divorce or the risk of being fined by your landlord mean that finally, and perhaps even reluctantly, domesticity falls to you. Equally, if you have run a home for years, you can find fresh ways to tackle everyday tasks. Often, these ideas will save you time and perhaps money too.

You can read it from cover to cover and perhaps plan how you would like your clean home to shape up. Or you can skip to any point in the book as you look for the advice and tips you need right away. Oops! Just sent your coffee cup flying as you turned a page in this book? Turn to the Appendix pronto. In plain, clear English, *Cleaning & Stain Removal For Dummies* is arranged so you can get the information that you need as quickly as possible.

Conventions Used in This Book

I use *italics* for emphasis and to highlight words or terms that I define nearby.

Translations into US terms, measurements, and temperatures are in parenthesis the first time they occur in a chapter. Be aware that conversions from metric measurements are approximate. For example, 5 litres is actually 1.32086 US gallons, but I usually just leave it at a gallon. This isn't rocket-science and a bit more or less soap or water won't make a difference to your results. On the occasions where precision is important, rest assured I'm precise with the conversions.

Foolish Assumptions

In putting together this book, I made a few assumptions about you, the reader, and your cleaning needs. Here's what I assumed:

- ✔ You know a clean room when you see one.

- ✔ You like where you live, but you know you'd enjoy it a whole load more if keeping it clean were more easily achievable.

- ✔ You're ready to put a regular effort into caring for your home. You may be thinking, 'I'll give it a go for a couple of weeks.'

- ✔ You have personal experience of stains ruining a favourite garment or piece of furnishing. You're looking for a handy reference that will tell you what to do next time, so that a spill will not become a stain.

- ✔ You're familiar with elbow grease.

- ✔ You know there is much more to life than cleaning! So whilst you want to spend time and energy keeping special things sparkling, you also want to take shortcuts to lessen the grind of shifting everyday dirt.

How This Book Is Organised

This book is divided into six parts so that you can swiftly see the information you need at any moment. Each of these parts is broken down further into individual chapters with smaller sub-headings, allowing you to find your way directly to any sub-topic you may want to browse. For example, you don't have to wade through information about cleaning hardwood floors if your home is carpeted throughout. The following sections give a brief summary of what I cover in each part of the book.

Part 1: Getting Your Hands Dirty: Cleaning Basics

This part of the book introduces you to the many benefits of maintaining a clean home. I give you advice on choosing the right equipment and materials, plus tips that will save you a great deal of effort and often money as well.

Chapter 3 gives you a room-by-room guide to what needs to be done, and how often. Daily and weekly lists make keeping on top of your cleaning simple. You decide whether you want to spend ten minutes a day, two hours a fortnight, or significantly longer cleaning your home, then turn to this book to show you how to get maximum results from your time commitment.

Part II: Cleaning Your Home Top to Bottom

The chapters in this part look at ways to clean the contents of your home, including furniture and furnishings as well as the walls, floors, and ceilings.

I devote an entire chapter to each of the wet rooms – kitchen and bath – so that you can confidently keep these rooms thoroughly clean and germ-free.

Part III: Keeping Up Appearances Outside

Here the focus is on the walls, windows, and doors of your home that are exposed to the weather. You'll find how to carry out the different cleaning needs caused by exposure to rain, wind, and heat.

I offer a chapter on paths, patios, decking, and driveways as well as one on caring for your vehicles.

Part IV: Cleaning Special Items and in Special Situations

If you have ever looked at an object you own and been at a loss as to how to safely and effectively clean it, I aim to show you the answer here. I cover everything from sporting equipment to musical instruments and stereos. I also give you a

Chapter 1

Recognising the Value of Cleaning Well

*I*magine arriving at a sumptuous hotel. The facilities are impressive, the food staggering, and the bedroom the ultimate in plush. But ugh . . . you notice stains on the red velvet carpet, your wine glass has old lipstick on the rim, and there's grime on the gold taps. Would you recommend the place? Absolutely not! You don't want to stay a moment longer than you have to in a place that isn't clean.

By contrast, take the feel of freshly laundered sheets, the ease of putting together a meal from a hygienic, uncluttered kitchen, or the anticipation of ending a tough day with a long, hot bath in relaxing surroundings.

For quality of everyday life – those fresh sheets – you need to keep your home, furnishings, and possessions clean. Few experiences depress more than waking up to dirt. For health reasons, basic levels of cleanliness are a must. Germs – bacteria, viruses, mould – reproduce rapidly if they're not destroyed by timely cleaning.

Finally, a clean home becomes a welcoming haven. Sure, it takes effort and discipline to maintain. And new items you buy for your home may bring with them fresh cleaning challenges.

Accidents mean that you always need to treat stains, too. But like getting the bathroom how you like it, getting your home right gets easier and easier. Your home won't ever run itself, but it may feel like a close thing.

Reaping the Surprising Benefits of a Clean Home

Clean regularly and effectively and your place won't only look great, you also enjoy these additional benefits:

- **Fewer home accidents:** In the UK, almost three million home-accident injuries need hospital attention every year. Falls, the number one home accident, frequently happen as people trip over clutter or spills that weren't immediately cleared up.

- **Fresher air:** You eliminate unpleasant odours and promote easier breathing for anyone who has allergies or asthma.

- **A greater profit when you go to sell your home:** It's a fact that clean homes sell faster and for more money than dirty ones.

- **Lower furnishing bills:** With proper care, carpets, upholstery, and curtains may last up to twice as long as those that aren't tended to.

- **Lower restaurant bills:** If the kitchen's under control, you're more likely to enjoy cooking and eating at home.

- **More spontaneity:** Whether it's inviting friends back to your place or getting romantic exactly when the mood strikes, you can go with the moment if you're confident of a clean, welcoming environment.

And don't forget to experience a daily dollop of smugness! Sure, anyone *can* keep a clean home, but you actually *do* it. You can consider yourself one step ahead of all those others who are too lazy, disorganised, or time-pressed to make the effort.

In a nutshell, the three benefits that sum up the importance of keeping a clean home are

✔ A pleasant living environment

✔ A hygienic and germ-free living space

✔ The feel-good factor

Setting Your Cleaning Priorities

Cleaning, insomuch as it includes neatness and a way of presenting your home, is also a highly personal subject. What is general tidying-up in one home appears to be overkill to another family that prefers to keep its trinkets out on show. Decide on your priorities and clean to suit these. There is no right or wrong, excepting that clear work surfaces are quicker to clean.

Get to know, too, which items and surfaces in your home you absolutely must keep spotless. Myself, I like the sugar bowl lid to be speck-free and I remove lint from the tumble dryer after every session. But I haven't got a thing about cleaning the sink overflow like my sister, or using a cotton bud (cotton swab) to spot clean the tripmaster (trip odometer) button on the car, like a former housemate.

The point is: If it's important to you, then it deserves your time and attention. If it isn't important to you, then ease up a little. Life is too short and too much fun to wash and drip-dry a pleated lampshade when vacuuming the dust away is enough.

Finding the Time to Clean

A dirty kitchen is daunting. An entire house desperate for a clean is enough to make most of us reach not for the broom but for the front door! Little and often has to be the maxim of a good cleaning regimen. However busy your day, you can always find ten minutes somewhere without resorting to the depressing set-the-alarm-earlier suggestion.

Top of my time-finders are having a cereal bar as breakfast, recording TV programmes I think I want to watch (it's amazing how many I don't bother to watch after all), and arranging meet-ups with friends using e-mails rather than chatty phone calls.

Absolutely Not Just Women's Work!

It took computers to make using a typewriter keyboard a unisex skill. Cleaning in the home continues to be done largely by women, even when both partners work or have retired. Physically, mentally, emotionally, practically and, increasingly, financially there are no good reasons for this.

Focusing on the areas of cleaning that each of you enjoys or does best saves time, gets better results, and dramatically cuts domestic rows. You may want to consider a one month you, one month me approach to say, ironing and bed-making. Or you might make time the crucial factor: every other Sunday, do a two-hour blitz together. But the smartest way to improve your relationship is take on board the household jobs that you know your partner really hates. The foundation for lifelong marriage isn't putting the bins out (and cleaning the inside with dilute chlorine bleach). But it sure helps.

The point is that cleaning won't shout out at you in the same way an empty stomach lets you know it's time to cook. There are exceptions – having no shirts for work propels most of us towards that pile of dirty laundry. But mostly things have to be bad indeed for smells, stains, or a state of chaos to stop you in your tracks. For the most part, you may have to use self-discipline to keep on task.

But there are bonuses. Unlike other chores – mowing the lawn, for instance – cleaning breaks effortlessly into small time-chunks. Putting the lawnmower away after only two strips is annoying and leaves the grass looking unsightly. However, in just five minutes spent cleaning, you can blitz the bathroom and celebrate a job well done.

So is ten minutes a day enough? The answer is yes, if . . .

- ✔ You do a single longer session once a week.
- ✔ You're maintaining a clean home rather than bringing a dirty one up to standard.
- ✔ You make light demands on your home, perhaps using it mostly at weekends and evenings.

The sad news is that if you have children, pets, or work from home, ten minutes is not enough. You need to find five or ten more minutes each day for cleaning. But there's good news even here because if you have a family, it means that there are more people about to share the load.

Finding ways to cut your workload

The furniture, floor surfaces, and how you store your personal possessions have a huge impact on how frequently you need to clean. Choose wisely and you can significantly cut your work.

- ✔ Go for easy-care washable furnishings and floors.

- ✔ Avoid dust-traps by choosing furniture without grooves, and cupboards and glass display units over open shelving.

- ✔ Take good care of your things. It's only after it gets scratched that a wood table or linoleum floor becomes a dirt magnet.

- ✔ Whenever you buy something new, ask the shop assistant how to keep it clean and how to treat stains. If the assistant merely smiles and shrugs, walk away.

Let me give an example of how just one buying choice can save you a working day a year. A painted louvred door can take 20 minutes to clean thoroughly because you need to run a gloved finger along each slat. If the door's in a high dust area, such as a kitchen, you need to clean it every two weeks. In contrast, a plain door takes a minute to wipe clean. With no crevices for dust, you can simply wash down every other month. Multiplying out the time, the cruel fact is that just one louvred door takes an amazing 8 hours and 34 minutes a year longer to keep clean. Multiply this throughout your home to understand how radically the things you buy affect your cleaning.

You can also cut your workload if you:

- ✔ Get others involved in the cleaning. Even children can be motivated to help out, possibly with the promise of pocket money. Even a three-year-old can clear a floor of toys to get it ready for sweeping.

- ✔ Pay for help. Either have someone come regularly or get a cleaner in for a catch-up cleaning session.

✔ Avoid situations that create mess. Parties, pets, and visiting children are obvious ones. (See Chapter 16 for tips on dealing with kids and pets and Chapter 17 for advice on hosting.)

✔ Make more use of the garden. Eat and entertain outside in summertime.

✔ Choose cleaning products that you don't need to rinse. You can cut the time you spend on cleaning sinks, walls, and floors in half!

✔ Buy the best-quality cleaning materials and equipment. A good-quality dustpan and brush means you get all the dust in with one or two strokes instead of chasing dirt around the floor trying to get it up.

✔ Clean when you feel refreshed and energetic. If you're tired before you start out, you're bound to be slower and less effective.

✔ Throw away unnecessary clutter and store possessions in drawers or closed containers.

Offering shortcuts for busy people

It's not just time, it's remembering that you should be doing something domestic that can be the problem. So try these memory joggers.

✔ Buy sufficient bed linen so that you can change sheets on a set day each week, even if you don't have time to wash them until later.

✔ Get your cleaning supplies from a supermarket that offers online groceries. After you place your first order, the items appear as 'favourites' next time, so you can simply log on to top up stocks.

✔ Keep a timer by the washing-machine. Set it for the length of the wash programme and take it with you as you go about doing other chores. When the timer rings you know you've washing to unload.

✔ Use a fabric pen to mark initials on the inside of children's clothing. This saves time on sorting washed clothes.

✔ Get out all the cleaning products and equipment that you need at the start (assuming no children or pets are about).

You save on trips up and down stairs, and it's hard to forget to do the windows today if the squeegee's right in front of you!

✔ Start a cleaning file, either on cards or on the computer. Include special-care instructions and manufacturer helpline phone numbers and Web sites.

✔ Cheat a little and stretch all the filter-change dates for vacuum cleaners, water softeners, and so on to the same date. This way, you're far more likely to remember to take the necessary action.

Treating Stains and Repairing Damage

Ongoing cleaning is good, but it's only by being on the ball when accidents happen that you get to live in a home that isn't marred by stains and marks. It doesn't matter how debris-free a just-vacuumed carpet is. You won't notice how attractively your vacuum swept the pile if all you can see is a blue spot where a pen got crushed underfoot and leaked ink all over the beige carpet.

The possibility of stains gets a lot of people uptight, which is a real shame. Where's the fun in life if you're too wary of spills to offer guests beetroot (beets) or chocolate fondue, or you limit your small child to just two friends on his birthday, because having a whole young crowd over is sure to be the death of the carpet.

The thing to bear in mind about spills is that most of them do not become stains. And many of those that do don't have to stay stains forever. Take that ink, for example. With the right solvent, it's history.

In the chapters on stain removal I show how getting to a problem quickly and then behaving gently and with extreme persistence pays off. Likewise, whilst a scratch on a new piece of furniture is never cause for pleasure, it absolutely doesn't warrant trimming the cat's claws. In the chapter on scratches, rips, and scuffs I show how the same techniques of gentle persistence win through.

Chapter 2

Equipping Yourself

. . . .

In This Chapter

▶ Getting the right tools

▶ Selecting the most effective cleaning products

▶ Recognising the importance of storage

. . . .

*I*magine trying to cut grass without a lawnmower or putting up wallpaper without a paste brush. How about trying to bake a cake without any flour or changing a plug without a screwdriver? The mere idea is ridiculous! You have to have the right tools and the right components if you want to do any job properly – including cleaning. You can't clean your wood floor without a mop and a cleaning solution that works on wood surfaces. You can do more harm than good if you don't use the right cleaner and the right type of cloth to polish your silver.

In this chapter, I tell you about the brushes, mops, and sponges, the polishes, solutions, and soaps you need to clean your home and possessions safely and effectively.

Brushing Up on Brushes, Brooms, and Mops

Whilst cleaning products (which I cover in the next section) dissolve grime and grease, it's the equipment that takes the dirt away – sponges and mops actually produce clean surfaces. They also help you get the job done effectively and efficiently, so it's worth a bit of your time and energy to make sure you have the proper tools.

Getting good-quality equipment saves you money. Better-quality sponges, carpet washers, and so on need less cleaning solution and do the job better and faster than cheaper, but inferior equipment.

Table 2-1 shows all the basic tools you need to clean your house and remove stains. (Well, maybe not every tool. I talk about vacuum cleaners and carpet cleaners in Chapter 5 and address outdoor equipment in Chapter 11.) The table also gives you recommendations for what to buy and how to care for your cleaning aids. Figure 2-1 shows you what all these tools (most of them anyway) look like.

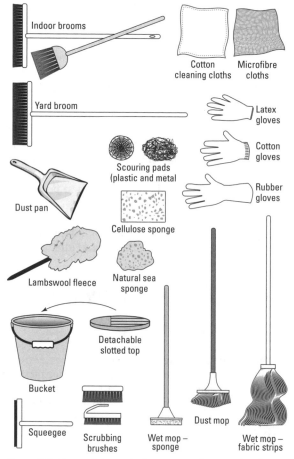

Figure 2-1: Some of the tools that you need to get cleaning.

Table 2-1	Cleaning Equipment		
Tool	*Materials*	*Uses*	*Buying Tips*	*Care and Storage*
Brooms				
Indoor broom	Bristle, nylon	Sweeping bare floors; removing cobwebs in ceiling corners		Wash often in warm soapy water – be sure to jig the broom head up and down so that the water loosens all the dirt. Shake off excess water and air-dry. To stop bristles bending under the weight of the handle, store upside down or hang.
Outdoor broom	Bristle, straw	Strong sweeping power for floors that won't scratch such as concrete.		When bristles start to lose stiffness, rinse in salty water and air-dry.
Dustpan	Metal, plastic, rubber	Conveying sweepings from the floor to the rubbish bin.	Check base carefully for any edges that could scratch a hard floor. Avoid metal for wet areas as the dustpan may rust.	Replace the dustpan at the first sign of wear.

(continued)

Table 2-1 (continued)

Tool	Materials	Uses	Buying Tips	Care and Storage
Cleaning cloths				
Cloth dusters	Lint-free cotton	Use with or without polishes or cleaners to clean all types of surfaces and materials.	Buy any colourfast colour. Dusters don't have to be yellow! Have at least six quality, lint-free fabric dusters so that you can start each time with one that's completely clean.	Machine-wash with no fabric conditioner; tumble dry.
Specialist cloths	Made of microfibres that lock in dirt and moisture to give instant shine without chemicals.	You can get specialist cloths for specialist jobs, such as polishing metal.		Machine-wash, air-dry
Lambs-wool	Fleece	Forget feather dusters! A lambs-wool duster grips dust rather than flicking it elsewhere.	A longer handle enables you to dust higher.	Wash in warm soapy water. Air-dry thoroughly.

Tool	Materials	Uses	Buying Tips	Care and Storage
Gloves	Cotton, latex, rubber	Protect your hands from chemicals and the general wear and tear that comes with cleaning. In addition, you won't leave finger marks as you work and can withstand hotter water, so you can do chores such as washing the dishes more effectively and hygienically.	Choose rubber gloves for all tasks that involve water and strong chemicals. Buy a size larger than you need so that they go on more easily and you can wear thin cotton gloves underneath, or dust some talcum powder on your hands before putting on the gloves to help with sweaty hands. Machine-washable cotton gloves are suited to dry, dusty jobs or for extra protection when you're cleaning items with sharp edges or possibly splinters. Disposable latex gloves can make a revolting clean-up, such as a pet accident, less grim.	Launder cotton gloves, rinse and air-dry rubber gloves, and toss out latex gloves.

(continued)

Table 2-1 (continued)

Tool	Materials	Uses	Buying Tips	Care and Storage
Mops				
Dust mop	Fringed cloth that may be treated with a permanent wax	Dusting floors, car interiors, vinyl blinds.		Wash in the machine only when absolutely essential. Use mild soap and no fabric conditioner. Rinse and air-dry. Store in its original sealed plastic container.
Wet mop	Fabric strips, sponge	Cleaning floors with water-based solutions.	Sponge mops give faster coverage and can sweep if used dry. Fabric-strip mop heads let you spot rub dirty marks out.	Wash mop head thoroughly to get rid of smelly germs and encase sponge mop in an airtight plastic bag to stop it drying. Wash cloth mop head in the washing-machine with mild soap and no fabric conditioner. Peg it out with the washing on a fine day. Store on a hook or in the cleaning cupboard.

Tool	Materials	Uses	Buying Tips	Care and Storage
Bucket	Metal, plastic	Holds cleaning solutions and rinsing water.	Plastic is lighter to carry and less likely to scratch floors than metal. Go for cheap pails with sturdy, comfortable handles. The bucket needs to be wider than your mop, but there's no big advantage to square, supposedly mop-friendly buckets. Have at least two to mop floors faster, as you can fill one with sudsy water and one with rinse water. If you use a fabric mop, buy a slotted top, so that you can wring out the mop.	Rinse thoroughly and air-dry.
Scouring pads	Metal, plastic	Great at getting off hard-to-shift dirt, especially burnt-on food on pots and pans. However, metal and some plastics may scratch softer surfaces.	Generally, you're safe with materials that are tougher than the scouring pad.	Rinse out thoroughly then squeeze excess moisture and air-dry. If left in water, metal scourers may rust.

(continued)

Table 2-1 *(continued)*

Tool	Materials	Uses	Buying Tips	Care and Storage
Sponges	Cellulose; natural sea sponge	An everyday option for mopping kitchen spills, washing dishes, and wet cleaning through the house.	Make use of the fact that cellulose sponges are cheap by having plenty and changing them frequently. When a natural sea sponge is no longer smart enough for bath time, let it join your cleaning equipment.	Germ spreading is a huge issue with sponges – they provide the perfect damp breeding ground. Avoid cross-contamination by keeping sponges for set jobs, the bathroom basin, for example. Rinse out thoroughly to prevent odour build-up and clean your sponges each day. The quickest way is to drop them into the dishwasher. In the sink, disinfect in diluted bleach solution or squirt with antibacterial washing-up liquid and let the sponge sit in this. Never simply rinse a sponge that smells: It needs a disinfectant cleaning, or it is time to get a fresh one.

Tool	Materials	Uses	Buying Tips	Care and Storage
Squeegee	Sponge and rubber	Gets into window corners in ways cleaning cloths can't.	Buy two sizes to suit your window sizes.	Wash briefly in soapy water, air-dry.
Scrubbing brushes	Bristle, nylon, plastic	Loosen dirt on floors, clothes, and fabric laundry, so that it can then be washed or dusted away.	Bristles can be short but they must be stiff and thick-set. You need a range of sizes. A basic assortment is a large plastic-bristled brush reserved for floors only, a long-handled toilet brush, and a regular scrubbing brush for the laundry. Useful extras include old toothbrushes, perfect for smartening tile grouting, and a natural-bristle brush for shoes and clothes.	Soak bristles in soapy water to loosen dirt. Don't soak wood brush handles lest they expand or split.

When purchasing mops, brooms, and other long-handled tools make sure that the handle height is comfortable. If you're short, choose a wooden handle that you can saw to fit. Whatever your stature, an extension pole that you can attach to dusters or brushes can come in handy both inside and outside the house. In general, make sure that handles handle well. You'll brush up faster with a dustpan that has a comfortable grip.

As the materials column in Table 2-1 shows, brush and broom bristles can be made from any number of materials. Match the bristle material to the job at hand. Soft, long nylon bristles don't scratch hard floors, but in a scrubbing brush, you want short, stiff, thick-set bristles that hold up under heavy elbow grease.

You can wash many cleaning materials in your washing-machine, but don't use fabric conditioner. Conditioner coats a material's fibres, thereby reducing the dust-attracting ability of dust cloths and mop heads and making them less absorbent. Being able to wash cleaning cloths helps ensure that you can start each cleaning session with a completely clean dust cloth. When you find your cleaning cloths are losing their fluffiness, just add a cup full of white vinegar to the final rinse. The vinegar cuts through any remaining grease and leaves them extra fluffy.

Steel-wool pads that are impregnated with soap have extra strength to get at dirty ovens and non-stick pans. Once opened, wrap the pads in aluminium foil, so they don't rust.

Polishing Up with Pastes, Sprays, and Cleaning Solutions

Elbow grease used always to be the good cleaner's best tool. But today – hooray – you can bid farewell to muscle power and say hello to cleaner living through chemistry if you choose to. You can employ a host of branded products that make fast, lightweight work of dissolving grime. You don't of course need to buy all of them.

Table 2-2 contains all that most homes need.

Table 2-2 **Cleaning Solutions**

Type of Cleanser	Uses	Cautions
Abrasive cream cleaner	Contains tiny granules to add friction to the cleaning power. Use to get stubborn marks off smooth, hard surfaces.	Can scratch worn enamel or worsen already scratched acrylic. Check that it's safe for enamel before using on the bath.
Furniture polish	Ignore silicone-based sprays designed to coat the surface and go for liquid and creams that penetrate into wood.	Can visibly darken wood. Be sure you are okay with this before you begin.
Liquid bleach	Use it neat to clean toilet bowls and indoor and outdoor drains. Dilute (50 millilitres [4 tablespoons] to 5 litres [1 gallon] of water) for floors and worktops.	Eye and skin irritant. Never mix with other cleaning products as this could release dangerous toxic fumes.
Liquid multi-surface cleaner	Use on worktops, sinks, basins, and hard surfaces around the home.	May contain dilute bleach and, if so, shares its cautions.

(continued)

Table 2-2 (continued)

Type of Cleanser	Uses	Cautions
Metal polish	Buy specialist products to suit the brass, copper, and silverware in your home. Chrome doesn't need a metal polish: a microfibre cloth is sufficient.	Always work in a ventilated room. Avoid breathing closely over metal polish.
Spot stain remover	Fast action for accidents on fabric and carpets	May not be colourfast. Do a small test patch first.
Toilet cleaner	Down the pan and under the rims of the bowl	Never mix with bleach and always flush several times before using another toilet cleaner.
Washing-up (dishwashing) liquid	Any cleaning that calls for mild, sudsy water including floors, cloths, toys, ornaments (decorations), and much more. However, all will need thorough rinsing.	Dishwasher tablets and powder are skin and eye irritants. Never directly hold dishwasher tablets. Some washing-up liquids contain bleach. Bear this in mind when using as a cleaning tool on delicate surfaces. Bleach-free varieties are available, so have a good look at the label.

Manufacturers sell cleaning products by linking them to specific chores or surfaces and making you think you need ten separate products just to clean the surfaces in your kitchen. For example, say you pick up a chrome cleaner you saw advertised. Reading the label, you notice that the chrome cleaner also cleans stainless steel and plastic. Then you check the label of the multi-surface cleaner you already have and find that it too would clean your chrome! Sometimes specialist cleaners save you time and elbow grease; I'm here to say that generally one cleaner works on many surfaces.

Compare unit prices before you buy. You may find that a cheaper cleaner does just as well as one three times the price.

If you want to get your cleaning done quickly and efficiently and want to cut the physical grind of scrubbing and scouring, go straight to the cleaning aisle at the supermarket. Pick up as many specialist cleaners as comfortably sit within your budget and you will gain vital time-savers by using products that don't need to be rinsed, or act in seconds rather than minutes, or are pleasantly scented. However – always go small. Once opened, a cleaner will lose its strength and needs to be replaced within a year.

Mixing up a multi-purpose cleaner

For less than five pence for the entire bottle, you can make an efficient cleaner for all the hard surfaces in your home that can safely withstand bleach without risk of damage or colour fade. Zap it over sinks and baths (unless they're enamel), kitchen worktops, ceramic and plastic tiles, and plastic rubbish bins.

Never, ever use this solution with an ammonia-based cleaner. The mixture of bleach and ammonia produces toxic fumes that may send you to hospital or even prove fatal. Follow these steps to make your concoction:

1. **Buy a large heavy-duty plastic spray bottle.**

   You can find appropriate spray bottles in any DIY store – look in the gardening section – or try a gardening store.

2. Fill it with

- 500 millilitres (ml) (1 pint) of warm water

- A generous squirt of washing-up liquid *or* a tea-spoon of bleach-free washing-powder

  (The item below is definitely an AND. There would be very little cleaning power without any bleach.)

- 30ml (2 tablespoons) of liquid bleach – economy bleach made up from sodium hypochlorite is fine.

3. Use the spray pipe on the lid to give the mixture a stir.

You can spray this generously onto your chosen hard surface. Follow up by rinsing the surface using a dampened cloth or sponge. Most surfaces can air-dry, but you need to rub metal with a cloth if you want to get a good shine.

Germs breed fastest in wet environments. So if there is a risk that the surface won't dry in a reasonable time, wipe it with a clean cloth or a paper towel.

Once bleach is diluted it quickly breaks down (mostly to salt and water), so you need to use up this solution in a day. Because it is so low-cost, that's no problem. When you finish cleaning, take any leftover solution and go give an outside drain a treat!

Bleach can damage fabrics and porous surfaces. Always check that a surface is bleach-safe by testing it out on an inconspicuous spot. Use a cotton bud (cotton swab) to wet the smallest area, then leave it to air-dry. You can tell that a surface is not bleach-safe if you can see a colour fade or the surface looks pitted or feels rough to the touch.

Some surfaces you can't use bleach on include:

- **Enamel:** When bleach sits on enamel that's already showing wear, it can take off the shine.

- **Fabric treated with special finishes:** It can cause fading and take shine off the finish.

- **Leather:** It can cause fading.

- **Marble:** It can pit the surface.

> ✔ **Metal:** Don't spray chrome or gold-plate taps. Sloshing past the metal drain plug is okay, just don't let the solution pool on the drain – wipe the plug dry.
>
> ✔ **Silk:** It can rot fibres.
>
> ✔ **Wool:** It can rot fibres.

If in doubt, use a mild cleaner, such as diluted washing-up liquid, instead. You can still fill this into the spray bottle, for quick easy cleaning.

Going green with alternative cleaners

Commercial cleaning products often get the thumbs down in cleaning books. Somehow, using a lemon to shift scum from a metal tap is seen to be that bit more wonderful than reaching for a can of bathroom mousse. The trade-off, however, is time and effort versus a clean, green feeling.

I'd like to throw in some praise for most things chemical. Using quality branded cleaning products saves you significant time and effort, principally because you don't need to rub commercial cleaners in, and if you do have to rinse them, you can do that quickly without waiting 30 minutes and then repeating. If you choose to go the natural route, prepare to squeeze citrus fruits and make up pastes and solutions.

Just because a product is natural doesn't mean it's gentle. You can damage surfaces with green cleaners. The humble lemon can fade fabric and leave streaks on untreated wood.

Health concerns may dictate that you avoid the strong chemicals in commercial cleaners. Asthmatics in particular have good reason to avoid irritants that may make them struggle for breath.

Environmentalists are concerned about the effect that all the toxins in commercial cleaning products may have on our planet. Scientists continually discover that more and more chemicals pose potential cancer threats. The latest ban is on fifty products used indoors to kill flies and moths. What you cheerfully spread onto your kitchen worktops today may be on the health hazard list tomorrow. If you want to avoid those dangers, you may want to test out the natural cleaning solutions in Table 2-3.

Table 2-3		Natural Cleansers	
Ingredient	*Properties*	*Uses*	*Tips and Cautions*
Bicarbonate of soda	Deodorises; absorbent; gently abrasive	Clean and deodorise the fridge (leave a small pot to neutralise food odours); remove stains from hard surfaces, such as crayon and ink from painted walls; mix with water to form a paste to polish silver or clean the grout between kitchen and bathroom tiles.	By weight it's pricier than top-brand scouring powder, so don't use more than you need.
Lemon	High acidity makes it an excellent grease cutter and stain remover. Good bleaching ability	Remove soap scum and limescale from taps, rust marks and fruit-based stains from white fabric, tarnish from brass and copper; disinfect hard surfaces that can safely withstand bleach, such as untreated wood chopping boards	Bleaches out coloured fabrics.
Salt	Abrasive and absorbent. Cheapest scouring powder you can buy!	Shift stubborn stains from worktops; provide extra power on hard surfaces such as food baked onto a casserole dish; unblock drains	Can rust metal; creates a permanent damp patch, so never sprinkle it on a wine spill on a carpet

Ingredient	Properties	Uses	Tips and Cautions
Vinegar	Cuts grease; dissolves scum	Shine windows and glassware; cut scum in showerheads, dishwashers, coffeemakers; remove mildew from plastic shower curtains; clean vinyl floors; replace fabric conditioner	Boiling strengthens the stain-removing properties, but splashes of cold, concentrated vinegar can acid-burn your hands, so take care; Use distilled *white* vinegar. The brown variety is cheaper and just as good a cleaner but the smell lingers and lingers.

To get more juice from a lemon, cut it in half then pop into the microwave for 15 seconds. You can use this tip whether you're cooking or cleaning with this little yellow fruit.

The magic of microfibres

The maker of E-Cloths claims you can cut at least 80 per cent of the amount of chemicals used to clean your home by using his microfibre cloths and mop. Wipe over any hard surface and the millions of tiny synthetic fibres contained in each cloth take up dust and dirt. Wet the cloth, and you can shift grease, too. The result? A surface so clean and totally dry that it shines.

Suitable for anywhere that doesn't need disinfecting as well – you wouldn't use these cloths for the toilet – microfibres are one of the big cleaning success stories of the past two years. Cost is around £5 per cloth.

The shine factor makes them particularly satisfying on stainless steel and chrome and on mirrors. After each job, simply toss the cloth into the washing-machine on a hot programme.

Look for bicarbonate of soda in your local chemists or pharmacy (sold as an antacid) – it's cheaper here than in the supermarket (sold as a cooking ingredient).

Storing and Using Strong Chemicals Safely

Don't underestimate the dangers of cleaning products, especially those that contain chlorine or ammonia. Wonderful cleaning solutions can cause not-so-wonderful damage to your possessions and to yourself. Many cleaning solutions can burn your skin and, if swallowed in sufficient quantity, prove fatal. Each year in the UK, 28,000 children under five years of age go to the accident and emergency department of their local hospital after accidental poisonings in the home.

Getting technical, it's the pH of a substance that makes it caustic. So whilst most people know that acids burn, you may not realise that strong alkalis are also harmful. The pH scale runs from 0 to 14, so a pH around 7 is neutral and won't hurt your skin. Blood, milk, and washing-up liquid all have neutral pH. Most cleaners are alkali because they work to neutralise and so shift grease and oils, which are mild acids. Exceptions are cleaners used to clear up rust, limescale, and hot caffeine drinks. All these items are alkalis, so they need acid-based cleaners to shift them.

If a cleaner has a high or low pH, take care. A pharmacy can sell you test strips to determine the pH of a cleaner, but there's no need to go this route. I'm simply telling you about acids and alkalis because it makes the whole process of why cleaners work easier to understand. And keeping that acid-alkali idea in your head makes it easier to understand why a particular stain remover works on what seems like two different stains. I come back to this some more in Part IV.

Working safely

The precautions you need to take to keep yourself and your possessions safe from cleaners are mainly common-sense guidelines. When working with chemicals follow these tips:

> ✔ Always read the label and accurately follow dilution and safety instructions.
>
> ✔ Open windows to ventilate where you are working.
>
> ✔ Wear gloves and eye protection if advised. Protect your clothes and surfaces from splashes.

Oven and drain cleaners are the most powerful cleaners. Take extra care when using these products.

Do *not* mix cleaning products. Combining chemicals won't make a super-cleaner and can produce toxic gases. The best-known example is chlorine bleach and ammonia, which you should *never* use together. If one cleaner doesn't produce the cleaning or stain removal power you hoped for rinse away (or, if you're cleaning the toilet, repeatedly flush) all traces of the first product before beginning again with cleaning agent two.

Storing for safety and savings

How and where you store your cleaning supplies can have a big impact on your health, safety, and pocketbook. By treating cleaning chemicals with respect, you can prolong the life of your cleaning tools and add to your quality of life by gaining peace of mind and monetary savings.

Create high, strong storage for chemicals in the rooms where you need them. For example, a small shelf that you can purchase for around £2 at a DIY store is all you need in the bathroom. Paint a plain wood one to match the wall and your toilet cleaner and bathroom bleach are safe and close to hand.

Making cleaning chemicals last longer

Once opened, most cleaners slowly lose their power. Bleach, for example, is only at its best for three to six months. This relatively short life is a good reason for sticking to multi-purpose cleaners and disinfectants rather than buying specialist treatments that could sit in your cupboard for years losing potency. Good storage techniques, however, help both cleaning products and your equipment last longer. So why not try these tips?

✔ Wrap soap-filled scouring pads in foil to prevent rusting.

✔ Make soap last longer by keeping it in a soap-dish with drainage holes, rather than on the sink side where it may sit in a pool of water.

✔ Keep chemicals in a cool, dry cupboard.

✔ Seal open packets of dry cleansers such as washing-soda to avoid clumping.

✔ Add a few grains of salt to stiffen the bristles when you wash an outdoor broom.

Creating good storage

Ideally, you should set aside a cupboard entirely for cleaning – under the stairs is perfect. Inside your cupboard use hooks and simple shelving to keep everything – except the vacuum cleaner – off the floor.

If you have children, choose a cupboard to store chemicals and fit a bolt on the door. Do not simply rely on keeping chemicals in childproof bottles. These are designed to resist opening but cannot keep out a determined child. The design aims to buy you time, but they're not foolproof locks.

To store a broom, fix into the wall two long nails, about 10 centimetres (4 inches) apart, and hang the broom-head on them. Use the same system for sponge-mops. Sew on a loop to a corner of dusters, so that they can hang up in your cleaning cupboard. I use old hair scrunchies.

Fabric mops, once thoroughly dry, can be detached to sit on shelves in the cupboard. Save space by choosing multi-fit tools. Dustpan, brush, and mop can all share the same handle.

Keep liquid cleaners in a handled tool carrier or pail, so you can take them with you as you work around the house.

Empty plastic food containers make simple storage boxes for brushes, cloths, and unused sponges.

Remember to clean out the cleaning cupboard now and again! An under-the-stairs cleaning cupboard can easily become dank. Leave the door open whilst you clean, provided there are no children at home.

See your supplies more easily by hooking up a light. You can get a portable battery-powered lamp from pound shops.

Chapter 3

Talking Timing and Techniques

- -

In This Chapter

▶ Figuring out how often to clean

▶ Using the best methods

- -

*U*sing your eyes, and in some cases your nose too, is one way of knowing when to clean. But if you'd rather stay one step ahead of the grimy carpet or the smelly sink, then you need to figure out a routine that fits both your home's particular cleaning needs and the time you have available. Modern life means that this is often a compromise. In this chapter, I give advice for when to clean, as well as sharing techniques that make the work you do more efficient and faster.

Deciding on Cleaning Frequency

Previous generations had a neat answer to the question of how often you should clean: every day, from dawn until dusk, would be about right so long as it was the hired help who wielded the broom. Even 30 years ago, keeping up appearances meant homes had to be clean enough to be seen at any time and a rigid cleaning agenda kept. So front steps got scrubbed by rote, rather than by whether they needed doing.

Today, it's reasonable to clean your home as often as it needs, accepting that these needs change along with the seasons (a blustery autumn brings a lot of dust inside) and how you happen to be using your home during a particular time (as a bed-and-breakfast during the winter holidays, for example).

Periods when your home needs more cleaning include

- Autumn and winter, when shoes bring in dirt and mud and closed doors and windows keep it trapped inside.

- The permanent arrival of more pets or people (especially children) who bring with them the need for more frequent cleaning that bears no relation to their size. One tiny baby – one gigantic clean-up operation.

- Guests are staying and you have raised expectations of what you believe to be clean enough.

- Renovations – DIY projects, even when confined to one room, have a knock-on effect of creating dust and mess throughout the home.

- Sickness in the household, especially if a family member has a condition that suppresses their immune system or is receiving a treatment, such as chemotherapy, that decreases their ability to fight infections. You need to step up on hygiene and disinfecting work.

- Your home is up for sale and you have potential buyers touring through it periodically.

- Summers and holidays when everyone's off work and school. If the whole family is around the house all day, they can create a whole load of mess to clean up.

For me, as mum to three children at primary school, the distinctions are clear-cut. In term-time, I may be the only person to walk across the living room all day. Following up with a daily vacuum would be a ridiculous waste of both time and electricity. But in the holidays, when a caramel carpet has to endure trains, trucks, kitten heels, and chocolate snacks, then I need to get busy with the vacuum daily.

Clearly, at the base lie important health safeguards. A dirty bathroom, for instance, is a health hazard. But given that a thorough cleaning takes a good deal of time, you need to balance the pleasure and well-being a clean house gives you against the impact it has on the rest of your life. At the extreme, it's pointless having shiny silverware if cleaning it makes you too exhausted to entertain and use it!

You are the best judge of how often your home needs clean-ing, because you're cleaning it to meet your standards as a reaction to what dirt and dust life throws at your home.

However, unless you're giving home to a pet zoo or running a day-care nursery, your lifestyle is not the most important cleaning variant. Instead, your home's contents determine how often you need to clean. And the good news, of course, is that to a large extent these can be changed. If you want to cut cleaning – and who doesn't – consider these simple changes:

- ✔ Go for durable surfaces when you fit new kitchens and bathrooms.

- ✔ Replace worn items throughout your home. Old always takes longer to clean, because you have to do so with care, and because once the surface has become pitted, it takes longer to remove the dirt.

- ✔ Anything that comes in a single, large panel or unit is quick to clean. Consider the time it takes to clean between the grout on small tiles with a fast sweep across a uni-formly flat surface, and you know what sort of worktop to choose.

- ✔ Have adequate storage. Put items away in closed drawers where they stay dust-free, rather than on open shelving that draws dust.

- ✔ Paint in colours that mask dirt: on walls cream is forgiving where white never can be.

- ✔ Open windows on the quiet side of your home: lessen the dust and dirt that comes in with passing traffic.

- ✔ Set clean house rules for children, pets, and visitors. Taking off shoes in the porch and keeping the dog down-stairs both dramatically cut clean-ups.

- ✔ Restrict eating to as few rooms as you can.

- ✔ Buy great-quality cleaning appliances.

Some areas of your home need cleaning attention more fre-quently than others. Table 3-1 gives you a chart detailing how often to clean each room in your home.

Table 3-1	Room-by-Room Cleaning Frequency Chart
Room	*Frequency*
Bathroom	Daily for hygiene; all surfaces fortnightly (every two weeks)
Regular bedrooms	Air daily; clean weekly
Guest bedrooms	Monthly
Halls	Twice weekly, more often in wet weather
Kitchen	Daily for hygiene; all surfaces fortnightly
Living rooms	Vacuum daily as needed; clean weekly
Dining room	Vacuum and clean weekly, or less often if you use it only on special occasions
Stairs	Vacuum fortnightly; vacuum uncarpeted stairs on hard floor setting or sweep twice weekly

Doing your daily duties

You wouldn't dream of getting up and dressed without first paying attention to personal hygiene. So think of the small amount of morning attention your home needs as a little like washing your face and combing your hair. Think how uncomfortable you'd feel if you didn't do these tasks – and how much of a tangle your hair would get into by the end of the day. A home that's been slept and lived in needs its morning fast fix, too.

Your morning cleaning routine is one you can do with your eyes still half-closed:

- ✔ Throw back the covers as you get out of bed. This exposes the bedclothes and mattress to the air and helps dissipate moisture you sweated into it during the night. If there's room, take the covers right off and pop them top-side down over a chair or onto the floor.

- ✔ Do a lightning sweep through the living rooms, removing any mugs, newspapers, post, shoes left out yesterday and stowing them where they belong.

- ✔ After breakfast, put the covers back on the bed, plump up the pillows, and lay out nightwear.

With your evening meal giving you energy, run through the following daily jobs before relaxing with your partner or settling down in front of the TV or any other fun activity.

- Sweep the kitchen floor if you prepared or ate a meal there that day.

- Empty waste bins from around the home into the kitchen bin and take combined rubbish out to the dustbin.

- Clean the toilets. Brush off any dirt sticking to the bowl and wipe both the top and underneath of the seat with a disposable toilet-cleaning wipe. If cost puts you off using wipes, a cloth reserved especially for this purpose is okay; spray disinfectant onto the cloth, not the seat, and wipe top and underneath. Before you go to bed, add toilet cleaner so that it can sit in the pan during the night.

- Check bathroom towels and change them if needed.

- Pick up clothes, hanging them up or depositing dirty ones into the wash basket. On work and schooldays, set out what you'll all wear tomorrow.

You can always find little cleaning jobs to do whenever you have a few minutes. Some tasks that you can, and should, do anytime you have a chance include:

- Wiping kitchen surfaces with antibacterial cleaner and a fresh cloth. Sink, worktops, and table need attention after every meal.

- Doing dishes. Either hand wash after each meal or stack dirty dishes in the dishwasher. Run either the rinse cycle or the complete programme if the machine is full.

- Wiping sinks with multi-surface spray.

- Cleaning pet dishes and the floor around them. Check cat-litter tray and clean if necessary.

Discovering why two weeks are better than one

Life is busy! For an increasing number of us, it simply isn't realistic to say we'll devote a decent time-block to cleaning each week. How about spending two hours every fortnight? Now that's a whole load more achievable.

A fortnightly checklist builds in leeway for all the other things that crop up in a busy life, yet stops you from sliding into awful habits. It isn't, however, a substitute for doing mini-cleans of your home throughout the week as time allows.

You probably want to do some of the tasks on this list more frequently than once every two weeks – perhaps even twice a week. But the point of this checklist is to make sure that you consciously go round every fortnight and check that each area is up to speed. If they're not, this is the time you set aside to get them done!

The general checklist, which you may copy if you like, follows. I list the chapter that tells you in precise detail how to carry out each cleaning task in parentheses.

❑ **Bathrooms** (Chapter 7): Thoroughly clean the entire bathroom

❑ **Floors** (Chapter 5): Vacuum carpets – up to twice-weekly in halls and high-traffic areas – and sweep or spot clean hard floors

❑ **Furniture** (Chapter 8): Dust ornaments and furniture; vacuum upholstery

❑ **Kitchen** (Chapter 6): Include fridge, worktops, cooker-top, backsplash, sinks, and appliances

❑ **Lamps and light fixtures** (Chapter 8): Check lamps, light shades, and light bulbs

❑ **Laundry** (Chapter 18): Wash any loads you haven't had time to do and take care of items that need special attention

❑ **Living rooms** (Chapter 4): Clean 'dry' rooms – lounge, dining, bedrooms, home office

❑ **Outside areas** (Chapter 11): Shake doormats, sweep out porch and patio, in summer

❑ **Pet homes** (Chapter 16): Shake out pet baskets and clean animal cages

❑ **Windows, mirrors, and blinds** (Chapter 10 and Chapter 4 for blinds): Wash windows that need attention. Check window blinds. Tackle any marks and stains that have appeared

Clean little and often and you'll enjoy a home that's mostly clean most of the time! Waiting two months until it's filthy and having a major go means a clean home only occasionally. For seven weeks in eight, you're putting up with dirt.

Incorporating Effective Techniques

If you're baking fruit scones, it's a disaster if you use a food processor to beat up the sultanas (raisins) and cherries into a thousand pieces rather than folding them in with a spoon. You rarely have to worry about overdoing it in your cleaning habits. As long as you get the cleaning solutions and equipment right, there isn't a wrong way to wash a wall or scrub a floor. But there is a technique to follow if you want to achieve optimum results. In the following list, I share with you what works for me:

- ✔ Start at the far side of the room when you wash a floor or shampoo a carpet, so that you don't walk back into the clean or wet area.

- ✔ Use a handled tray to help dust shelves. Off-load the items on a shelf whilst you clean both the shelf and the ornaments.

- ✔ Wash walls from top to bottom and you'll be able to wipe away drips as you go along.

- ✔ Use long, firm one-directional strokes when you sweep and use hand-sized bristle brushes. Resist the temptation to rub quickly back and forth, as this can simply rub dirt back in.

- ✔ Make your duster into a small pad and keep turning it over so that you always present a clean section to the furniture.

 Certain techniques can save you time and effort. Use the following tips to help do both!

- ✔ Spend the first 15 seconds in a room you're about to clean looking around. Train yourself to home in, not on dirt or stain problems, but on areas that *don't* need attention this time around. The mirror has no smears or dust? Great. You just saved yourself three minutes!

✔ To sweep a room using the fewest brush strokes, start at each corner and work to the centre. Only then get out the dustpan.

Using these tips, specific to certain jobs or tools, can help your cleaning go more easily:

✔ **Dustpan:** Wiping a dustpan with a damp kitchen roll (paper towel) makes dirt stick to it more readily.

✔ **Cleaning solution:** Apply what you need to a cloth rather than directly to the surface to be cleaned to reduce the amount you use and save your furniture from getting over wet or just over-exposed. Remember your rubber gloves if you have sensitive skin!

✔ **Cobwebs:** Take care to lift off cobwebs. Get your duster brush under the web and gently lift it off intact to prevent bits of web breaking free to stick on the ceiling or suck them up quickly with the long attachment on your vacuum-cleaner.

✔ **Rooms:** Begin on one side of the door and work your way around. When you return to the door, you know you're done.

Going room by room

Take it from the top, says the musical conductor. It's also the best way to work through your home. Follow these steps to work through your home quickly and efficiently:

1. **Start on the top-most floor, cleaning 'dry' rooms first and then doing upstairs bathrooms just before you move down the stairs.**

2. **Clean the stairs moving downwards.**

   It's more effective to stand below on dirty risers and sweep dirt towards you. But if working backwards makes you dizzy – don't! Always put safety before cleaning perfection.

3. **Do the hall next.**

   Typically, it's the dirtiest dry space in the home, so doing it now stops you from traipsing dirt into other rooms. However, be prepared to give it a quick final vacuum when you finish.

4. Go to living rooms and the dining room.

Dust the highest shelves first, so you get dust that falls onto lower shelves as you clean the upper ones. Dust tables and dining chairs. Plump cushions on the sofa and lounge chairs and check removable cushions for small items that have strayed down the sides: The TV remote is a classic, but you may find less savoury offerings, like food crumbs, coins, and small toys.

Clean the floor last.

5. Move onto downstairs wet areas to clean the bathroom and utility room.

6. Finish in the kitchen.

End by making yourself a cuppa!

Play beat-the-clock to cut the time you spend on each room. Most of us work faster when we're aware of the time. Set a portable kitchen timer for six minutes as you enter the bedroom. When it rings, you're done. If you fancy getting competitive, next time set it for five minutes and see if you can achieve the same results. Using a timer has the dual benefit of reinforcing in your mind how quick cleaning can be – a spare five minutes really does count!

Making a day of it

By tradition, the truly big clean of the year is done in spring because the worst of the dirt and dust caused by chimney fires is over. Especially if you work outside the home, your major clean is likely to be dictated by when you have time off. Don't let the fact that it's winter stop you if this is when you can allocate the time. However, if you're less pressed for time, there are good practical reasons for having a major clear-up in spring:

- ✔ Serious cleaning calls for ventilation. You want to keep open all the windows without freezing.

- ✔ With the central heating off, you can clean radiators and surrounds.

- ✔ Carpets dry quicker with good ventilation.

- ✔ There's more chance of a good breezy day to air duvets and curtains on the line.

So how far should you go with a major clean-up? For most of us, time is the big factor. Even in a full day, two people working flat out won't get to every surface. In the days before, look thoroughly over your house to see which of the jobs listed in Table 3-2 needs attention most.

Table 3-2	**Jobs to Do on a Major Clean**
Quarterly/Twice-yearly	*Annually*
Remove food and clean food cupboards	Clean behind heavy furniture
Shampoo high-wear carpets	Shampoo bedroom and dining carpets
Wash appliance filters	Clean cooker hood filters
Thoroughly clean windows and frames	Wash down walls (some every other year)
Defrost fridge/freezer	Sort out major cupboards for charity shops or rubbish
Treat hard floors with permanent polish or wax	Launder or have laundered curtains and duvets
Dust blinds	Wash fabric blinds
Clean oven (monthly, if high use)	Clean fireplace
Take out books to dust	
Take down and clean light fittings	

To make the best use of your time:

- ✔ Start your day with the physically demanding tasks. Don't try to do the heavy lifting late in the day when you're worn out — you just increase your chance of getting hurt.

- ✔ Intersperse physical jobs with sit-down clean-ups, such as brushing out a fireplace.

- ✔ Allow sufficient time to clear up. Set a time to stop working and stick to it.

Part II
Cleaning Your Home Top to Bottom

"If I could just get him to wipe his feet before entering the house, it would cut my cleaning day in half."

In This Part . . .

Professional cleaners always work top to bottom because it saves on time and cleaning fluids. So that's what I do in these chapters. With the focus on the inside of your home, I offer chapters on ceilings, walls, and window treatments, right down to how to keep clean every type of floor and floor covering. Then it's on to two grime hotspots – the bathroom and the kitchen. Reading through this part gives you advice on cleaning all the interior surfaces of your home.

Chapter 4

Cleaning Ceilings, Walls, Radiators, and Window Treatments

● ●

In This Chapter

▶ Talking timing

▶ Washing down ceilings and walls

▶ Cleaning curtains and blinds

▶ Coming to grips with hot spots – from radiators to fireplaces

● ●

*L*et's hear it for cleaning jobs that need to be done only now and again! Every day, the walls and ceilings of your home – plus the curtains and blinds that partly line them – absorb airborne particles of dust, dirt, and oil. Mostly the dirt is brought in through windows and doors. Or it's caused by everyday activities such as cooking greasy foods or smoking. But the good news is that, unlike floors which need very frequent attention, you need to reach out or up to clean these big boys only now and again.

In this chapter, I look at easy ways to do just that. For problems with specific stains on walls, window treatments, and ceilings go to Chapter 20 which addresses household stains, or look up a specific staining substance in the Appendix to find hints for removing it.

Figuring Out Frequency

Typically, you may want to clean blinds every other month and curtains each year. Washing down walls and ceilings can be an annual task, except in rooms that see heavy action such as the kitchen and bathroom. Here, you may want to get wiping every other month. Fireplaces and radiators are an annual chore as well.

But these are just rough averages. Naturally, specific stain problems make you want to get cleaning right then and there.

Exactly how often you clean depends on the location of your home – places near traffic need infinitely more cleaning than those in open country – and who lives there. The ceilings of homes where people smoke need attention every six months. For non-smokers, it's more like every two years.

Cleaning Walls and Ceilings According to Covering

The real trick in cleaning walls and ceilings is to stay dry yourself and not to get walls and ceilings too wet. As well as adding to your comfort, it makes sense to go easy on the water because too much water may start to wash away water-soluble emulsion (latex) paint (which is what practically all ceilings are painted with). You can go more heavily with the gloss and oil-based paints you may find on picture rails, skirting boards (baseboards), and fancy trims. But there's no real need: Over-wet walls are more likely to dry in streaks. Up on the ceiling, too much water just means unnecessary extra mopping, as well as a wet head and arms!

To prevent yourself from getting soaked while you work, wear a hat – a baseball-style cap that has a back-flap is ideal as it also gives your neck protection from drips. Stop water from running back down your raised arms by wearing sports sweatbands if you have them. If you don't, loosely tying a dry flannel (washcloth) around each wrist absorbs the drips.

If you're trying to wash away the yellow tinge that forms over time, especially on the ceilings, in a room where people smoke – stop now. You can't wash that away; you need to repaint. But before you paint, use an alkali-resistant primer or an all-purpose stain block as these stains can come through a new coat of paint.

If you hit mould, washing it off isn't sufficient. You need to paint on a biocide solution (available from DIY [hardware] stores) to prevent it growing again.

Kitchen ceilings are prone to develop a greasy film. Extractor (exhaust) fans take away dirt and grease that otherwise accumulate on the kitchen ceiling and contribute to this film. Unfortunately, most people don't use their fans very often because they hate the noise. But turning on the fan for even 15 minutes as you leave the kitchen helps cut down on ceiling grime and therefore makes your cleaning life much easier.

Erasing grime from emulsion surfaces

You need only a very weak detergent solution for washing emulsion surfaces – 60 millilitres (ml) (4 tablespoons) of soap in about 5 litres (a gallon) of hot water. Any multi-purpose liquid cleaner is fine. You can buy cleaners sold either as liquids or as highly concentrated liquids (follow the dilution directions on these). Choosing one with a mild fragrance can make the task more pleasant. With this mild mixture, hand irritation shouldn't be an issue, so you may want to wear cotton gardening gloves to absorb extra water rather than hot and heavy rubber gloves. Sugar soap washes walls well too but is much more expensive than the detergent you use for occasional cleaning. Save the sugar soap for special occasions such as when you're about to repaint and want to remove all trace of detergent residue.

I find a sponge mop best for washing ceilings. For stubborn spots, you can tie a towel over the mop to get added rubbing power. When washing down walls, you can get closer using a sponge (an old natural sponge that's too tatty for the bathroom works well).

Whether you're using a mop or sponge, keeping it well wrung will help prevent streaks.

Give yourself a clear area for working, thus avoiding tripping over whilst working. Move electrical items well out of the way, or anything else that may be upset by dripping water.

The first step in cleaning is dusting to remove the light surface dirt. Using brushed lambs-wool is perfect.

In cleaning a ceiling, start by imagining you're on a cleaning task you do often such as mopping the kitchen floor. Take your mop or sponge right around the perimeter, going tight into the corners where the ceiling is likely to be dirtiest. Wring out your mop or sponge, dip it into your cleaning bucket, wring again, then work across your ceiling in quarters, going backwards and forwards in lines in each section. If your ceiling is such a height that you need to stand on some steps, you may find it easier to imagine you're tackling a chessboard of small squares. Avoid long mop strokes that could cause you to overreach and overbalance.

To wash a wall, start at the top of the wall and work your way down. That way, you can wipe away drips that run away from you. I suggest that you first wash the top along the whole length of the room – this is the tiring, stretching bit. Next, divide the wall into manageable vertical sections. Then, for each section, do the skirting board (baseboard), and a few centimetres (inches) of wall directly above it, as this is dirtier and takes longer to get clean.

Next, look for any particular stain problems and marks on the wall, and tackle them – around the light switches may be especially grimy. If necessary, spot clean these with a drop of neat multi-purpose cleaner on your sponge; look in the Appendix for how to tackle any identifiable stain.

Then, it's on to the easy bit that you can whip through – the middle section of the wall. Work along in easy up-and-down sweeps, overlapping slightly with the top and bottom sections that you already washed.

Repeated washing down in dirt hot spots like the hall and lounge (living room) can wear away the top layer of emulsion paint, making it appear dull. So be prepared to repaint after a handful of washes.

Attacking artex ceilings

What dust traps! Only cleaning enthusiasts would choose to put in a ceiling that's full of dirt-accommodating grooves, which is exactly what artex is. Unfortunately, adding water only grinds in the dirt. The best way to clean artex is with gentle suction. Use the soft brush attachment on your vacuum that sweeps as it sucks to gently tease dirt away.

If the ceiling is really appalling and you have no choice but to use water, keep it as delicate as you can. Use plain warm water – no detergent – and a soft sponge, well wrung out. To avoid mould take extra steps to dry the ceiling quickly, such as using an electric fan-heater, turning up the heat and directing the fan at the ceiling.

Wiping down wallpaper

The only type of wallpaper you can safely wash is vinyl. Even with vinyl, unless the care label says it's scrubbable, use as little moisture and pressure as you can.

To wash vinyl wallpaper, use two buckets. Fill one bucket with a warm, soapy solution made from 20ml (1 tablespoon) of multi-purpose cleaner per 5 litres (1 gallon) of water. Put warm, clean water in the other bucket and use it to rinse your sponge so that you never bring dirty suds up to the paper.

Rinse and dry afterwards. For rinsing, use a slightly damp sponge, blotting it over the area you just washed. To dry the walls turn up the radiators or use an electric fan-heater so that the work is done for you. If this isn't possible, you can lightly towel-dry the walls. But take care: wet paper is fragile, so press the towel against the wall to blot up moisture rather than giving the wall a quick rubdown.

With non-vinyl wallpaper, the most you can do is spot clean. To do this using dry materials, you can try to soak out the grease and grime that make your wall look dull. You will need patience. Hold a clean, absorbent cloth, or about four sheets of kitchen towel (paper towels), against the wall, then iron the cloth or sheets on a very low heat setting. The heat loosens dirt and oil, which the towelling absorbs. Another neat trick is to rub a slice of white bread against the paper which may draw out the grease element of the stain.

Every month or so, vacuum wallpaper walls using the soft-brush attachment and you may never need to wash them.

Tidying Window Treatments

Curtains add colour, shape, and definition to a room. But it's easy not to notice how everyday dirt dulls their ability to do all of these things. When you do clean them, you get the sheer joy of seeing once again exactly why you chose a particular design and fabric texture.

Although dry-cleaning businesses often offer discounts on curtain cleaning in January, it's far better to wait until May to tackle both dry-clean-only and washable curtains. Both need to be fully aired, and you can do this more easily when you can open patio doors and windows. Also, you want to peg out larger washable curtains on an outdoor clothes-line.

Blinds are fine to do all year round, and those in kitchens and bathrooms need frequent attention. So let your eyes tell you when to clean.

(For tips on cleaning the windows themselves, head to Chapter 10.)

Considering curtains

Curtains take a lot of abuse from many angles:

- ✔ Sunlight beats down on them, fading their colour and weakening their fabric.

- ✔ Smoke, dirt, and other pollutants become entwined in the fibres, making them smell and dulling their lustre, but sometimes hiding other defects.

- ✔ Dirt acts as a cover for natural bleaching from sunlight and cleaning it away may make your curtains look worse. So think twice about washing the drapes in a conservatory or sunroom.

Take extra care with old curtains, even if they carry a care label that says they're machine-washable, as they may be too damaged to wash safely.

Brocade and ribbon trims can get dirty ahead of the curtains. Spot treat them with dry-foam upholstery shampoo. On the other extreme, pelmets (valances) and other types of trim may get dirty more slowly than the curtains themselves. This is no reason not to wash them when you clean the curtains, though. Clean all the major curtain components at the same time so that one item doesn't look fresher (or more tired) than the others.

Using the washing-machine for washable curtains

If your curtains and your washing-machine are a good match, go right ahead and let them get together, being careful to follow the care labels on the curtains. If any part of your washable curtain is going to shrink, it's generally the lining. Detach the lining first if you're worried, then hand wash the lining or do nothing to it. If you forget to take off the lining and it does shrink, you can snip it off after washing the curtains and just stretch the wet curtains back to their regular size.

If the lining is very colour-stained, stitch it back inside out.

To safely wash washable curtains, follow these steps after you take them down:

1. **Remove the curtain hooks.**

2. **Check the weight of each curtain against the maximum wash-load weight recommended for your machine.**

   One full-length curtain can easily weigh the maximum amount your machine can handle. (See Chapter 18 for the weights of various washables.) A pair may need two loads.

3. **Add the amount of washing-powder (laundry detergent) recommended on the container for maximum soil.**

4. **Select a gentle wash cycle.**

   Remove promptly afterwards to cut down on creasing.

When the curtains come out of the machine, you may have to stretch them back into shape before hanging them on the line to dry. Even if your curtains can stand up to the washing-machine, the dryer is almost guaranteed to be the end of them, so let them air-dry.

Wet curtains are extremely heavy, so if you have two parallel wash lines, lay the curtains over both.

If the curtains need ironing, do it whilst they're still damp. Iron the inside of the curtain, pressing the seams flat.

Use upholstery shampoo to clean fixed pelmets, taking care not to get them too wet. Towel dry.

Dry-cleaning non-washable curtains

Dry-cleaners typically charge by the surface area of curtains, so a big room means a big price. If, when you get the curtains home again, you can detect the smell of cleaning solvents, you need to air the curtains before hanging them back up, particularly if they are destined for a bedroom. If they are returned to you on a peg-rail, an easy way to air them is to hook the rail onto the curtain rail by your patio doors, and let the breeze work its magic. Pegging on the clothes-line is of course a standard option. Do not be tempted to get the smell out by using the tumble dryer – the solvents used in cleaning your curtains are flammable and pose a fire risk even if you use the no-heat option on the dryer.

If your curtains have a dry-cleaning code, you can use a machine programme at the self-service dry-clean machine at a launderette for a fraction of the cost of taking them to a dry-cleaner. Once home, hang curtains outdoors until the smell subsides.

You can also get curtains dry-cleaned in your home, whilst they're still hanging on their poles. This is a good choice if you have fitted pelmets that need doing as well.

Hand-washing net and voile curtains

Delicate sheers need special handling, but are easy enough to hand-wash in warm, soapy water – the bathtub makes an ideal washbasin. Rinse them in cold water then fold the curtains vertically to carry them outside to hang on the line. Take them in when they're still damp and hang up at once.

Take all steps to avoid creasing, as the creases can become permanent. If white curtains have yellowed, try using a bio-detergent or net-whitener, which you can purchase at most supermarkets and department stores.

Adjusting blinds

When dressing your windows, you can hang a variety of blinds in place of, or in addition to, curtains which can hang stylishly in front. Types of blinds include:

- ✔ **Roller:** Made from a window-sized piece of stiffened fabric or vinyl that is stored on a roller at the top of the window when the blind is drawn up.

- ✔ **Roman:** Made from fabric, these blinds lift up in horizontal folds. They're usually individually made to fit living-room or kitchen windows.

- ✔ **Venetian:** Typically horizontal slats of high-shine plastic or metal, venetian blinds may also hang vertically and be linked by chains (in which case, they're usually referred to as vertical blinds).

Cleaning the different types of blinds requires different methods, which are explained in Table 4-1. The first step for each method is to let the blind down to expose as much surface as possible.

Table 4-1	Cleaning Methods for Blinds
Type	*Cleaning Method*
Roller	Leave the blind hanging and try vacuuming with the soft-brush attachment; if this isn't enough, sponge the fabric with upholstery shampoo.
Roman	Have a professional cleaner come in to clean them.
Venetian	Open the slats. Wearing dampened colourfast cotton gloves, start at the top and run the glove across each slat. If the blinds are desperately dirty, take them down and wash them with soap and water in the bathtub lined with a towel. Rinse and towel them dry, re-hang them, then dry them again slat by slat with dry gloves.

For less than £3, you can buy a Venetian-blind duster that whips through dusty slats with soft fluffy fabric prongs.

Cleaning Your Home's Hot Spots

Radiators, fireplaces, and boilers (furnaces) are clearly tasks best done in summer. Fireplaces can be a slog, but the rest are five-minute wonders. Table 4-2 lays out cleaning methods for radiators, boilers, and electric-heater fans.

Table 4-2	Cleaning Heat Sources
Item	**Cleaning Method**
Radiator	Frequently vacuum the central grooves with the crevice tool of your vacuum. To periodically dust the back, lay a cloth on the floor under the radiator, tie a duster onto a measuring stick, and use the stick to push dust down onto the cloth. Be sure to take a look above your radiator at the same time: heat can cause passing dirt to attach to the wall along here. Wash it off with a soapy sponge.
Boiler (Furnace)	There are no user-safe parts inside your boiler. A registered professional should clean the inside as the major part of a boiler's annual service. Simply polish outside with a soft cloth.
Electric-fan heater	Never get any electrical appliance wet. Hold the vacuum's crevice tool about 6 centimetres (2 inches) away from the unplugged fan and move in the direction of the grooves/blades.

Frequently-used fireplaces need the grate cleaned frequently, but don't fuss about getting out the fine, bottom layer of ash that can so easily spread into the air and on carpets. Do one total clear-out at the end of winter, when you won't be using the fireplace again for some time.

Clean a fireplace *only* when you're certain that the ash is utterly cold and can't re-ignite. The morning after a cosy fire-lit evening is too soon. The fire may not have gone completely out until the small hours. Also take care in disposing of the ash. Warm ash that comes into contact with paper or plastic can re-ignite and cause a house fire.

To do the dirty deed, don gloves and a dust mask to protect yourself, and shut the room's windows and doors.

Your big aim in cleaning the fireplace is to stop ash flying up to scatter over you and the room. Scoop or very gently brush the ash into an enclosed dustpan. Just dampening the dustpan helps the ash stick to it. To empty the dustbin, go outside and tip the ash into a sealable bag and put out with the rubbish.

HEPA vacuum filters are fine enough to filter ash dust, but don't use them for that purpose. Ash can clog the machine.

To clean the hearth, using a stiff brush is always better than washing with water. So keep it dry to remove smoke and soot marks. You may have to be very persistent to get out large soot marks, but it can be done. Vacuum with the soft-brush attachment then brush with a stiff-bristle brush.

If you are using your fireplace for open fires, have your chimney swept professionally at least once a year. This will improve efficiency, cut down on smoke in your home, and prevent chimney fires.

If staining that remains bothers you, wet the soot patch with water, then sprinkle on salt, let it dry, and brush off vigorously.

You'll want to clean the fireplace surround once a year after you clean the fireplace itself. How you clean the surround depends on what it's made of:

- ✔ **Brick:** Use a specialised fireplace cleaner, then apply a brick/stone sealant.

- ✔ **Cast iron:** Remove rust with wire wool (steel wool), then clean using a sponge dipped in soapy washing-up water. Rinse and dry promptly and thoroughly.

- ✔ **Ceramic tile:** Use a mild abrasive cleanser on really dirty tiles, taking care not to scratch any glaze. Rinse the abrasive off, then dry and polish with a cloth.

- ✔ **Marble:** Use a commercial polish specifically designed for marble annually. Products give either a matte or shiny finish. Do not use abrasives or chemical cleaners on marble as it's very easy to damage the surface.

✔ **Stone:** You can use a strong bleach solution if necessary, but test for colour fade on a hidden spot first. For speed, clean large areas using a sponge, then scrub at stubborn spots with a stiff brush.

Unused grates can get rusty over summer. So, after the last fire of the year, rub the grate with lubricant such as WD-40 to prevent the problem.

Chapter 5

Standing Up to Floors

• •

In This Chapter

▶ Vacuuming and attachments

▶ Washing carpets

▶ Caring for hard floors

• •

*M*uddy boots, dirty paws, dusty shoes, and greasy feet all bring dirt into your home. Add to that airborne dust and soil that breezes in from windows and doors and it's easy to see why floors demand so much cleaning attention.

Whatever floor surfaces you have, two simple practices help cut your cleaning:

✔ First, tackle it dry. Grease bonds to carpet fibres immediately but dust and general grit don't. If you sweep and vacuum regularly, you take away the dirt before it combines with water or oil to stick quite literally to the floor.

✔ Secondly, get a mat. Better still, get two – or even four. Placing a mat on either side of both front and back doors significantly reduces the amount of soil that gets inside. Place mats lengthways so that both feet have to tread on them before reaching the carpet.

It takes years for children to get in the habit of wiping their feet. So make it easy on yourself and them by choosing mats that you can shampoo.

This chapter looks at regular care for all the floor surfaces you're likely to have in your home. When you need to shift stains from them, turn to the Appendix and look up the specific stain.

Undertaking Vacuuming

The disappointing news for perfectionists is that you may have to go over the same spot of carpet up to seven times to remove all soil. But for the rest of us, vacuuming is a high-speed chore, though you shouldn't just rush through it. You have to go slowly enough to give the machine time to suck up the dirt.

Vacuum *last.* Dust, polish, make the beds, clean the walls if they're on the schedule – do all your cleaning tasks *before* you run the vacuum. That way you catch up any dust and dirt your cleaning knocks to the floor.

Before you start, get clutter off the floor. Be on the lookout for items that may jam the machine. Wearing an apron with pockets gives you a handy place to dump stray items.

On a carpet, start by the door and work your way across the room, going back and forth. You need to overlap each strip by a little, because your vacuum doesn't clean absolutely up to the edge of the machine. (Many people have a habit of pushing back and forward in lots of mini-movements, as they might sweep a floor. This takes longer and means you miss bits.)

Go tight into the corners every third vacuum if you have fitted (wall-to-wall) carpets. Doing the corners takes a bit more effort and, frankly, isn't called for every time you clean. You may need a combination of the crevice nozzle (for tiny spots) and the dust-brush (when suction alone isn't enough). Doing a big room can mean hard, on-your-knees work, so do this first and then stand up and leisurely vacuum as normal. By contrast, if you're vacuuming wood or hard floors, you need to get into the corners every time because dirt and dust collect in corners.

Vacuum rug fringes by moving from the rug towards the end of the fringes. Going the other way will suck up the fringes and can jam the moving parts of your vacuum.

Wood floors scratch easily. When vacuuming a wood floor, check the vacuum's wheels before you start and wipe off any grit that could mark the floor. Remember to switch off the beater bar or choose the hard-floor attachment if your machine has one. Always vacuum in the direction of the planks.

If your vacuum suddenly sounds different, stop immediately. Unplug it, then check for blockages. Typically an odd noise is caused by something caught in the brush bar. Continuing to use the vacuum whilst it is blocked in any way will burn out your motor or other moving parts. Check your manual for advice on undoing the brush bar to remove foreign matter. Don't stretch for that extra metre and risk damaging your machine or tripping over taut flex. Stop and plug the vacuum in again at a closer socket.

When you're in a dash, it's absolutely fine to do just the high-traffic walkways.

Making good use of attachments

Any modern vacuum comes with a load of attachments designed to help you clean specific parts of your home with ease. Making use of these attachments makes good sense. Following is a list of the most common attachments and their uses:

- ✔ **Brush attachment:** The long, soft bristles of this tool are set around an oval suction hole and are perfect for delicate cleaning. Try it on blinds, fabric lampshades, and special rugs. It's also good on paintwork.

  You can also dust decorative ornaments with the brush. If these are small or exceptionally delicate, be on the safe side by fitting a quick safety net. Pop a leg cut from an old pair of tights (pantyhose) or a knee-high nylon sock over the brush and secure with a fabric hair scrunchie. You reduce the vacuum's suction power and eliminate the danger of objects disappearing into the cleaner.

- ✔ **Crevice attachment:** This long, shaped pipe brings strong suction to awkward corners. Ideal for skirting boards (baseboards) and the floor around the toilet. It's also good for reaching up high. Use it to suck away trapped ceiling dirt.

- ✔ **Floor attachment:** A large brush that mimics the standard cylinder cleaner brush and is generally the same size. It may have a setting for hard floors. Use it on areas where wheeling your vacuum is difficult. But in a typical home, you may not use this attachment that much.

    ✓ **Stair attachment:** This neat tool is shaped like a scaled-
    down version of the hose on a cylinder vacuum. It has
    strong, even suction that gets into tight corners and so
    helps you do stairs (obviously!) plus sofas, curtains, and
    small areas of carpet.

Figure 5-1 shows the various vacuum attachments.

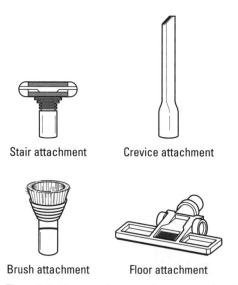

Figure 5-1: Vacuum cleaner attachments make cleaning easier.

You can only clean with clean equipment. So it makes sense
not to move straight from a dirty job like cleaning blinds onto
a delicate one such as vacuuming a curtain pelmet. Instead,
take a good look at your attachment as you finish a particular
task. The brush attachment is particularly prone to getting
lint trapped within the bristles.

Choosing the right vacuum cleaner

Upright vacuum cleaners are large machines that you push in
front of you. Carpets get clean because a brush bar beats out
the dirt, which the machine then sucks up. This action also
grooms the carpet. You can also turn off the brush bar and
use an upright on bare floors.

In the past decade, huge improvements have been made in the brush bar and tool attachments. If you can handle one and have a large or busy house, an upright is always the top choice.

Uprights do have a few flaws, however:

- ✔ **Height:** If you're tall, you'll stoop, which can make a bad back feel worse.

- ✔ **Power:** May pull the threads from Berber carpets. Check with your carpet retailer about using a cylinder vacuum.

- ✔ **Size:** Can't get into small corners. For a pristine finish, you need to use the attachments.

- ✔ **Weight:** They're often too heavy to carry upstairs.

Never use an upright cleaner above you on the stairs. It could topple and cause injury. Keep it on the ground floor, then take just the hose and the stair attachment up to the top stair and work back down.

Cylinders are small, fairly compact cleaners on wheels that follow behind you as you use the attached hose. The cleaning power of a cylinder vacuum comes mostly from suction. Cylinder vacuums are lightweight and compact, which makes them easy to use on the stairs and a candidate for a second vacuum to keep upstairs. Their small size makes them easy to store and their mobility and design mean they can get into tight corners and clean right up to the carpet edge.

Cylinders are arguably less effective than uprights, and they don't groom the pile on carpets as well. But if cost is a concern, budget models sell for under £50.

Sometimes your vacuum pulls up a thread, particularly in shag and twist piles. Simply snip it back to the correct height.

A vacuum is probably the most important electrical cleaning tool. So if you want to go top-model on one appliance, this is it. Features worth paying extra for are:

- ✔ **High-level filters:** These trap microscopic particles including pollen and dust mite droppings that aggravate asthma and allergies. The best filters are marked HEPA (high efficiency particulate air).

The filter is only as good as the bag emptying system. There is no point sucking tiny allergens into your vacuum only to breathe them in as you empty the vacuum bag or canister. A bagless cleaner, for example, can give you a lungful of dust as you empty it out. If you're asthmatic or have allergies, chose a vacuum with a sealed disposable bag system. With such a system, as you go to change the bag, it automatically seals so no dust can escape.

✔ **Bag-free cleaning:** Though not for asthmatics (see the preceding bulleted item) a bag-less vacuum gives you full suction throughout your clean, saves time and hassle in emptying the dirt, and you don't have the expense of buying bags.

✔ **Pet hair features:** All decent vacuums get pet hair off the floor. A truly pet-owner-friendly vacuum offers a better way to get fur off stairs and sofas. Some models have a rotating brush that fits to the vacuum hose so you can beat then suction fur from seats, stairs, and car interiors.

Cleaning your vacuum cleaner

Before inspecting any moving part of your vacuum ensure that the vacuum is unplugged.

Keep the wheels clean to avoid marking your floors or adding dirt to your carpet instead of taking it away. Check the wheels before you plug in the machine and wipe off the wheels with either a wet or dry cloth. If you take the vacuum outside to do the car with the hose attachments, stand the base on a carpet mat.

Change and wash filters as your model dictates. Be sure these are scrupulously dry before replacing. Stand them near, but *not* touching, a radiator for at least 12 hours.

To remove threads and coils of hair caught in the brush bar, carefully snip across at intervals then gently pull free. Bizarrely, the quickest way to clean a dirty brush attachment is to use another vacuum tool. Simply undo the brush attachment, clip on the crevice tool, and go along the brush bristles, suctioning up dirt.

Giving new carpets extra care

Unless you buy a premium all-wool Axminster, you can expect a canister full of fibres when you first vacuum a new carpet. Polypropylene and nylon straight-pile carpets are possibly the worst in this regard, but don't worry; it's all perfectly expected. Your carpet is not falling apart and you won't be left with bald patches.

In fact, it's a good idea to vacuum more frequently in the first month of a new carpet. Giving the fibres a beating helps release and remove gluing chemicals that cause that new-carpet smell. Opening the windows frequently is a more significant way to get rid of this odour, however.

Emptying the vacuum bag or bagless canister is an opportunity for developing good cleaning habits. Take bags, and the canisters of bagless containers, outside to empty them. The newest models have trigger switches that empty straight into the bin. Take care to avoid breathing in the dust.

- ✔ **For lift-off canisters:** Hold a bin bag tightly across the rim of the canister then invert carefully to empty. Leave at least 10 seconds for dirt to slowly drift into the bag before you take it away. Seal and bin outside.

- ✔ **For vacuum bags:** Aim to never let the bag get above half-full. A bag bursting with dirt dramatically cuts the efficiency of your vacuum. Follow the manufacturer's removal instructions, taking care to pinch tight the top so that no dust can escape. Drop immediately into a rubbish bag, seal, and bin.

Washing Your Carpet

However often you vacuum, there comes a day when the carpet looks dull. Grease from cooking, food spills, and body oils cannot be vacuumed up. It needs either to be dissolved in the wet, sudsy solution of a detergent or lifted dry by chemical absorption.

People often put off carpet cleaning thinking it's a major heavy-weight of a job. Only painting ceilings is worse! But actually having a carpet-cleaning machine out on an 12-hour hire gives you the motivation to tackle not just the floors but all those other cleaning/home maintenance tasks you never get round to, such as unsticking the sock drawer (rub candle wax on the runners and you're done) or descaling the iron. Low physical effort jobs sit neatly with the push and sweat of carpet cleaning and give you something to do whilst you take regular breaks. So go on – make a day of it!

Stains are dealt with fully in the Appendix, but for periodic washing you face two choices: getting in professionals – top choice is a wet high-pressure steam-and-water extraction method that costs around £20 per room – or to do it yourself. You can hire a machine from a DIY (hardware) store or super-market for around £30 to £50 per day including cleaning solution. Or you can buy your own carpet-cleaning machine.

Deep cleaners are worth having. These shoot a high-pressure spray of hot tap water and cleaning solution deep into the base of your carpet. Almost immediately, this is extracted out by the machine to give carpets that are dry to the touch in an hour or so.

You can often apply stain protector to your carpet via a carpet cleaner. Some carpet shampoos add stain protection as they clean.

Give traditional combination wet-and-dry cleaners a miss. Although you get a cylinder vacuum and a carpet shampooer, they are bulky and awkward to use. The vacuum function is usually fine, and the shampooer may be okay for regular fresh-ening up, but they don't remove soil from deepest fibres.

To get great results from a carpet washer, use these tips:

> ✓ Before you begin, spot test with a correctly diluted spot of solution to check for colour and shrinkage. Leave the solution to fully dry then compare your spot with the rest of the carpet. Look for any colour fade, or for pile that now looks visibly shorter, or distorted. These are signs of shrinkage.

> ✓ Dilute shampoo as instructed. Using a stronger solution only increases the likelihood of leaving detergent residue in the carpet and won't give you cleaner results.

> ✓ Use warm water on wool to avoid shrinkage.

✔ Spot treat bad stains first. Pre-treatments are sold along-side the shampoo.

✔ Start from the far side of the room to avoid walking on the wet parts. Carpets are weaker when wet and your footprints can permanently depress the pile.

✔ Go slowly. The water extractor needs time to work.

✔ Make this a two-person job, or take regular breaks. Emptying bucket after bucket of dirty water is tiring.

✔ Open windows and doors to speed drying time. Turn on central heating as you finish.

Take two pieces of identification with you when you go to hire a carpet cleaner. Most stores insist on seeing items with your address on, such as a driving licence and utility bills. Go pre-pared and save a double journey!

Caring for Non-Carpeted Floors

Dents, liquid spills, and scratches are your big problems with hard and semi-hard floors, and I deal with these problems in Chapter 21 and in the stain-removal appendix. By contrast, regular cleaning is a breeze. All you have to remember is that it's typically a two-step job. First, sweep away dust and dry dirt. Then clean. The specifics are in the following sections.

Skip the sweeping and go straight to the mopping and all you do is turn dry soil into wet grit that scratches the floor.

Laminate

Laminate floors are often DIY projects. So whilst individual planks are factory sealed, gaps between the laminate planks and the edge of your floor aren't. If you get too much water into these gaps, the planks may lift up.

To clean laminate floors, your choices are:

✔ **Dry-mop** using an electrostatic mop especially for lami-nates. You can choose from several brands that attract the dust that so easily sticks to laminate.

✔ **Vacuum** with the brush bar setting off.

✔ **Sweep** with a soft broom.

For bedrooms and living rooms, any of these methods should be enough. But for laminates in the kitchen, follow up with a just-damp mop. If the floor is especially dirty, use a specialist cleaner. Alcohol-based mop cloths help get rid of tough dirt yet evaporate quickly.

Avoid using polishes, general floor cleaners, or multi-surface cleaners. Anything containing detergent dulls the floor.

A steam mop can be a good investment if you have several laminate floors. It's safe to wet your floor with steam because within 30 seconds it's dry again. You may be able to use your steam mop to clean windows and sofas as well as clean and kill germs on all your hard floors.

Ground-in dirt may mean you get desperate for a liquid wash. If your room has low humidity, you may well get away with using a gentle soapy wood cleaner. But you must mop-dry afterwards. I've done this for years in my kitchen, where an AGA cooker provides constant dry heat, with no board lift-up.

Linoleum and vinyl

The difference between linoleum and vinyl is that vinyl is totally man-made whereas linoleum is made from natural fibres. Both make waterproof, hard-wearing surfaces for the wet rooms in your home.

To clean either surface, follow these steps:

1. **Vacuum or sweep to pick up grit.**

2. **Use your favourite floor cleaner, a detergent diluted to instructions, or a homemade multi-purpose cleaner.**

   Go easy on the water by wringing thoroughly before you put your mop onto the floor.

   Use two buckets – one with cleaning solution, one with plain water. Keep your bucket of detergent solution fresh and make it last the entire floor by dunking the mop in the plain-water bucket after every sweep of the floor, wringing it out, then dipping it back into the soapy water.

3. **Rinse thoroughly by mopping the floor with clean water.**

   Again, take care not to get the floor overly wet.

Twice a year, get up a glossy finish by coating the floor with a water-based polish designed for vinyl or linoleum.

Wood

Wood floors present a quandary. They're the ultimate in hard-wearing surfaces – go round a stately 19th-century home and you're likely to see many original boards. Yet if you don't clean them correctly, they can warp, rot, and become permanently stained. The big enemy is water. Mop up spills promptly and if you have a wood floor kitchen, go easy on the kitchen tap to avoid splashing.

The simple beauty of a wood floor deserves special attention. To keep wood floors looking great on a daily basis, use the following tips:

- ✔ Avoid scratches. Table and especially chair legs can scratch a wood floor. So fit protective pads using colour-fast felt on the bottoms of chairs. When you move furniture around, make it a two-person job and lift, don't push.

- ✔ Pay attention to the shoes you wear. Take high heels off at the door! Stilettos bearing down onto the floor can cause dents. It's not automatic – typically a heel needs a worn, sharp bit to make a mark. But why take the risk? Wear trainers (sneakers) with non-marking soles.

- ✔ React to spills and stains promptly and properly. Wipe up spills promptly with a soft, just-damp cloth. Scrape up solids ever so gently using a blunt knife. Always follow the grain as you work.

- ✔ Be sparing with the wax. When the floor dulls, try buffing with a soft cloth before you get out the wax. With patience, and a lint-free cloth folded up into a smooth, thick pad that you can rub and rub again, you can generally bring back the shine.

✔ When you really must wax again, stick to high-use areas that need it. Wax build-up dulls the floor, and when you put on too much, the only way to deal with this is to strip it off and start again. So save yourself a deal of work by not re-waxing corners or low-use parts of the room.

Table 5-1 presents types of wood floors and how to clean them.

Table 5-1	Cleaning Wood Floors
Type	*Method*
Polished wood	Sweep only. Do not wax because it makes the floor slippery.
Sealed wood	Sweep with a soft-bristle broom – daily if you can manage it – and damp mop from time to time.
Unsealed waxed wood	Sweep and reapply wax as needed; in a well-used room, and if you love your floor to look good, this might be every three months. But every 6 to 9 months is acceptable if you're time pressed. Liquid wax is easiest. It's elbow grease, not a heap of product, that gives a great result.

Every few years, when unsealed wood gets too dark and greasy, use white spirit (turpentine) to strip off the top layers of wax. Go easy on the stuff – it's a heavy-duty chemical, so wear gloves and a protective mask as you work. Add a few drops of white spirit to a thick wad of old white rags and rub down the floor to remove surface wax. Apply fresh wax the next day.

Tiled floors

Tiled floors can be a doddle to maintain. Slate flagstones, granite, and ceramic tiles are generally sealed to protect them from water and stains. Quarry stone is fine as it is, although you may need to buy a specialist stain remover, which you can find at specialist tile shops.

To clean a tiled floor, follow these steps:

1. **Sweep or vacuum.**

2. **Wash with mild detergent, diluted as instructed on the label.**

In a small room such as a bathroom, it can be as quick to get down on the floor and use cleaning rags. But if you'd rather stay upright, a cloth-strips mop is better than a sponge one. The latter seems to encourage water to collect in the grouting.

3. **Rinse with water.**

4. **Air-dry, keeping pets and people out.**

Tile, especially ceramic tile, is very slippery when wet. Take care as you clean, and if you can't be absolutely certain that no one will nip into the room in the next 30 minutes, dry the floor with an old towel.

Get at dirty grouting when it needs it with diluted bleach (10 parts water to one part bleach is a safe, frequently recommended dilution). You can go up to 1 part bleach to 3 parts water, but only if you take good care to protect yourself from splashes and wear gloves. For speed, pour the recommended diluted solution into an empty squirt bottle then pipe the solution along the grout line. Rinse thoroughly.

Cork

Floor tiles are typically factory-sealed to shrug off stains. Basically, you're cleaning the sealant on the top, not the cork. To do so, follow these steps:

1. **Sweep up dirt.**

2. **Damp-mop.**

Take care not to over-wet edges where the tiles have been cut to fit around basins, for example. Very wet cork can crack. If you do cause a flood, soak up as much of the moisture as you can with your mop or an old towel, then open the windows and turn on the radiators to lower the humidity and dry things out.

Chapter 6

Scouring Everything and the Kitchen Sink

*P*ay someone to clean your home and the kitchen is where they want to start. They know that attention to detail and an organised approach will have you gushing with gratitude. The kitchen is my favourite room to clean, too. I'm no fan of some elements – rubbish clear-outs and oven gunk are icky – but more than any other room a just-cleaned kitchen brings a transformation. Just 45 minutes – an hour tops – and you get a room so good that you'll feel like a child eager to break into the plastic wrap on that neatly boxed toy and get down to play.

This chapter covers how to clean every surface and appliance that's likely to be in your kitchen and provides essential information on keeping your kitchen hygienic. A thoroughly clean kitchen doesn't just look good, it's sanitary and helps cut the risk that you'll get sick too.

Embracing Reasons to Be Clean

Each year in the UK there are 10 million cases of food poisoning. And 80 per cent of these food-borne outbreaks are picked up in the home, not that dodgy take-away place so many of us put problems down to.

The infections are caused by a mix of bacteria and viruses that are always around wherever there are domestic pets, people, raw food, and water. Now, low doses of these micro-organisms are fine: Your immune system shrugs them away as naturally as breathing. But when they multiply, which they do in warm and especially wet places, they overwhelm your body's defences. Babies and the elderly are the most susceptible, but anyone can get sick from contact with a major contamination.

The chief culprits in passing along these micro-organisms are food that isn't properly stored and poor hygiene standards by those handling the food. Food handlers who don't follow good hygiene procedures risk spreading their germs to the foods they handle.

According to research, the cause everyone knows about – food that isn't cooked or reheated enough – actually lies behind just one in ten food-caused tummy upsets. So it doesn't matter how burnt you like your steak if it's served up on a germ-laden plate.

The most important element in avoiding food-borne illness starts at the sink. As you cook and clean thoroughly, wash with soap then dry your hands frequently, using a hand towel – not the tea towel you use to dry your pots and pans.

Choosing disinfecting over simply cleaning

A surface can be spotless but still be home to millions of germs. Ordinary cleaners are designed to dissolve grease or provide abrasive action, but not to disinfect. A *disinfectant* actually kills microscopic bacteria and virus-carrying organisms. Of course, in rubbing a surface or drying it afterwards, your cloth naturally takes away plenty of harmful organisms, though it does nothing to stop those it leaves behind. Boiling water kills germs, but until you can have a heat-resistant robot do your housekeeping, this isn't practical. A hand-held steam machine is a tool you can use now to kill germs, but again, it's not practical for all situations and surfaces.

The simplest way to kill germs is to choose cleaners with built-in disinfectants. Use them on all the high-risk spots in the kitchen and through your home. Most kill more than 99 per cent of harmful micro-organisms in the house. But they don't do it in a split second. You must leave the solution in contact with the surface for the time it says on the bottle – three to five minutes is typical. Otherwise, you're just cleaning, not disinfecting.

You can make your own disinfecting solution with bleach and water. The traditional choice is *chlorine bleach,* which actually contains sodium hypochlorite, not chlorine. It has that swimming-pool odour and quickly takes the colour from any carpet and clothing that it splashes on. *Oxygen bleach,* which contains hydrogen peroxide, is as strong as chlorine bleach but colour-safe for most fabrics and carpets. Some companies now make versions that have a pleasant fragrance – no bleach smell. But no matter how nice it smells, bleach remains a skin and eye irritant so be careful when you use it.

To make a solution for worktops, sinks, and floors, add 60 millilitres (ml) (4 tablespoons) of bleach to 5 litres (1 gallon) of water. To make a soaking solution to disinfect dishcloths, mop heads, and so on, add 20ml (1½ tablespoons) of bleach to 5 litres of water. If you're soaking overnight, 10ml (2 teaspoons) of bleach is sufficient. Remember, any diluted bleach cleaner only lasts a day, so don't make more than you need.

Balancing cost and cleanliness

Absorbent paper towels are the ultimate in sanitary. But using them to dry everything is pricey. So make colourfast cotton dishcloths sanitary in the hot wash cycle. Don't keep using the same cleaning cloth over and over. Instead, keep a stack in a drawer, and once the one you're using becomes wet, throw it in the laundry and pick up a fresh cloth. When you've got enough, toss the pile of used cloths into the washing- machine on the highest heat setting.

Recognising the most important areas to clean

There are certain areas in your kitchen which are the most likely to have harmful micro-organisms. You need to take special care with these items.

Because germs love water, *thoroughly dry* the surface of each of the following problem areas with a clean cloth or paper towel after you clean it.

✓ **Chopping boards:** Clean with an antibacterial spray before use and during use when you switch foods. Ideally, keep one board for raw meats and wash this with dilute bleach (1 part bleach to 9 parts water).

✓ **Eating and cooking utensils:** It's the hot water, not the washing-up liquid, that kills germs on your pots, pans, plates, and cutlery (silverware). If you can tolerate only lukewarm water, consider switching to a dishwasher.

If you can't do the dishes right away, cut germs by scraping off food, but don't leave pans or dishes to soak if you won't get back to them within two hours – stagnant water is a breeding ground for germs.

✓ **Inside the fridge:** Stay on top of drips and spills. When raw meat drips on a shelf, for example, spray an antibacterial cleaner onto a cloth, not the fridge shelf, or use an antibacterial wipe to clean the spill. Always store raw meat at the very bottom of your fridge so that any drips will not contaminate your other food.

✓ **Sink drainer (dish drainer):** Wipe with dilute bleach or antibacterial cleaner after each use. Dry thoroughly.

✓ **Worktops:** Use an antibacterial spray labelled safe for food-preparation areas on surfaces where you prepare food.

Because bacteria and viruses grow in pooled, stagnant water, the kitchen black spots listed here can turn into reservoirs of germs. Take special care to clean and dry these areas:

✓ **Plughole (drain) and U-bend in the sink:** Pour around 60ml (4 tablespoons) of neat bleach down the sink. After three minutes, run water, then dry plughole.

✓ **String-mesh dishcloths and sponges:** Soak in very diluted bleach (20ml [1½ teaspoons] to 5 litres [1 gallon] of water in a bucket). You can do this in the sink (and so disinfect the sink, too), but only if you're confident that the metal on the plughole can withstand this – bleach may tarnish the metal.

✓ **Wet tea towels and fabric cloths:** Machine-wash on hot with bio-powder or liquid.

Good hygiene isn't about cleaning *more;* it's about targeting *hygiene hot spots,* the areas where keeping things clean helps keep you well.

Cutting the Clutter to Cut the Work

Kitchens are so satisfying to clean because a good deal of the work is actually restoring order to chaos – not really cleaning at all!

Put away as much as you can before you start to clean. Ordered worktops look great and are more likely to stay clean. It's no hassle to wipe over a clear worktop, whereas lifting jars, cups, and yesterday's post is too much effort to bother with.

 Get it off the worktop with hooks. Use self-adhesive ones for lightweight things such as aprons, towels, plastic bags, and so on. Screw metal hooks into the wall or cupboard to hang cups and utensils.

Only some people are born neat. But everyone can cheat by creating both a clutter drawer and a clutter cupboard in the kitchen. Having a holding space for paperwork and action figures and the other stuff that gets left on the table, and a cupboard for hard-to-store-away dishes and equipment you plan to use again later (in a heat-wave, the blender that crushes ice qualifies!), is a simple way to a visually tidy the kitchen.

 Each time you clean the kitchen, start at a different place, then go steadily round in a full circle. Everyone cleans their first section to perfection, then runs out of time to whip along the final stretch of worktop. This approach evens things out.

Cleaning Your Kitchen Surfaces

Hopefully, your kitchen worktops (countertops) and units are the ultimate in hard-wearing, able to withstand strong and effective cleaning. But you can't guarantee it for a fact. Many kitchens are designed to look wonderful but their ability to withstand a good cleaning is way down on the list.

If you can't identify a surface, err with caution and avoid bleach. This means checking all bottles of multi-surface cleaner, as many include bleach as an ingredient.

For sheer speed, it can be tempting to zap the same product on every surface in the room, but only surfaces that come into direct contact with food need antibacterial protection. A standard multi-purpose spray, which is cheaper and may have more stain-shifting power, is the better choice for other areas.

The worktops that you prepare and perhaps eat your food on need to be kept as hygienically clean as possible. Table 6-1 runs through the best ways to disinfect various worktop surfaces. Be sure to choose an antibacterial cleaner, rather than a simple antibacterial spray. Sprays are designed to disinfect freshly cleaned surfaces. Using them on small areas such as telephone key pads or toilet handles is fine, but why make twice the work for yourself in the kitchen, when you're covering large areas.

Table 6-1	Cleaning Worktop Surfaces
Surface	*Cleaning Method*
Granite	Use an antibacterial spray cleaner. Dry thoroughly.
Laminate	Use an antibacterial spray cleaner. Dry thoroughly.
Marble	Wipe with a soapy (sudsy) solution from a bowl of mild washing-up liquid – the kindest ones for marble work surfaces are those sold as being kind to your hands! Rinse it away completely. Detergent residue dulls marble. Avoid acidic cleaners as they eat into the surface.
Tile	Use a multi-purpose spray or microfibre cloth.
Sealed wood	Use a very dilute bleach solution of 20ml (1½ tablespoons) of bleach in 5 litres (1 gallon) of water on stubborn grime, working quickly so as not to let the bleach change the colour of the wood.

It's easy to neglect cupboard and drawer fronts during your regular cleaning session. Yet frequent attention makes your kitchen look smart and inviting. Table 6-2 tells you how to clean each surface.

Table 6-2	Cleaning Kitchen Surfaces
Surface	*Cleaning Method*
High-shine resin	Use only soft cloths that won't scratch. Wipe to remove dirt before getting at stains with a dab of washing-up (dishwashing) liquid.
Laminate	Use a non-abrasive multi-surface cleaner, taking care not to let any drips dry hard.
Sealed wood and veneers	Dilute 30ml (2 tablespoons) of a soap-based wood cleaner in 5 litres (1 gallon) of lukewarm water and wipe the entire surface, then buff with a soft cloth. There's no need to rinse. Polish occasionally with a light liquid wax if you like a shiny effect.
Unsealed wood	Unsealed wood is not a good choice in the kitchen. The wood darkens as it ages no matter how often you dust it. If you use water to clean it, the wood may warp. My advice is to preserve unsealed wood's good looks and colour by sealing it with a light varnish.

Doing the Dishes

You had just a light meal and a drink, yet whether you wash by hand or machine, it seems you always have a stack of dishes to clean. The following sections tell you how to be most effective no matter which method you use.

Washing up by hand

Being organised can save you time and trouble. Clear the plate rack (dish drainer) before you begin. Stack everything that needs to be washed on the other side of the sink according to type – collect glasses together, cutlery, bowls, and so on.

Go heavy on the hot tap water and easy on the washing-up liquid. Hot water, not soap, kills germs. Using a scrubber, carefully clean each item.

Do glasses first – holding them by the stem – only if you can stack them safely out of the way and won't risk chipping or breaking them by bumping them with the plates that follow. If you have an enamel sink, you may want to protect glasses and fine china by lining the sink with a tea towel. Leading hotels give glassware a final vinegar rinse for added shine. But this works only if you then dry the glasses promptly with a linen cloth.

In removing baked-on food, try to avoid overnight soaking. The stagnant water is a germ-laden pool in the making. Soaking in cold water for 20 minutes or so whilst you wash everything else up should be enough time to loosen the food. If not, sprinkle salt on your pan scourer to add extra abrasion.

You can try lifting off stuck-on foodstuff with a wooden spatula or a blunt knife, though with a knife you run the risk of scratching the plate or bowl or whatever.

You can sometimes shift tough, baked-on food by covering it with water and briefly heating the pan or returning the casserole to the oven.

To prolong the life of cast-iron pans and pans coated with a non-stick finish, use a pastry brush to coat the surface with vegetable oil after every sixth wash.

Rinse with fresh, hot water. Hot water evaporates faster than cold, which means that dishes dry quicker and with fewer smears if they're rinsed in hot water. With double sinks, rinsing is easy – you use one sink for washing and fill the other with hot water for rinsing. If you have just a single sink, pile clean, soapy dishes into an empty washing-up bowl after you wash them, and when you have a decent number of items waiting to be rinsed, drain the soapy water from the sink, fill it with fresh hot water, and rinse off your dishes. Using the hot tap instead is okay if you're doing a small wash-up session. It just uses more water and of course makes the soapy water progressively hotter. Simply hold washed, soapy plates under the running tap, then stack them to dry.

Loading the dishwasher

The secret of using a dishwasher is in the stacking. Dishwashers aren't miracle machines. Unless the jet spray of water is able to reach every portion of the plate, spoon, glass, or whatever, it can't clean it. So read the manual for stacking advice. If you can't find the manual, crouch down to your machine and look at the spray arm. Gently spin it and check that everything you have loaded would get wet.

Tips for loading your dishwasher:

- ✔ Scrape plates before loading. This is a dishwasher, not a waste disposal unit! Rinsing first is, however, a waste of time.

- ✔ Secure delicate items on the top rack. Alternating cups with glasses prevents scratching.

- ✔ Mix up cutlery in the basket. An all-spoons-together approach produces scrappy cleaning.

- ✔ Stack everything so that water can run off freely. For example, invert cups and casseroles.

When you empty, do the bottom first. That way, any drips you spill as you empty the top basket won't matter.

Modern dishwashers have all sorts of settings. So you may want to get out the instruction manual. In general a lower water temperature means the machine uses less electricity and helps your dishes last longer. A higher temperature is better for grease and stain removal.

Standard dishwasher tablets contain a strong detergent. But detergent isn't enough to give your plates a sparkling finish or to keep your machine running smoothly and without risk of limescale blockage – very important if you have very hard water. So you need to buy two additional products:

- ✔ **Dishwasher salt**: Add this separately, every sixth cycle or so, in the salt dispenser which you find on the inside base of the machine according to packet instructions. Salt softens the water before it enters the machine so that it is better able to take up the dishwashing powder – and also protects your machine's plumbing from limescale.

- ✔ **A rinse agent:** Sold as a liquid that you pour into a chamber inside the dishwasher at the start of each cycle, a rinse agent helps reduce streaks and spots that often appear as dishes dry.

An alternative to buying three separate products is to use a three-in-one product that combines detergent, water softener, and rinse agent. But these don't suit all machines or you may need more or less of one ingredient.

What you mustn't put into dishwashers:

- ✔ **Aluminium pots:** They may darken.
- ✔ **Antique and hand-painted china and gold-rimmed pieces:** The glaze may fade and the gold chip.
- ✔ **Cast iron:** It may rust.
- ✔ **Cutlery handles made from bone or wood:** The glue may loosen.
- ✔ **Lead crystal and decorative glassware:** It may dull over time and lose pattern definition.
- ✔ **Plastics that aren't labelled dishwasher-safe:** They may melt.
- ✔ **Wooden spoons and bowls:** Prolonged wet can warp the wood.

You can wash both silver plate and stainless steel cutlery, just don't let them touch each other. If they do, transfer between the two metals can leave silver tarnished.

Be aware that repeated washing makes designs fade and shortens the life of eating and cooking utensils.

Maintaining your dishwasher

Clean out dishwasher filters – ideally after every wash. You don't need to get the grease off, just stuck-on bits of rice and so on. If you don't clear it off, that gunk just flies back over the dishes.

Wipe dirty seals dry with paper towelling.

Now and again, take off the water spray arm and check that it isn't clogged (sweet corn is a likely culprit). Use toothpicks to carefully unblock any logjams.

A capful of white vinegar keeps shut-up smells at bay. Pour some in on a day when you're not going to use the dishwasher and leave it to sit in the machine. You can also buy branded leave-in freshener blocks.

Troubleshooting

Dishwashers are a blessing and a curse! The short and far-from-complete list that follows tells you how to take care of some of the most common dishwasher problems. Your dishwasher manual should have additional advice.

- **Cups still tea-stained:** You're not putting enough cleaning powder into your machine. Add dishwasher salt, as described in the preceding 'Loading the dishwasher' section, or switch to a premium dishwasher powder and avoid light wash settings.

- **Detergent residue or half-dissolved tablets left in the machine:** This indicates that hot water isn't getting through. Check the spray arm for blockages and clear them out with a toothpick. Also, tablets can be too much for small machines. Switch to powder.

- **Too many suds:** Use less rinse-aid in the dispenser. Also, scrape away egg- and cheese-based sauces, as too much protein in the machine causes over-soaping.

- **Wet plates and glasses:** Add more rinse-aid.

- **White film on inside of the machine and glassware:** Descale the dishwasher with a limescale remover.

Shining Up Major Appliances

Get out the rubber gloves and be sure to give yourself sufficient time to do a thorough job when you decide to tackle your kitchen appliances. Unlike the worktops and sink, appliances can always wait that extra day or so when you're time-pressed. But there's no point at all in half-cleaning a cooker (oven). However, the good news is that with appliance cleaning, one thing doesn't have to lead to another. It's absolutely okay to deal with just one major appliance each time you clean.

Keeping the fridge clean and cool

It's rare to find a fridge that needs manual defrosting these days. Still, the drip vent at the back may collect gunge and cause ice to form. If you can't readily see the drip vent, look just above the main shelf, or move shelf racks. As you clean out the fridge, the raised temperature of having the door open should make any ice lumps melt. If not, encourage them free with a spoon. Don't use anything sharp.

If you have sensitive hands, wearing cotton garden gloves (machine wash them first) can stop you suffering from the cold as you clean out the fridge. Even if you're lucky enough to have a large icy beast, fridge cleaning isn't a long job – 15 minutes max. So there's no need to worry about leaving milk and other perishables exposed to the warmer air. You leave them out longer during a meal.

Make it easy on yourself by emptying just one shelf at a time. This saves the need to free up an ocean of space on the work-top for food. Simply get out a large tray, then stand one shelf's worth of food on it, and you're ready to clean. Of course doing it this way means you've got to be a tad more careful inside the fridge.

Starting from the top shelf, take out food and clean shelving with a damp cloth. If the shelves are stained, take them out and wash them at the sink with washing-up liquid. Be scrupulous about using clean cloths and water!

Gunge can collect in vegetable and meat drawers if you've been less than quick to throw out an ageing lettuce or to mop up leaked juices. When ordinary soapy water doesn't do the trick, try using a little olive oil on colour stains. For stuck-on foods: scrape up using a plastic spatula.

A tablespoonful of bicarbonate of soda (baking soda) in an old coffee-jar lid left on a shelf absorbs odours for up to a fort-night (two weeks).

The exterior can get grubby fast, so wipe it each week with a damp cloth, then dry thoroughly. Use a light oil, such as WD-40, to get off stubborn marks. Wash well afterwards, to remove any odour. You can get back that showroom shine by using a light, liquid wax polish every few months. Be aware, however, that making it shine also makes it show up surface dents, and most older fridges have plenty of these.

Annually, pull out free-standing fridges and use the crevice attachment to vacuum the coils at the back.

De-icing freezers

Defrost the freezer the day before you need to do a big shop, and do it when the freezer is at a low ebb. Aim to fit all the frozen food you have into one cool-box (cooler). Accept that you might lose the odd ice cream to melting.

To clean a freezer, follow these steps:

1. **Switch off the freezer.**
2. **Pack the cool-box with food.**
3. **Leave the door ajar and wait for ice to melt and catch any run-off.**

   - For upright freezers, stand a towel on the floor and place a deep tray on the bottom shelf to catch drips – an oven-roaster tray is ideal.

   - For a chest-type freezer, look for the drainage chamber, open the valve, and place a washbowl underneath.

   - Putting saucepans of hot water on the shelves speeds up melting.

4. **Use a very mild, odourless cleaner to wipe down the insides.**

   You can buy a cleaner recommended for fridges or use warm water mixed with bicarbonate of soda – 1 pint of water to 1 dessertspoon (teaspoon) of bicarb.

5. **Dry thoroughly with a clean lint-free cloth.**

Operating on ovens and other heating elements

It's essential to follow the manufacturer's instructions when cleaning your oven. In particular, you need to know whether your oven has a self-cleaning lining that cleans without chemicals. Instead, matter is burnt off at high temperatures (you may have to be very patient here, we're talking hours).

If you don't have your manual, most companies have a Web site (usually www. the brand name.com) you can check. If that doesn't work, at www.creda.com you can download around 1,000 manuals!

When you're sure you have to clean the oven yourself, reach for a specialist oven cleaner. But be careful. Oven cleaners are among the most caustic and toxic substances allowed for home use. Follow all cautions. Wear gloves and ventilate the room when you apply the cleaner. Don't save these precautions just for when you take it off later.

Protect your floor by laying down several layers of newspaper to catch any drips. If the grill pan fits totally inside the oven, apply cleaner to this too.

Asthmatics or anyone who can't tolerate these caustic chemicals can use the little-and-often method of sprinkling bicarbonate of soda on oven spills and grime, then rubbing with damp wire wool (steel wool). This gets at the worst dirt, but you don't get shine.

When you splash or spill while cooking, immediately sprinkle some salt on the mess and carry on cooking. When you come to clean up you'll find that the salt has absorbed the oil or fat and your spill is easy to clean up.

If you can take out the glass in the door, soak it in diluted detergent. Use the same soapy water for the oven racks and scour off any remaining marks with an abrasive pad or wire wool.

The following list tells you how to clean various other heating elements:

- ✔ **Gas hob (stovetop):** Check the manual to see whether the pan-supports and wells are dishwasher safe. If they are, pop them in the machine, otherwise, dot a thick, abrasive cream cleaner (rather than simply a liquid cleaner) onto a cloth and wipe.

- ✔ **Glass top, halogen, and ceramic hobs (stovetop):** Do not use chemicals on these types of cooker tops, as they may impair how well your cooker can radiate heat. Consult the manual that comes with your cooker for complete cleaning instructions. If you don't have a manual, a damp cloth will have to do it all. In emergencies, when there is a big spill, use a plastic spatula (but not whilst the surface is still hot) or a hob scraper, sold especially for your oven type. Regularly apply hob conditioner, sold by your cooker company, to glass.

✔ **Microwave:** Get into the habit of wiping the insides, especially the roof, after each use with a cloth dampened in soapy water. Soapy water also cleans the removable bottom plate.

Never scour the insides. Soften tough deposits by steaming half a lemon in a bowl of water for 15 minutes. You can then shift the gunk with your rubber-glove-clad fingers. The lemon has the added bonus of removing smells as well.

Don't get the outside controls wet; wipe them with a barely-damp cloth.

✔ **Sealed hotplate:** Be certain the hotplate is turned off. Use a soap-filled steel-wool pad following any circular lines within the hotplate, rather than cutting right across them. Wipe over using a clean cloth, then warm the hotplate for a few seconds to ensure that it dries. This prevents rusting.

Brush hotplates with a bristle brush. Polish vitreous enamel fronts with a mild abrasive paste. Treat stubborn marks with concentrated washing-up liquid. Damp-wipe stainless steel lids or buff with microfibre cloth.

✔ **Aga and range cookers:** Ovens self-clean, which is just as well since they're never turned off so they're never cool enough to clean. Remove large oven-floor deposits with a very stiff bristle brush with a wood handle – plastic might melt! Clean racks in soapy water in the sink.

Many cooker manufacturers sell their own specialist cleaners. Although you pay more – up to double – having exactly the right cleaner may bring you peace of mind.

Taking Good Care of Small Appliances

Toasters and kettles especially can have extremely short working lives. Rarely worth repairing, you need to look at replacing them every two years. However, regular cleaning can help to prolong their usefulness as well as save your otherwise clean kitchen from a worktop eyesore. Because they're small, these appliances are easy to overlook at cleaning time. Each month, make a point of checking for visual grime that means it's time for a spruce-up.

Washing toasters and sandwich-makers

Toasters and sandwich-makers aren't tricky to clean, just remember to unplug them before you do and never immerse either one in water.

If the toaster has a removable crumb tray, chances are you can wash the tray on the top rack of the dishwasher – but check the manual. If not, up-end the toaster over the rubbish bin to remove crumbs.

To clean a sandwich-maker, lift out the plates if possible and clean them in soapy water. Dry scrupulously. If the plates in your sandwich-maker cannot be removed, you have to be more patient. When foodstuff is completely dry, pick off carefully using your fingernail or a plastic spatula. Then, to wash, use a squeezed-out soapy sponge so that you don't flood the machine with water. If needed, soak the plates by laying them on top of a paper towel that has been lightly wetted with your soapy solution. Rinse with a damp cloth. After every ten washes, take a pastry brush and very thinly coat the plates in vegetable oil to protect the non-stick coating. Never immerse the machine in water.

Treat the exterior of both machines to a thorough wipe with a microfibre cloth. It's a neat way to bring up shine. As an alternative, a spray-on chrome cleaner does a fine job at taking out greasy fingerprints, which is a toaster's biggest problem.

Descaling kettles and coffee-makers

Use a branded descaler every three to six months or when you first notice limescale deposits in the kettle or at the top of the coffee-maker. Switch off at the plug and half fill the kettle or coffee-maker with water. You need to leave room for the descaler to fizz up! Be safe: Boil two lots of water in the machine before drinking from it again.

Diluted distilled white vinegar makes a slow yet effective descaler for a fraction of the cost of commercial products. Pour 200 millilitres (1 cup) of water and 200 millilitres (1cup) of distilled white vinegar into the kettle or coffee-maker and leave overnight. In the morning, tip solution away, then boil the kettle with fresh water and discard that water, so that the water you drink is not tainted.

Freshening food processors, mixers, and blenders

Increasingly, the toughened plastic bowls that form the base of food processors, mixers, and blenders are dishwasher safe, though clear plastic may become cloudy after repeated machine washing. *Never* wash the section housing the motor – damp-wipe it only.

Safety is crucial with the attachments. Work out a safe drying place for processor blades before you start – don't just leave razor-sharp blades on the drainer.

Clean processor bowls and blender jugs where they live. Half fill the container with warm water, add a drop of washing-up liquid, then turn on the machine and let it clean itself! If the bowl is stained by foodstuffs, processing ice cubes should shift even carrot and beetroot residue.

Usually, dried-on cake mix or orange-juice pulp is the most difficult to clean. To ensure that you always wash bowls out immediately, fill a sink with hot, soapy water *before* you begin.

Tackling Kitchen Rubbish

Everyone argues about whose turn it is to take out the rubbish. Unfortunately, I can't offer any solutions to that age-old issue, but I can offer ways to make bins and garbage disposal units less nasty.

Getting the best of bins

When choosing a rubbish bin, for hygienic reasons it has to be a pedal-operated bin because your hands don't make contact with the bin lid, so there's zero chance of transferring germs. But if you prefer bins with swinging or lift tops, regularly wipe over the lid area with an antibacterial solution or wipe.

Daily emptying is ideal. Wipe down with cleaning wipes. Before replacing a bin bag, sprinkle some bicarbonate of soda in the bottom of the bin to absorb smells and moisture.

Pay more for quality bin bags that are the same size as your bin and you should scarcely need to wash the bin. Spilt garbage or liquids due to poor-quality bin bags mean frequent clean-ups.

The fastest way to clean a plastic bin is to stand your cleaning solution inside it! Dilute some of the multi-purpose cleaner you use on your worktops and let the lid soak in this too. You can then use a rag mop to clean up the bin sides. Tip carefully into the sink and rinse. Dry thoroughly before putting in a fresh liner. You can give the outside of the bins the same wash treatment. Afterwards, wash the mop head in a diluted bleach solution.

Bin experts Brabantia don't recommend cleaning inside at all: If you use their bins with the right-sized liners a wipe of the stainless steel exterior with an E-cloth (a microfibre cloth) is sufficient.

Paying attention to waste disposal units

Flush with clear water after every grind. Use a diluted multi-purpose cleaner as a degreaser unless your manual suggests a specific cleaner. To get rid of smells, pour a generous slug of distilled white vinegar down the hatch, wait two minutes, then flush with water. If you have stuck pieces of food, throw in a few ice cubes: as they crush they'll break up any food particles.

Chapter 7

Bringing Brilliance to the Bathroom

● ●

In This Chapter

▶ Developing good cleaning habits

▶ Following a step-by-step action plan

▶ Treating then beating bathroom condensation

● ●

*Y*ou can eat out all day. You can relax in the garden, rather than the lounge. But you can't skip the bathroom.

Because most bathrooms are shared by everyone in the household, you have to be that bit more scrupulous about cleaning. If you only have five minutes in a day to clean, head for this room.

People who get sick and suffer from diarrhoea and vomiting obviously spend a lot of time in the bathroom and are likely to leave behind germ-carrying organisms in the toilet, the air, and on bathroom surfaces. Visitors aren't likely to tell you about a touch of tummy trouble. You just have to be thorough, as a matter of course. The stomach health of your household depends on a clean bathroom.

Bathroom hygiene hot spots are areas in your bathroom where you're at the highest risk from micro-organisms that can make you sick. The key spots are door and toilet handles, facecloths, hands, light-switches, taps, and towels. Surprisingly, the toilet itself comes last of all these other items. That's because you don't come into contact with the toilet's two germiest places – under the rim and under the water.

If someone in your household is ill, issue them with an 'I am sick' towel and have them and only them use it for the duration of their illness. This will prevent spread of illness.

Beginning with Bathroom Basics

Take good care of your bath, basin, and toilet and, except for the taps, they will need changing only because you grow tired of the design or decide to upgrade to a whirlpool bath or walk-in shower.

Baths fitted 40 years ago can still look like new and they can also be returned to a sparkling state. This is exactly what you want to hear if you've just moved into a place with a grimy bathroom. However, this happy news comes with a caution. Using cleaning products that are not suitable to your particular surface can cause permanent damage. In particular, you could get colour fade and weaken the structure of the coating.

Scrubbing different surfaces

Your bathroom is made up of loads of different materials – most of which are supposed to gleam. Table 7-1 fills you in on the characteristics of various surfaces and can help keep you out of hot water.

Table 7-1	Bath and Sink Surfaces and Surrounds		
Surface	**Characteristics**	**Likely Fitting**	**Cleaning Tips**
Acrylic (plastic)	Lightweight, keeps room temperature. Practically all budget and DIY-store baths are acrylic.	Bathtubs, sinks (especially in cloakrooms [half-baths]), shower trays (floors)	Avoid abrasive cleaners because acrylic scratches easily. Instead, use a liquid cleaner or a mild cream cleaner if it specifically says that it is safe for acrylic. Keep on top of the cleaning: It's especially easy to get a build-up of soap on acrylic. Be careful not to drop sharp items — the acrylic may be very thin. A sharp or hard object (a razor or a metal can of hairspray, for example) may crack the bath, meaning you have to get a replacement.
Cast iron/steel	In terms of cleaning the metal doesn't matter because both get a top coat of enamel. This is what you clean, so see the entry for *enamel*.		
Enamel	Solid and shiny! Briefly feels cold to the touch (that's the metal underneath the enamel coating).	Older (pre 1970s) bathtubs and sinks and expensive modern baths	Take care! Use only products that state they are safe for enamel. Avoid acid-based cleaners (and limescale fighters) as they can eat into the enamel. Over time, the enamel coating can wear thin. Your plumber can advise you if professional re-enamelling is an option.

(continued)

Table 7-1 *(continued)*

Surface	Characteristics	Likely Fitting	Cleaning Tips
Porcelain	A top choice for sinks and toilets. Not found in bathtubs. Heavy, solid items falling into the sink may chip the edge, so watch what you put on that windowsill!	Sinks, toilet cisterns, and pans	It's hard wearing and can stand gentle abrasives. The most delicate part is the plughole, which can discolour if strong cleaners are left to pool.
Ceramic tiles	Smooth, hard-wearing, water-resistant.	Used as splashbacks to sinks and baths and as water-resistant, hard-wearing wall coverings	A doddle to clean and can withstand most all-purpose cleaners. Rinse then buff dry with a smooth cloth to bring up shine.
Glass/toughened plastic	Slick, shiny surfaces.	Used for shower screens, shelves, and mirrors	Prone to smearing and getting coated with soap scum. Easiest choice is a specialist daily shower spray, but you have to use it at once, whilst the glass is still wet. Otherwise, use the glass cleaner you'd use on your windows.
Resin-bonded	Solid, with flecked appearance. This mix of stone and resin is tough and hard-wearing.	Shower trays	Use gentle liquid bathroom cleaners and rinse off, using the shower attachment.

Making cleaning easier with good habits

Bathroom cleaning is quicker and more pleasant in a room that has sufficient storage to keep lotions, make-up, razors, and toothbrushes off window ledges and sink edges. Buy a wall cabinet with a door and encourage everyone to store their bathroom articles in it. You can take out the contents and clean this cabinet semi-annually rather than cleaning monthly as you need to with open shelving.

Bacteria multiply in wet conditions. Besides, damp flannels (washcloths) smell, so always rinse yours clean, then air-dry – but not, I beg you, over the side of the sink. I know it's a popular choice, but an awful one for so many reasons, including the fact that it's unsightly and it invites others to use a flannel that should be for one person only.

So be discreet. Hanging your flannel on a rack on the bath is okay, but using a new flannel each time you wash solves the problem and is infinitely more hygienic. Keep a laundry basket in the bathroom ready to receive used flannels as well as towels and clothes changed at bath time.

Other tips to make the bathroom look neater and easier to clean include:

- Buy a soap dish with a drip tray: China looks prettier than plastic and you can simply stick it in the dishwasher periodically.

- Choose bath bubbles over oils for an easier-to-clean tub. Acrylic tubs are most prone to rings, so wipe them down after every bath.

- Lift out plastic slip mats to dry every day: They can mark the bath if left in permanently, because bathroom heat may stick them to the bath. Also, water gets trapped underneath and promotes the growth of germs and mould.

- Recharge your shaver in another room: You may have to buy a two-pin adaptor plug, but you avoid the unsightly look and cleaning inconvenience of a shaver dangling in front of the mirror.

- Hang towels on a towel-rail, not the side of the bath.

✔ Change towels and bath mats frequently – twice weekly if you can. Having two complete sets in different colours may jog your memory on changing. It also makes it easy to launder the whole lot at the same time, thereby avoiding leaving a mangy towel behind.

Fit a simple high shelf that children can't reach for the toilet cleaner and spare loo roll. If you've space, also stack extra towels and flannels here.

Always send children back to pick up the towel they left on the floor, or empty out the sink, or do anything else they forgot to do! One day, these will become automatic habits.

Pick up the free perfume samplers from beauty counters. They make great bathroom fresheners that smell a whole load classier than most room sprays. Perfume can stain, however, so dot it onto the extreme corner of a towel or spray it into the centre of the room with care, avoiding fabric curtains, wood, and anything else that can't handle an alcohol-based liquid.

Keep a box of disposable plastic gloves in the bathroom for any truly ghastly clean-ups. It's not over-the-top to wear a mask over your mouth and nose when you're clearing up after someone's been sick. This type of protection can help you face what has to be a thorough cleaning and disinfecting job. In addition, if you can't handle a smell, dab a little vapour rub under your nose to mask the smell.

Making the Bathroom Sparkle in a Hurry

Every bathroom has lots of surfaces to cover. But five minutes a day is easily enough time to get to them *all*. This point was proved to me during a family holiday at the beach. Five people, three of them sandy children, all used a bathroom without a cabinet. Yet – I timed this – the cleaner had it sweet and spotless in three minutes. Like a hotel cleaner, it's a routine that you need to do daily. The steps a bit further on tell you how.

You can keep everything you need in one side of a tool/cleaning caddy, so that the other side is free for any rubbish you need to take out of the bathroom. A rigid-plastic carrier with a central divider and carry handle is your best choice. Stock your caddy with

- ✔ **A fast-action bathroom mousse (foam spray):** You may have to decide between a fast-acting cleaner that has a strong smell or one that you have to leave on for five or ten minutes to work at its very best.

- ✔ **Flushable toilet wipes:** These are great for freshening the seat. Some brands keep surfaces hygienically clean for up to 12 hours.

- ✔ **Fresh cleaning cloths:** Old terry-cotton flannels (wash-cloths) are perfect. They don't scratch or leave lint and can be machine-washed afterwards.

- ✔ **Microfibre cloth:** For mirrors.

- ✔ **A small plastic rubbish bag:** To either take away rubbish or replace the existing bag.

- ✔ **Thick liquid toilet cleaner:** For the toilet, obviously.

- ✔ **Two pairs of rubber gloves:** Designate one pair strictly for cleaning the toilet.

After you assemble your cleaning materials, you're ready to go. Use these steps to get a brilliant bathroom:

1. **Clear soaps, flannels, nail brushes, and so on off the sink and bath ledge.**

   Popping them into the empty side of your cleaning caddy is quickest.

2. **Spray your chosen bathroom cleaner around the sink, onto taps, and at the base of the shower tray.**

   Every other day or so spray the bathtub as well.

   Some bathroom surfaces, particularly if they're old and worn, can't safely withstand multi-purpose bathroom sprays. Check the container to see whether the cleaner is safe for your surface. Some sprays can weaken enamel coating over time. When in doubt, use a special-ist cleaner or washing-up liquid for bath surfaces.

   Whilst the cleaner works to dissolve oil and dirt, move on to the toilet.

3. **Pull on the rubber gloves you use just for toilet cleaning.**

4. **Wipe the flush handle, then the lid and seat (both sides) with disposable wipes.**

   Flush the wipes away, if it's safe to do so. If not, pop them into the plastic bag, seal the bag, and put it in the rubbish bin.

5. **Visually check the toilet bowl.**

   If you see no hard deposits or limescale rings, simply use toilet cleaner, squirting it slowly around the rim.

   The "Tackling toilets" section later on gives specific advice about toilets.

6. **Brush any matter away with firm, even pressure as you move the scrub brush briskly back and forth.**

7. **Take off the gloves to remove any chance of contaminating washing areas.**

   If you have sensitive hands, pop on your second pair of gloves.

8. **Using flannels – and the showerhead where it reaches – rinse cleaner from the bath, sink, taps, and shower tray.**

9. **Pull out any hair from the sink and bath traps.**

10. **Shine the sink with a clean, dry flannel.**

11. **Pop the soap and other paraphernalia back onto counters and ledges.**

12. **Wipe smears off the mirror and glass shower doors with the microfibre cloth.**

13. **Check the floor as you back out of the room.**

    Deal with any splashes, dust or hair debris, and so on with the flannel you just used to shine the sink. Dampen it just a little to pick up dust more effectively. Once a week take more time to clean the bathroom floor thoroughly. I run through the attention that different floor surfaces need to stay looking good in Chapter 5.

On *really* busy days, skip the shower. For hygiene, your priority is disinfecting the toilet seat, handle, and bowl. Cosmetically, a clean sink comes after that, with niceties like changing the towels way down on the list.

If guests arrive and you have zero time to clean, change the towels if you do nothing else, and open a vent window so that the room gets aired.

Tackling toilets

Inside the toilet bowl is where the germs gather – in the water and under the seat. Sanitising the toilet is the number-one priority for any cleaning session.

Two words on blockages: panic not. Many times these turn out to be no big problem. Often the double effect of pouring half a bucket (5 litres [1 gallon] or so) of water directly into the bowl at the same time as flushing creates enough impetus to get things moving again.

If that doesn't work, try

- ✔ Stretching a wire coat hanger into a diagonal, then pushing the hook down the toilet to get at the blockage. If it's one specific bulky item that's caused the problem – a child who wanted to see a soft toy float, for example – you're likely to succeed.

- ✔ Using a plunger to cover the base of the bowl then pump the plunger. To get this to work, you have to be able to create a suction seal around the toilet exit. Unpleasantly, this may mean removing toilet tissue and so on first.

Everyday techniques

Apply cleaning solution, brush, then flush to rinse. That's really all it takes to get a clean toilet. Sometimes, however, you may need a few tricks up your sleeve (or down your rubber glove).

Persistence should get everything clean. If the brush bristles aren't doing the job on hard deposits, tie a soft rag onto the brush, then get rubbing.

Always choose a gel cleaner over a powder. Gel clings to the sides and foams when you're using the toilet brush, making it easier to scrub stubborn spots.

Cleaning chemicals can ruin toilet seats. Once the plastic has colour spots or the wood is bleached out, it's time to get a new seat. Next time lift the lid before you squirt liquid cleaner so that the seat doesn't get splashed on from below.

Some people want to apply cleaner directly so that it sits in a concentrated way over stains. This entails emptying the bowl of water. Look around the toilet to see if you can find a valve that shuts off the water going to the toilet. Shut this off then flush the toilet to empty the water. If your toilet doesn't have such a valve, try one of these methods:

- ✔ Lift up the cistern lid, and find the *ballcock*. This large, inflated ball controls how your tank refills with water after each flush. Flush the toilet and watch what it does if you're not sure. Then get some thick twine and tie down the ballcock so that the tank cannot refill with water.

- ✔ If your toilet doesn't respond to this, use a bucket to bail out the water from the pan. (For hygiene, tip the water down the outside drain, rather than using the basin.)

When you finish cleaning, disinfect the brush by rinsing it in bleach.

Limescale – the nasty brownish stuff that forms rings in your toilet bowl when you have hard, mineral-rich water – doesn't build up only in the bowl, The cistern (tank) may get clogged with this too. If you live in a hard-water area, fit an in-cistern cleaner/limescale remover.

Overnight solutions

The continual standing water causes the bowl to develop limescale rings around the base of the bowl and around the rim. How bad they get depends on how hard or soft your water is. Hard water promotes the worst problems, and unfortunately, that's six in ten homes in the UK.

Bleach simply whitens these marks. It takes a limescale remover to shift them. Many limescalers fizz, mostly because bubbles and a powder-blue colour make it look like hard work is being done. The fizzy ones aren't necessarily more effective, though. The action is in the strong acid of the cleaner, so choose what suits you best. Some people actually use denture tablets. They fizz in water. They shift the problem. I guess if you use dentures, you already have the tablets to hand, so why not give them a try.

But keeping things conventional, you can generally let your toilet deep clean itself whilst you sleep by popping in some descaler before you go to bed. Always make sure the product recommends overnight use. Cleaners that contain bleach can mark the glaze on the bowl and fade coloured toilets.

Stepping into a spotless shower

One rule – and this is for everyone – clean up as you go. It's the last thing anyone wants to do, of course, but if you can bear to give that wet and steamy glass door a spray with shower cleaner or even simply a quick run across with a squeegee, you can beat smears and remove oil before it sets.

If you do have dried-on grease and soap scum, clean glass doors with a solution of mild detergent – washing-up liquid is fine. Towel dry, or use a squeegee.

Clean shower trays with bathroom cleaner and wipe dry.

Throw dirty plastic shower curtains into the washing machine on hot, using your regular detergent. This removes grease, mould, and soap build-up. Throwing some towels into the same wash load can help agitate the stains off truly dirty curtains. Adding a cup of white vinegar to the fabric conditioner dispenser may offer some protection against the shower curtain getting quite so encrusted again with soap.

Going for the sparkle

Why settle for clean, when you can have sparkle! When you've a spare few minutes, focus on an individual task and you'll be rewarded with a bathroom that gleams. Choose from the following list of jobs that take minutes but bring hours of satisfaction:

- **Ceramic tiles:** Tiles need to be thoroughly dry to shine – not always easy in the dampest room in the house. Get into the habit of rubbing splash backs with a towel just before you send the towel to the laundry basket.

✔ **Grout:** Grouting needs harder work. Use an old tooth-brush (and keep this absolutely with your cleaning kit!) and brush bleach-and-water solution on grout to restore whiteness. Rinse to finish.

✔ **Mirror:** Rubbing in a dash of washing-up liquid on a smooth cloth prevents mirrors from misting up so easily. Alternatively, steal a screen (window) wipe from your car.

✔ **Showerhead:** Unscrew from the shower and scrub with an old nailbrush. For stubborn hard-water scale, use a descaler per packet instructions.

Be sneaky and do two descaling jobs at once. Pop the showerhead into your kettle and descale both with one lot of solution.

✔ **Taps:**

• **Standard tap:** Line the sink with a plastic bag to catch drips, then wrap a paper towel soaked in liquid descaler around the tap edge and leave as long as instructions suggest. For a natural approach, half a lemon squashed up against the tap can loosen scale. Again, protect the basin.

• **Gold-plated tap:** Polish with a soft microfibre cloth. If recommended by manufacturers, use metal polish to ease away scratches. Thoroughly dry to avoid smears.

Treating and Beating Condensation

The drip-drip of water down the bathroom wall – that *condensation* is caused when hot steam hits cold walls. You've probably noticed that condensation is worst on outside walls and around the metal frames of single-glazed windows. It also happens most in bathrooms where poor ventilation means it takes ages for the room to dry after someone's showered or enjoyed a hot bath.

Now steam on the walls by itself isn't a big problem – providing that the walls are covered in water-repellent bathroom paint and that you can dry them sharpish by opening the windows or turning up the bathroom radiator. However, if condensation happens often enough and for long enough, the damp in the walls provides the perfect breeding ground for bacterial mould.

Mould (also called mildew) is actually a fungus. Especially if you have vinyl wallpaper or ordinary emulsion paint, it can burrow below the surface. Unless you have x-ray vision, you won't be able to see this undercover mould, so you have to make a judgement. If you've had mould for some time, or if the mould is in clumps rather than small dots, you can guess it's below the surface.

To get rid of mould, first kill it with a brush-on solution containing biocide, which you can get from DIY (hardware) stores. Next, repaint the walls using a fungicide paint recommended for bathrooms. Give the ceiling a coating of specialist paint, too.

To prevent mould:

- ✔ Cut humidity in the bathroom by running cold water into the bath before turning on the hot water. (This is safer, too, as you won't accidentally burn your skin.)

- ✔ Fit a thermostat to the bath and shower to control maximum temperature at the taps.

- ✔ Open the windows after you shower.

- ✔ When it gets misty, whip the towels off the heated rail to bring more drying heat into the room.

- ✔ Wipe down damp walls with old towels.

- ✔ Repaint walls and ceiling with specialist, low-moisture bathroom paint.

Chapter 8

Polishing Furniture and Furnishings

Dealing with furniture is where cleaning gets serious. If you choose the wrong way to deal with a particular piece of furniture you may ruin it, costing yourself big money!

Fortunately for you, this chapter is full of ways to clean your furniture safely and efficiently.

Basics for Burnishing Your Furnishings

Surprisingly, water is frequently your furniture's enemy number one. Plain, simple, straight-from-the-tap water is a prime cleaning solution ingredient, but too much of it can ruin upholstery and permanently stain wood furniture.

There is no set frequency for deep cleaning furniture or upholstery. In fact, less is better. Whilst deep cleaning removes grime and grease, it also subjects your furniture to extra wear and tear. Getting furniture too clean too often shortens the time it stays smart. In particular, stop to think before you clean something that's new to your home or something that's very old. It's a fact that years of accumulated dirt and dust can hold together fabric. Remove the soil and curtains – somehow, it always seems to be curtains – literally fall apart.

Keep the care instructions that come with sofas, flat-pack furniture, mattresses, and so on. Many of us hang onto the leaflets that come with electrical appliances but chuck everything else. The reality is that there's precious little you can do for a tumble dryer if it breaks, except call in the repair person, but you'll regularly want to refer to instructions on how to safely clean your sofa.

Whenever you think about cleaning a major item in your home, get the duster out first. This may be all it needs. When dry dusting isn't enough, move onto damp dusting. To add the least water possible, simply spray water onto your cloth. The trigger bottle you use to mist houseplant leaves is perfect.

In many cases, you may want to follow up on your basic dusting with the appropriate vacuum-cleaner tool. For fabric and hard, flat surfaces, vacuuming always beats dusting in effectiveness. With sofas and curtains, slip on the upholstery tool; use the crevice tool for wood and metal shelving.

Only if dusting or vacuuming doesn't shift ingrained dirt, or reveals a stain problem, do you move on to any other type of cleaning.

The big aim of cleaning is to take on the everyday light cleaning – all that dusting and vacuuming – more regularly so that you can keep the heavy cleans, which wear your furniture out as much as they do you, to a minimum. A few tips can make cleaning specific items easier:

   ✔ Carry a tray with handles when you clean desks, tables, and shelves. With somewhere safe to store things, it takes only a moment to empty that table-top and so give it a really good clean. Dusting around is never the same!

   ✔ Sticky fingerprints cluster on the sides of dining chairs and the edges of tables. Rub them away with a dampened microfibre cloth or soapy suds on a sponge.

> ✔ Have a favourite piece that you're really fussy about keeping clean? Get close and look at the surface from an angle rather than straight on and you'll spot any marks you've missed.

Caring for Upholstered Chairs and Sofas

If you want to keep your sofa looking smart for longer, wash your hair more often. In previous generations, oil – and in particular men's hair oil – meant the backs of chairs quickly became soiled and grimy. Even those linen or crocheted antimacassars designed to protect the backs of upholstered chairs only delay rather than prevent grease stains. Today, frequent hair washing and resisting leaning back in your seat if you are wearing hair gel or wax styling products minimises the problem.

However, sofas and chairs face a new danger – in food. All those TV dinners and snack foods are bad news for easy chairs and couches. The more you eat in front of the TV, the greater your risk of causing a big-time stain. Along with the convenience of TV dinners comes the usefulness of TV trays that sit on your lap as you eat. Use tables and napkins to help protect your furniture.

I examine general upholstery care in this section. For how to shift food stains, from chocolate to curry and other top culprits, see Chapter 19.

Washing washable fabrics

Technically, you can only really wash sofas that have loose covers. If you can unzip the seat cushions but nothing else – you can't remove the piece that goes over the back and arms – then you have a fixed-covers sofa that isn't strictly washable. The zips on the cushions are there simply so you can replace a seat cover when it gets worn.

However, I think these zip-on covers present a cleaning opportunity that's too good to waste. On both cotton and damask sofas I've always adopted a now-and-again approach to machine-washing the cushion covers, without any problems. But, if you want to follow my lead, you probably don't have any washing guidelines for your cushions, so you will have to determine for yourself whether the material is colourfast, and non-shrinking, and so on, and wash them at your own risk.

To stack the odds in your favour, wet a small, hidden area of the fabric (the underside of a cushion is ideal), then blot it with a white paper towel. There should be no colour transfer. To investigate for shrinkage, inspect your test patch when it dries to see whether it still lies totally flat. Any buckling indicates that the material may shrink in water. Sadly, the potential for sofa fabric to shrink is huge. Most, but not all, loose covers are pre-washed (and many say so on the care label). If they aren't, however, shrinkage can be substantial. Unless covers are roomy, you may want to consider dry cleaning covers that aren't pre-washed, if the care labels allows this.

Be aware that repeated washing of just the cushions may make them paler than the rest of the sofa. On the other hand, *not* washing your sofa at all generally leads to the seats becoming darker, as they attract the most grime. The best solution is to wash the cushion covers just often enough to keep them from looking grimy but not often enough to make them noticeably different from the back and arms.

For those couch covers that you do wash, follow the care instructions as to machine or hand washing. If you're washing coverings on your own initiative, use a low-temperature setting or hand wash. Partially dry them on the clothes line or in the dryer on low heat, but don't allow them to dry completely. Instead, put covers back onto the sofa when they're still slightly damp. This way, if you need to stretch them back to fit, you can do so easily. If you absolutely have to iron them, do so after they're back on the couch with the iron on the cool setting.

If you have a washable couch with fixed covers, use a water-extraction carpet cleaner (see Chapter 5 for information on hiring and using these machines) or spot clean stains as needed.

It is vital not to get sofas or chairs too wet. Fabrics such as cotton and linen are washable, yes, but they're often stretched across a wood or a wood-chip frame. If water seeps down below the surface of the fabric, mould may form deep inside the sofa because it never gets the chance to dry out. To prevent the fabric from getting too wet, concentrate on getting the cleaning solution, rather than the water, into it. Mix up upholstery shampoo as instructed on the package, then use only the foam to clean. Scoop up the bubbles and work these into the fabric with a soft brush. Rinse by using a slightly damp towel. Then take off the excess moisture by blotting dry towels over the sofa. Finally, turn up the temperature in the room to aid drying.

Calling in the professionals

Typically, velvet, velour, and brocade need to be professionally cleaned. You may see the letter *S* on the care label, which means *solvents only*, or, in other words: *no water.*

Take loose covers to the dry cleaners. Get fixed upholstery professionally cleaned in your home. (You may want to schedule this at the same time you do the carpets and curtains.)

Professionally cleaning items, even when they are washable, may be a smart move. Cotton chintz, for example, may lose its silky glaze in wet washing.

For everyday spot cleaning, buy a can of upholstery cleaner suitable for dry-cleanable fabrics. If you still feel unsure, spray the cleaner onto a cloth, then use the cloth to blot the upholstery.

Make furnishings last longer by closing the curtains in daytime to block out the sun. Sunlight, by fading fabrics, causes far more permanent damage than everyday soil and stains. If you don't want to close the curtains, place your furniture either directly in, or totally out of, the sun. Half-and-half bleaching looks the worst. If you can, regularly swap chairs around the room, so that you don't get left with one darker – or lighter – chair than the others.

Laving leather

Caring for leather is relatively easy: Just dust, then wipe with a soft damp cloth. Every year – or more frequently if the chair or sofa is in a room that is heavily heated – reverse the drying effects of heat by feeding your leather furniture with *hide food* or *leather furniture cream*, a specialist oil-based cream sold in furniture and department stores.

The use of hide food can darken pale leathers. To clean cream or white leather always choose a product specifically manufactured for such leathers.

With cream on your cloth, rub the food into the furniture, then wipe away excess with a fresh, clean cloth. Buff to a shine. Failure to rub off the excess makes your furniture look dull, and stains the clothes of anyone who sits on the leather! If you've the patience to split the job into two parts, you get maximum benefit if you apply the hide food at bedtime, then buff off the next morning.

As a fast alternative, you can now buy leather-cream impregnated wipes. Regardless of one-wipe-and-go instructions, always follow up by wiping again with a fresh clean cloth.

Handling Hard Furniture

It may be strong enough to hold a thousand books, but that wood bookcase is delicate too. And there's the rub of dealing with the hard furniture in your home. Some items can withstand a wash down in dilute bleach whilst others crumble under a drop of water. You can't go wrong with dry dusting. But why bother? If you've a large expanse to cover, getting out the vacuum attachments is quicker and more effective. Engrained dirt may need more effort than that, however, so here I look at how to tackle the variety of hard furniture surfaces in your home.

Cleaning cane and wicker

Blowing the cobwebs away is the best approach to cane and wicker. The weave of wicker is big on attracting dust and vacuuming with the nozzle attachment is the way to remove it. Overturn chairs and sofas to vacuum both sides. Use a hairdryer on cool to blow out any dust you can't get at with the vacuum nozzle.

Fitted versus free-standing furniture

Ask any cleaner, fitted furniture wins a popularity contest hands down every time.

In the bedroom, a floor-to-ceiling wardrobe means a whole load less surfaces to attract dust. Be sure to keep up the good work by keeping the doors closed so that clothes and shoes are protected from dust, also. In the kitchen, some people believe that free-standing units have their place, because you can pull them out to clean behind them. However, this opinion ignores the fact that no dirt can get behind correctly fitted furniture in the first place.

The main danger of fitted furniture occurs when it is poorly fitted or if it is attached to a wall that is not dry. Mould (which appears as black patches) may grow on a wet wall and will need to be treated – see the Appendix for advice on how – and sadly the fitting will also need to be taken down so that the fungus can be eliminated from the wall.

For persistent grime, use a nailbrush or old toothbrush dipped in the foamy suds from a bowl of washing-up liquid and scrub gently. Rinse with a damp cloth then dry with a separate cloth. Alternatively, a solution of soda crystals – 1 cup to 1 litre (1 quart) of water – loosens dirt and shifts grease with the added bonus of leaving a residue that hardens cane and wicker. This is good news if your cane seat has started to sag. In one job, you can clean and tighten the frame. Rinse using a fresh cloth and carefully rub dry, if you're not in a well-heated room.

Polishing metal

First, you need to determine whether what looks like metal really is metal. Sometimes plastic is given a metal-effect coating and sometimes metal is coated with an acrylic varnish. In either of these cases, you wash to suit the top coating. An acrylic varnish can take heavy-duty scrubbing and wet washing as needed, though a metal-effect finish requires more delicacy. Clean a metal finish with a mild solution of washing-up liquid, taking care not to saturate any joins or seams. Your furniture may be chipboard underneath the finish and may warp if saturated with water.

With true metals, the two risks are rust and scratches. If spoiling a smooth surface is the key issue, wipe with a sponge dipped in the foam from a solution of washing-up liquid and water. Think how carefully you clean a car, and aim to do the same. To remove rust, which typically accumulates on cast iron, use a stiff wire-brush. Be aware that you may leave scratch marks if there is grit on your brush or on the metal surface.

Be scrupulous about drying metal. Unsealed metal plus prolonged water equals rust.

Working on wood and wood-effect items

Check the finish before you start cleaning wood. Wood furniture is made from everything from the finest teak and mahogany to inexpensive chipboard. But, no matter what the actual wood is, when it comes to cleaning, all you care about is the finish because that's what you have to clean.

Mats and coasters are not old hat. Using them significantly prolongs the life of wood tables and dressers. For the ultimate protection of wood surfaces, go glass topped. Be sure to prevent scratching by putting white felt pads between the wood and the glass. Always avoid coloured felt, as the colour can come off onto your wood.

Sunlight fades more than fabric. If you have knick-knacks displayed on a table that gets direct sun, move the ornaments around to keep the colour crisp on both the ornament and the table.

Finding out the finish

The sideboard may be solid wood with an acrylic varnish on top. Conversely, that inexpensive table may well be chipboard with a synthetic veneer. The easiest way to find out which is to compare your item with others in the house whose composition you do know. Solid wood is significantly heavier than chipboard. You may also see the irregular, natural grain of real wood. And, if the item is old, it is likely to have a dent or two. The grain in manufactured chipboard is fairly uniform. There may be scratching, but dents are unlikely. At the corners, the veneer could be wearing thin, and you may glimpse the white, untreated chipboard.

If you determine that a piece of furniture is solid wood, but you're not sure whether it has a wax or polish coating, do a quick test. Apply a drop of white spirit (turpentine) to a white cloth and rub a hidden spot of the piece of furniture. If you get marks on your cloth, the wood is covered with oil or wax. If the cloth stays clean and the wood shiny, then it's protected with a varnish.

Aside from bare softwood, the most delicate wood is that which has been simply waxed or oiled. Popular examples are thick pine kitchen tables, antique furniture, and designer items.

Practically all mass-produced modern wood furniture is treated with a wood stain and given a varnish to protect the wood.

Though you probably want to paint or stain bare wood, keep in mind that wood that is simply stained is as vulnerable to damage as untreated wood. It may splinter if you rub it against the grain, and it's likely to swell if it gets soaked. The only difference between wood that's stained and untreated wood is that a dark or bright stain hides more marks. You need to varnish wood to really protect it.

Cleaning the finish

For everyday wood care follow these tips:

- ✔ Dust in the direction of the grain. Years of doing this help hold onto distinctive patterns in the wood.

- ✔ Any soft cloth will do, but clever cloths made from micro-fibres scoop up and hang onto dust so that you don't merely shift it somewhere else.

- ✔ Go easy on the spray polish. Over time, polish residue dulls wood. Many people reach for the spray can simply because they love that just-polished smell. If that's you, get an air freshener and give your wood a break.

For specific problems, such as watermarks, turn to Chapter 21.

Table 8-1 gives you advice on cleaning various wood, and wood-effect, furniture.

Table 8-1	Cleaning Methods for Wood Furniture
Type of Finish	*Method*
Paint	Neat washing-up liquid is an effective grease and stain shifter on this hard-wearing surface.
Stain	Damp dust only, if possible. Otherwise treat as unsealed wood.
Unsealed	Wash down with water or a soapy washing-up liquid solution, applied from a cloth, not directly on the wood. Rinse and dry promptly. Do not leave wet.
Varnish	Damp dust and avoid over-wetting precious items. Treat tough spots with a solution of diluted washing-up liquid. Polish with a chamois leather cloth or spray polish, applied on a cloth.
Veneer	Clean with care. The fine top layer of wood may or may not be varnished and a thin varnish can easily bubble up in water. If unsealed, damp dust only. If covered with a hard-wearing synthetic coating, wash sparingly with a sponge dipped in soapy washing-up liquid. Rinse and dry.
Wax	Detergent dulls the wax, so use soapflakes instead. Buy a ready-mixed soapy wood cleaner to make this easy. Make up the solution and dip your cloth into it. Don't get the table overly wet. Dry with a soft cloth.

Use beeswax polish only on wood that hasn't been lacquered. The lacquer prevents the wax from penetrating, so why waste your time simply smoothing it on the top?

Varnished or lacquered wood is able to withstand mild cleaning products provided that you use minimal water. Take care not to soak the wood or, worse, let a wet cleaning solution gather on the surface.

Very dilute white vinegar removes surface stickiness on antique furniture. Add a few drops of vinegar to a cup of water, then dip your cloth into the solution and wring it out.

If you want to improve air quality, the dusty places that you can't see are as important as those that you can. Fresh, dust-free air in bedrooms means a better sleep and an end to morning sneezing. So use a step-stool and a duster on a pole to dust the tops of wardrobes and other tall dust-catchers. Or why not cheat if your wardrobes have a top pelmet (valance)? Simply drop sheets of newspaper onto the top of your wardrobes and every so often carefully lift off the papers and drop them and the dust that's with them into the rubbish. You'll need to do this with care, however, otherwise you'll set off a dust storm. So take a large tray with you and stand on a step-stool in front of the wardrobe. Lay a clean sheet of newspaper on top of the dusty one. Fold the edges of both papers into the centre – and drop the lot onto your tray, ready to parcel up with the rubbish.

Keeping Lights Shining

Stop paying for electricity you don't benefit from! Dust on lamps and lampshades – as well as on light bulbs – seriously dims your rooms. The heat from the bulb draws dust to the shade and only periodic cleaning – every other month is good – gets it off.

Don't forget to clean the light bulbs themselves, which get dustier than the shades. Wipe over them with a microfibre cloth.

Take lampshades off before cleaning them so that you can get at both sides. Vacuum robust fabric and plastic lampshades with the crevice attachment. For delicate shades made of paper, use the brush tool.

When vacuuming isn't enough, take fabric lampshades to the bathroom. Stand them on a plastic mat in the bathtub and clean them very gently using a sponge dipped in a solution of washing-up liquid. Rinse with a damp sponge and dry them with a hairdryer on the lowest setting if necessary. Only put back shades that you are certain are totally dry.

Never wet paper shades. If dusting won't do, consider replacing.

If you have wall- or ceiling-lights with glass fitments, consider buying a proprietary spray that lets you clean them *in situ*. Taking down glass fittings can be a big task, so save this for every six months or so at a time when you're not rushed. Always turn off electricity. The skill is remembering how to hang it all together again afterwards.

Chandeliers can be deceptively heavy, so consider making this a two-person job. Lay thick material on the floor, under the light. Carefully undo your fittings and lay them on the fabric. Wipe over every surface with a microfibre cloth, or a slightly damp linen cloth. Refit with care.

Turning to Bedding

Dust – and horribly enough the dust mites that are its chief component – is the main reason to clean beds regularly.

You cannot eliminate the microscopic creatures that are dust mites however fastidious you are about cleaning. They thrive inside both mattresses and pillows, feeding on the tiny particles of skin you shed each night. However, you can trap them inside the mattress and pillow by using an anti-allergy mattress and pillow protectors. Sold principally for asthmatics and those with dust allergies, these protectors are made from an exceptionally close-knit synthetic fabric that keeps mites and their debris inside the bed. Unlike vinyl, the fabric is breathable, so you don't feel you're lying on a plastic cover. In fact, the only difference you may spot between these and conventional covers is the initial cost. You may pay up to four times the price of standard pillowslips and mattress covers. Having one, however, doesn't lessen how often you need to clean the bed underneath.

I talk about cleaning the various parts of a bed in the following sections, but all beds have a few things in common, so first, look to the basics:

- **Metal frames:** Dust, then check for rust spots. Brush away any you see with a stiff wire-brush and paint with sealant to prevent it reappearing.

- **Wood slats:** Dust, periodically checking that screws are tight.

✔ **Divans:** Brush away fluff, then vacuum using the upholstery tool. Do not wash the fabric! It is hugely difficult to dry, and you risk damaging what, in the cheapest beds, may be a cardboard casing set on a wood frame.

Messing with mattresses

When you change the sheets, air the mattress. Doing so takes away any stale odours that have collected in the mattress, meaning a fresher night's sleep for you. Open the bedroom windows to let in as much air as possible. Even in winter, 30 minutes with the vent windows open and the bedroom door closed won't chill out your home. Make it a habit to take off the sheets and go do something else before you come back to replace the bedding. It doesn't have to be a cleaning thing, of course. Slipping off to shower and eat breakfast is ideal. For the ultimate in airing, each summer carry your mattress into the garden to let it sit in hot, dry sunlight for an afternoon.

Once a month, when you're changing sheets, strip off the sheets, vacuum your mattress, then turn it over so that the head now sits at the foot and the underside becomes the top side. Turning your mattress helps it wear evenly. New mattresses need to be turned weekly for the first two to three months, and monthly after that break-in period. After turning the mattress, vacuum the new top side. You'll sleep much fresher for it.

Don't flip new-style mattresses that have a comfort-top of padding above the springs.

Using a removable mattress cover helps keep your mattress clean for longer, even if it does mean one more piece of laundry. However, if you choose not to have one, and especially if you take breakfast or late-night beverages in bed, food and drink accidents may happen. Additionally, mattresses can take a hammering from a variety of bodily fluids that seep through sheets. I deal fully with cleaning stains from mattresses in Chapter 20 and address specific stains in the Appendix.

Fussing with futons

Turn futons weekly to preserve the evenness of the filling. Read the care label for cleaning instructions. Only polyester futons can be safely washed – and you'll need a very large machine. Cotton-filled futons need dry cleaning.

Plumping up pillows

You want to rest your head someplace clean and cosy. So unless you adopt a yearly throw-away-and-replace approach, cleaning pillows is a must. Your feather pillow tells you when you're overdue for laundering – disgustingly enough, it get heavier due to all the dust mite droppings inside! Prevent that unpleasant thought by washing your pillow every 6 to 12 months.

Washing pillows can mean a surprising amount of hassle. So give yourself longer between washes by using a pillow protector. You don't have to spend money, just use an old pillowcase under the top one.

Table 8-2 goes through the various types of pillows and how to clean them.

Table 8-2	Methods for Cleaning Pillows	
Material	*Cleaning*	*Special tips*
Foam	Sponge with soapy water. Don't immerse.	Don't squeeze out. Dry slowly indoors or out of direct sun outdoors.
Feather	Machine wash one at a time (because they're so heavy when wet).	Peg on an outdoor line to dry. Be patient. Even with regular shakes, drying may take three days! Find a warm undisturbed drying place: Use an airing cupboard if you have one, otherwise leave it on a towel on the floor in front of a radiator. Make sure it's completely dry before you sleep on it.
Polyester and hollow fibre	Machine wash on delicate cycle; tumble dry.	Shake and stretch back into shape before drying to avoid lumps.

Regularly air feather pillows outside on dry days.

When you simply can't wait for a feather pillow to line-dry, you may be driven to use the dryer. Do so at your own risk. A wet pillow may be too heavy a load for your particular dryer's drum. Putting a child's machine-washable trainer (sneaker) into the drum at the same time helps balance the load.

Snuggling up to duvets and eiderdowns

Few beds these days boast plain old blankets. Chances are you snuggle down under a *duvet (comforter)*, a cotton envelope filled with feathers or synthetic fibres. And maybe you also have an *eiderdown*, an often patchwork cover that sits on the top to look good and, if you're desperate, add extra warmth.

Most synthetic-filled duvets can be machine washed. But the sheer weight and size of a bed-sized cover filled with feathers or synthetic material turns duvet washing into a bit of a trial. A single may easily fit the washing machine tub, but you may need to use an extra capacity launderette machine to wash a king-size duvet. Tumble dry on low heat, removing now and again to shake the filling.

Feather and down duvets are best professionally cleaned. Their weight when wet makes cleaning them with water impractical and air drying them, which is the safest drying method, can take a week or longer.

However, if spills, sickness, or children's wetting means you have to do something, it's perfectly possible to launder a feather duvet in the machine (if it fits) or the bath (if it doesn't). Gently scrape off soil and spot treat stains first. For example, rinse through blood stains with cold water. (See the Appendix for relevant stain instructions.)

You save a great deal of drying hassle if you soak just the stained sections of the duvet. Use a mild detergent solution (it needs to be mild for the sake of your acrylic bathtub – the duvet itself can withstand most detergents). Rinse, adding a few drops of disinfectant if you're clearing up after vomit.

Bathtubs aren't designed for prolonged exposure to detergent. If you're worried how your bath may react to a duvet-washing session, use an absolutely safe solution such as bubble bath or washing-up liquid. However, if you use either of these, you need to rinse the duvet three or four times afterwards.

To dry, ideally use the clothes line outside. In winter, spread the duvet out in front of (but not touching) radiators, then finish in the airing-cupboard or somewhere else warm and dry.

Eiderdowns need only occasional washing, especially if you use them as intended – as pretty day-time covers for your bed that get removed at night. Their size means the two options are either professional cleaning or washing in the bath, if the fabric is washable.

If you're prepared to use a sunny day this way, a children's paddling pool makes an ideal washtub for duvets and eiderdowns. Start early (you'll need maximum outdoor drying time). Instead of the outdoor tap, connect the hose to downstairs sink-taps to fill your pool with warm water and add non-bio detergent. Get the whole lot done at once and add extra cleaning power by walking around the pool and all over your soapy washing with bare (clean!) feet. Imagine you're at the vineyard, crushing the grapes, as you agitate the dirt away. Remember to use fresh water to rinse. To finish, squeeze out excess water by rolling up each duvet as tightly as possible without wringing, then peg onto the line.

Part III

Keeping Up Appearances Outside

"You'd be surprised how much a fresh coat of polish and some new laces increase the resale value."

In This Part . . .

Step outside your home and the line between cleaning and maintenance becomes very thin. If you don't clean indoors . . . well, you have to endure a dirty home. But fail to clear away dirt and debris that attaches to the outside of your home, and over time you risk suffering damage that can be costly and inconvenient to put right. I'm talking of the guttering that gives up under the load of two years of leaves and causes wood windowsills to rot due to water damage. How about the neglected front door that sticks and warps until one rainy day it doesn't open at all? Through chapters on how to care for external walls, windows, and doors, you can put into place simple care routines to keep everything running smoothly.

Garden paths, decking, and patios get the once-over as well. As well as how to clean for everything that surrounds your home, discover how to make the outdoor items you cherish withstand all the wind, rain, and sun Mother Nature throws at them. Finally – cleaning gets wheels. Only you know whether keeping the family bicycles and cars gleaming is a chore or a labour of love, so there are sections that show two levels of cleaning. So whether you're going for showroom perfect or just perfectly acceptable, you find clever tricks to get maximum results from the time you spend.

Chapter 9

Washing Up Outside

● ●

In This Chapter

▶ Washing outside walls

▶ Cleaning paint

▶ Shining doors and door knockers

▶ Getting gunk out of your gutters and drains

● ●

Spring is traditionally the time people look to cleaning up the outside of their home – it must be all those long Bank Holiday weekends. Yet it's autumn when your home truly needs its hatches battened down, preferably under a fresh coat of weather-protective paint.

From August, give the outside of your home a thorough visual check and decide whether you're going to do any major work before the cold sets in. You want to wash walls and apply paint or varnish in good weather. So it makes sense to get the equipment in early, then when the sunshine and the right frame of mind combine, you can get going. Some jobs, however, such as clearing the guttering, have to be done in the autumn.

If that never happens, seize the opportunity in spring. This is also the time to do jobs that will irritate you like crazy if they're not done. I'm thinking dirty white UPVC window frames, vinyl siding, patio furniture, and panelling that you have to look at all summer whilst you chill out on the patio.

Cleaning Winter Dirt Away

After the snow finally melts away, the wind and rain come to an end, and you see the sun for more than a minute at a time, your homeowner's heart turns to cleaning up your home's exterior. What's that? You say that's *not* your first springtime desire? Ah well, when you do get around to washing up outside, you can use the hints in this section to tell you how.

If you haven't the energy to cover all four sides of your house, give priority to those that face south and west. These receive the most sun and therefore weather most quickly. An exception to this is if you live by the sea. As you'd expect, the side of your house that faces the coast gets dirtiest, with salt deposits speeding up damage.

Pay special attention to any horizontal areas including decorative trims on windows and doors and porch roofs.

Pressuring dirt away from stone

Professionals use high-pressure water jets to wash dirty exteriors. But it's highly unlikely you want – or need – to spend the 48 hours plus it takes to have a pronounced effect. Using a pressure-washer attached to your garden hose is a quicker way to clean up smaller areas on any material that isn't prone to chipping under pressure. Stone, brick, and even concrete fascias are good candidates for the high-pressure treatment.

Pressure-washers look a little like cylinder vacuum cleaners, but of course instead of sucking up dirt, water comes out the hose. Before you buy, look for the figure that tells you how much pressure the water can get put under. Go for the highest possible – and get a machine on wheels – water is heavy! You can get pressure-washers from catalogue shops and DIY (hardware) stores. If it's giant power you need, you may prefer to go to the hire shop for an industrial model.

Don't use high pressure on pebbledash or other textured effects. These walls are best left as they are until it's time to redo the coating. Rendered (plastered) or painted walls can also be adversely affected by pressure-washers. New render can flake and old painted walls may chip and flake too. So test a small area before blasting with the pressure-washer.

Before you turn on the water, use a stiff brush to remove loose dirt from the wall. If you're just going to brush then power wash, use an extension pole to brush areas that you can't reach. It's easy to make a temporary one yourself. Simply tape your brush to a broomstick with strong tape (from the DIY store or use duct tape).

You may notice white deposits, most often seen on new-build brick and some stone walls in the first couple of years, especially as the walls dry out after heavy rain. These are mineral deposits that get drawn out to the wall's surface. Resist the temptation to wash them away – you'll simply bring more mineral salts to the surface. Instead, use a stiff wire-brush to sweep the walls clean.

Pressure-washing calls for surprising precision. You have to hold on tight to your hose otherwise it can get away from you! Your results are directly related to the time each spot of wall gets hit by the water. So moving steadily across, as slowly as you can, is a good way to get even coverage. As you'd expect, you may get splashed, so wear waterproofs or be prepared to change. Eye protection is important too. Go for swimming goggles if you don't have protective eye covering. As you pressure-wash, start at the top, then work on down.

Take care to keep the nozzle moving. Aim it too long on one spot and the power of the water could bore a small hole in your wall. You'll also want to steer clear of the windows and windowsills and any other parts of your wall you know to be delicate, such as a wood steps.

Pressure-washers come with extensions that make high places easy to get at. If you're going to go one step further and use a cleaning solution to tackle stains on your walls, you'll probably need to get out the ladder. I deal fully with ladder safety in Chapter 10.

You can clean seriously discoloured stone and brick with an acid-based wall cleaner obtainable at any DIY (hardware) store. Be sure to wear gloves and goggles and follow instructions with care. If there is mould growth, wash it down with a bleach solution – 1 part bleach to 4 parts water.

If the problem is contained to a few areas, try simply rubbing it away. Rub a dirty brick with a dry brick of the same shade to transfer its colour onto the brick on the wall. You can also use the same technique with stone: With stone, you need water to get colour transfer, so always keep your stone block wet.

Using bleach or a stain treatment on just one section of wall can quickly become a very big job because the change in colour means you then need to do the entire wall on that side.

Whenever you use chemicals, be sure to follow up with sustained rinsing – at least two minutes for every area. Walls are porous and may absorb cleaner beneath the surface so you have to make sure that the rinsing afterwards goes deep enough. Failing to totally rinse away chemicals leaves your wall vulnerable to attack by the acid or alkaline residue left from your cleaner.

Removing dirt from exterior wood and siding

Some parts of your home may have exterior walls that are neither brick nor stone. However, all exterior surfaces can take water – they wouldn't last long with the rain otherwise! So it's fine to get going with the pressure-washing described in the previous section. However, you need to add detergent to clean UPVC and aluminium surfaces. Look for a pressure-washer that has a compartment for cleaning solutions.

After washing a wooden wall – and when both the weather and the wall are totally dry – consider giving the wall an extra coat of protective varnish. Choose either ordinary wood protector or one with a stain if you want to go darker or different.

It is my belief that cleaning roofing is best left to experts and only started if there's a serious problem requiring maintenance. An exception is any low flat, ground-floor roofing. Mould growth here can substantially shorten the life of your shingle or asphalt surface. So climb up the ladder, observing the safety rules detailed in Chapter 10, and brush it off with a stiff, dry brush.

Washing Paint

Accept that cleaning painted windows and door trims is a slow task and you'll do a worthwhile job. Choose to do this job in the autumn so that you can take care of any problems you uncover before harsh winter weather does even more damage.

First, use old rags to take away the worst of the dirt. Feel free to rub vigorously, even if doing so causes the paint to bubble – quite likely with older paintwork. The winter weather does the same thing; you're just getting in first.

After the surface dirt is wiped away, wash the paint using a large sponge and an all-purpose liquid cleaner that doesn't need rinsing. Sugar soap is an expensive but effective choice.

Dry with clean cloths, and make a decision about which areas need paint. Certainly now's the time to do that because any area that needs repainting to protect the wood underneath from bad weather is now clean and ready. Simply rub down the to-be-painted patches with sandpaper, and you're ready to open up that can of waterproof exterior paint.

Working On Doors

Your door furniture – the knobs, knockers, and all – is real first-impression stuff, and making it count takes all of 15 minutes every month.

First, dust the door, reaching into the corners of grooves. Next, get to the grimiest bits – the doorbell, knocker, and the area surrounding the key. Use a quality, slightly damp cloth (for best results, choose a microfibre one) to rub away finger marks.

Apply cream metal polish or brass cleaner to the knob, knocker, and any other metal bits, and buff them to a shine with a clean cloth. Finally, whilst you're there with cloth and spray, give the once-over to any exterior utility boxes (meters). As ever in cleaning, it's going that extra metre (or in this case, meter!) that shows you care.

If your key has begun to stick in the lock, now's the time to fix that problem. Using the extension straw on a light lubricant such as WD-40, spray a few drops into the lock. Shield the door surface around the lock with a cloth as you turn the key both ways to remove any excess lubricant.

An annual clean with water and a mild liquid detergent is good enough for most doors, including those wood doors that have been stained or painted. Be sure to rinse off the solution, then dry thoroughly.

As you clean, and again six months later, make a point to check the condition of your wood door. Look for areas where the colour has started to patch or has lost its sheen. Then, once every three years or so, prepare to be so disappointed during this check-up that you decide to paint or re-stain.

Before you paint or re-stain, scrupulously prepare the door. Use a fungicidal wash to strip off any algae (most likely on north-facing stained doors) and at the same time see off dirt, too. Rinse and dry the door, then very gently sand any areas where the weather has worn away the previous layer of paint or stain. Rub the entire door with a nylon abrasive pad, then get painting. Take care to get the colour right: whilst it's impossible to lighten with stain, it's very easy to go too dark.

Clearing Out Gutters

In October, or whenever trees near your gutters are shedding their leaves in earnest, get out the ladder and clean the guttering. Before that, though, pay attention to water flow when it rains. Go outside and look for leaks and blockages in your guttering.

When you do the actual cleaning, use ladders carefully. See Chapter 10 for advice.

Use a garden trowel to scoop out the decaying leaves and wet muck that almost certainly is lining the gutters. Don't take a rubbish bag up with you to put the decaying leaves into. If you're using a ladder, or standing on a step, adding extra bags is a sure way to increase your risk of over-balancing. Instead, simply stand a wheelbarrow near your ladder and toss the muck into it. It's all ready then to wheel down to your garden compost bin. Finish off by flushing the pipes clean by using a hose with a spray nozzle.

Opening Drains

Your drains can become blocked with debris anytime of year and it is well worth walking round your home every month just to check that none of the drain covers has become clogged with leaves or rubbish. If they have, simply scoop all matter out, then follow with around 100ml of neat bleach down the drain.

Chapter 10

Making Windows Sparkle

*I*t's official: Window cleaning is the most hated household chore according to research by glass manufacturer Pilkington. So much so that one in five people surveyed don't bother to do windows at all.

Principally, a fear of ladders is to blame, and with good reason. In the UK, 26,000 people fall off ladders each year (though these people may have been painting, decorating, or clearing out gutters).

As well as looking at ways to get every style of window sparkling, this chapter looks at ladder safety and finds tools that do the job without the need for a ladder.

Washing Windows

Always choose a dull, overcast day to clean the windows. You can't see streaks in bright sunshine and hot temperatures may make your cleaning solution evaporate too quickly. That's not to say that you should pick the coldest, gloomiest winter day to tackle the windows. Cold that's severe enough for frost can make older windows more vulnerable to breakage as it hardens both glass and glass-holding putty. Clean too vigorously and you could have a smashed pane. Rainy days are an obvious non-starter!

Self-cleaning for people who don't do windows

Pilkington Activ is the world's first self-cleaning glass for domestic windows. An invisible coating on the glass works to keep windows clean and free from rain smears. It's perfect for conservatories, which can be such a chore to clean, and for hard-to-reach windows.

To get technical, the coating on the glass reacts with the UV rays that come from the sun (even on cloudy days) to break down dirt – even tough marks such as bird droppings and fingerprints. As a bonus, the coating causes rain to sheet rather than drop pitter-patter (and spot-spot) on window glass. So you don't get raindrop smears either.

At the moment, you pay around 10 per cent more for this clever glass. Check out www.activglass.com for stockists (distributors) and technical details.

Putting together a basic window-cleaning kit

Professional window-washers use surprisingly little equipment. To marry speed and safety, they typically prune their tools to one squeegee, one cloth, and for the dirtiest windows, a bottle of window-cleaning concentrate that gets diluted and applied to the cloth. All the fancy and not so fancy cleaning tips – such as using crumbled newspaper to buff glass to a streak-free shine – go out the window (so to speak). Only serious grime gets a professional to back down from the ladder for more window-cleaning concentrate. To be a fast and effective window-washer, the following equipment is all you need:

- ✔ **A good-quality squeegee with a flexible rubber strip:** Choose one that's 20 centimetres (8 inches) long for normal windows. For smaller or cottage-style windows, get a second squeegee small enough to fit the panes.

- ✔ **Washing cloth:** This is your main washing cloth. Microfibre is best. Spontex make Window Wonders, which are beautifully soft, but any soft, lint-free material – such as a quality dust cloth – will do.

✔ **Kitchen roll (paper towels):** Use this on extremely dirty areas of the window to save your cloth from getting grimy and unusable.

✔ **Plastic bucket:** A standard 5-litre (1 gallon) bucket is a good size to hold your cleaning solution.

✔ **A step stool:** You need this for reaching tall windows inside and ground-floor windows outside. To reach the upstairs windows from outside, you need a stable ladder. (See 'Looking at ladder safety' later in this chapter.)

✔ **An old toothbrush:** Use this to get grit from corners of older windows.

If you tackle windows that haven't been cleaned for years you may need an abrasive nylon scrubber to shift bird muck, paint slashes, and other such caked-on delights.

✔ **An apron with pockets:** It can hold tools if you're using a ladder – you need both hands free – and you can wipe your hands and squeegee on it.

Add the cleaning solution (see the next section), and you're set to go!

Choosing a solution

Glass is such a hard, yet smooth, material that nothing gets into it. Stains don't permeate glass, and unlike other solid surfaces such as tile, cracks aren't a problem because, if a window cracks, you automatically get a new one.

So when you clean windows all you need is a solution that dissolves grease so that you can shift that and any dirt that's become stuck in it. You can choose from a vast array of window-washing products, most of which work just fine.

Alternatively, you can make your own washing solution by adding one of the following to a bucket of water that feels hot to your hand but that isn't hot enough to burn you:

✔ 60 millilitres (ml) (4 tablespoons) of ammonia

✔ 1 tablespoon of soda crystals

✔ 30 ml (2 tablespoons) of vinegar

✔ 2 to 3 squirts of washing-up (dishwashing) liquid

For a fast fix for windows for when you want to just spray and wipe, choose either

- ✓ a commercial window cleaner, or
- ✓ a dilute-vinegar spray of 1 part white vinegar and 4 parts water in a trigger spray.

Spray your chosen solution very sparingly onto the window. Wipe over each pane of glass, being sure to take your cloth into the corners. Turn over the cloth so you have a fresh surface to buff up to a shine.

Don't be tempted to use spray cleaner on already-wet windows because it's tricky to dry without causing streaks.

Following a complete window-washing action plan

To begin, clean the frames. If you don't, dirt from here is ready to sweep back onto your clean glass as soon as it turns windy. Get right into grimy corners with an old toothbrush. This method is especially useful with old wooden window frames. With the brush, you can sweep out dirt without creating pools of water in the area and avoid speeding up the rotting process that may already have started in your wood frames. Use a brush to remove mud from the door tracks of sliding patio doors.

Grit can scratch plastic window frames (UPVC) so remove it with a dry cloth before wiping the frames with a soft, damp cloth. Unless there's particular staining, stick to water only. Washing-up liquid that doesn't get fully rinsed away can eventually cause the seals on plastic windows to decay. Painted wood or steel windows can take a stronger soapy treatment. Be sure to rinse and dry thoroughly afterwards.

With new windows, be sure to follow the manufacturer's guidelines for cleaning the frames. In particular, go easy on aluminium-coated frames with a wood-grain finish. Over time, even mild abrasives can scratch the finish.

Make a quick visual check of each window. If you can see loose dirt, you'll save time and effort by simply sweeping it away now. Adding water may stick the dirt more firmly to the glass. Using kitchen roll is fine, or you may prefer a soft brush if, for example, the window is close to a bush or tree and is covered with pollen.

Remove bird droppings at this stage to avoid getting gunk all over your squeegee. Droppings can be tough to shift by just rubbing alone, so soften them with a proprietary cleaner or a strong solution of washing-up liquid or washing soda crystals. Wait a few minutes, then wipe away with a damp sponge.

To clean glass, follow these two basic steps:

1. **Wet the window using a cloth which is first dipped into your chosen solution and then wrung out.**

2. **Use the squeegee to clear everything away.**

   Tilt the squeegee downwards, so your hand makes roughly a 45-degree angle up from the glass. Start from the top and work in overlapping sweeps, shaking and wiping the blade frequently.

   When you're cleaning both sides of a window, dry one side using horizontal strokes with your squeegee and the other by going up and down. When you spot a smear, it's easier to see which side of the glass needs extra attention.

   It isn't practical to squeegee small or raised panes, so use cloths to wipe off and polish.

Ideally, that's it. In practice, though, getting a smear-free finish isn't always so easy. When people say they hate washing windows, they actually mean they hate drying them. It can take several sweeps, and occasionally you may have to re-wet a section and start again. Alternatively, a circular rub over with old, soft T-shirt material can rub away the smear.

Steer clear of chamois leather unless you're incredibly patient. Yes, it makes a beautiful shine on car glass. But remember how long that takes and how many windows your house has.

Once a year, clean the window hinges, too. Lightly oil moving parts with a silicone-free lubricant such as WD-40.

In bathrooms and kitchens, adopt a clean-as-you-go approach. Make good use of steam raised by cooking or showering and squeegee it away before it evaporates leaving grease and soap scum residue on your glass.

Coming to grips with secondary glazing

A second layer of glass that fits in front of your windows is the traditional budget choice for draughty, older style windows. But the annual clean of this *secondary glazing* (similar to storm windows) is no picnic.

Always get help. Lifting out the inner pane of glass is a heavy, two-person job.

Concentrate your cleaning on the side that you can't get to when the glazing is in place – that's to say, the inside of your original windows and the outside of the glazing panes. (The opposite is true for storm windows – you focus on the inside of the storm window and the outside of your fixed window.) The other two sides you can do anytime you wash the rest of your home's windows. Believe me, just doing the two hidden sides is enough work for one session.

Lay some sheeting on the floor before you start so that you have somewhere to place each large pane of glass. Working very carefully, slide one pane away from the corner and, by tilting the right edge downwards, lift and manoeuvre it out of the top of the frame. Lay the glass safely onto your sheeting so that the side you want to clean is on the top.

Aim simply to dust. Once you add water, you up the risk of smears.

With the inside of your original window exposed, you can now get down to serious cleaning. First, vacuum dirt up from the sills and around the frame – there'll be plenty! Wash window frames if needed and dry them before cleaning the windows, using the methods I describe in 'Following a complete window-washing action plan'.

Replace the secondary glazing only when you're certain everything is quite dry.

Shining Skylights and Conservatories

Many skylights tilt inwards, making cleaning them from the inside fairly straightforward. However, because the room is typically dependent on a small pane of glass for much of its light, it's important to clean them very frequently. Also, dirt is more likely to get trapped on a slanting skylight than an ordinary vertical window.

Plastic skylights need special care. Follow the manufacturer's cleaning instructions. Avoid ammonia-based cleaners and use only water with a swish of mild washing-up liquid.

In cleaning terms, think of your skylight as a mirror rather than a window and clean it as frequently and as thoroughly as you do mirrored glass.

For speed, use a disposable glass-cleaning wipe, taking care to get into the corners but avoiding the frame, especially if it's wood grain.

Cleaning conservatory glass is quicker with an extra wide squeegee (around 45 centimetres (18 inches). Even if you're tall, use a step-stool to clean top vents and windows. You can see more clearly at eye level and do a better job when you're not stretching upwards.

To clean a sloping conservatory glass roof, stand on a stool and power wash it much as you would a car roof. Use a hose and brush attachment to sweep away dirt and debris.

Setting Up Ladders

Using a ladder safely is a matter of using your common sense and following a few safety rules, probably the most important of which is to pay attention and be mindful of where you are. Never rush setting up a ladder. Take care when you set it up, take special care as you climb up and down it, and take care when you lower the ladder and put it away.

Even if you do all you can to avoid using ladders and use alternatives such as extension tools to reach up to awkward places, keep safety at the forefront.

Looking at ladder safety

First off, make sure everyone knows what you're doing. The easiest way to fall off a ladder is to have someone open a window where you're working and startle you into falling.

The bottom of the ladder – that means both feet – needs to be on a solid level platform, and solid ground isn't nearly solid enough when it comes to supporting a ladder. Ideally, you can set up the ladder on concrete – perhaps you have a pathway running alongside your house. If you must set up over a gap in your flowers, put down a strong wooden board, wide enough for both feet of the ladder, then put the ladder on that.

Tilt the ladder fairly tightly up against the wall, aiming for an angle of around 70 degrees. Do not lean the ladder against a window or window frame. For maximum stability, it must be the wall. For a 6-metre (18 feet) ladder, that puts the ladder's feet roughly 1.5 metres (4½ feet) from the wall. Put a sandbag, or bag of garden peat or charcoal, or anything heavy in front of the ladder to help lock it into place as you climb. Having a second person assist you by holding the ladder can be a great help. They can also look out for passers-by or traffic. However, if you plan on doing lots of ladder work, think about buying a stabiliser platform from a DIY store.

Stay flush with the ladder and face the wall all the time you're on the ladder. Resist the temptation to stretch out to the side to reach farther – reach only the length of your arm. Shifting around on the ladder may shift your centre of gravity and move the ladder out from under you. Accept that you'll need to climb down and move the ladder a good many times to clean the outside of upstairs windows.

Staying safe without a ladder

If you want to avoid using a ladder at all, you can simply work from inside, cleaning as much of the outside windows as you can. Be careful, though, and be alert to the possibility that leaning out too far may make you overbalance and cause you to topple out of the window.

Buy an extension pole for your squeegee, to enable it to reach upstairs windows whilst you remain outside on the ground. Using this awkward contraption is an acquired skill, however. There's always a 'more by luck than judgment' element involved because you can't accurately see smears on the windows from down below.

Because you'll be knocking off dirt and debris whilst looking upwards, always protect your eyes with safety goggles.

When you replace your windows, give a thought to cleaning when you choose new styles. Sash windows that open inwards, rather than the traditional style that slides up and down, can make cleaning the exterior of the windows from inside a whole lot safer.

Chapter 11

Sweeping Up the Garden Path: Decks, Driveways, and Patios

· ·

In This Chapter

▶ Keeping decks, patios, and gravel paths smart

▶ Finding ways to keep furniture clean

▶ Scraping off grills and other accessories

▶ Treating tools well

▶ Tidying greenhouses

▶ Taking care of the rubbish

· ·

Keen gardeners don't want to waste precious pruning or planting time by cleaning. Yet flowers aren't the only things that need attention outside your home. Taking task with the fixtures and fittings in your garden makes a tremendous difference to its overall visual appearance and to your overall enjoyment of it. What's more, whilst marrows or sunflowers can fall victim to the vagaries of the weather, cleaning is more of a science. Get the chemicals and instructions right and your paths won't fail to look pristine. Whether you want quick clean-ups when visitors are due or regular maintenance tips to keep your tools working from one year to the next, this chapter has the answers.

Dealing with Decks and Patios

A wealth of surfaces combine to make the outside of your home hard-wearing yet attractive and some definitely require a higher maintenance than others. But whilst you would cut your clean-up work considerably by converting everything to concrete, my country-girl's view is that just about every other outdoor surface – wooden decking, gravel drives, and individual (albeit concrete) paving stones – make the garden and car areas that bit more appealing.

Keeping wooden decking smart

The stunning decks so quickly put together on TV garden shows have inspired many thousands of imitators. On TV the chat is always how ripping up the lawn brings an end to all that time you waste mowing. What's left unsaid is that decking needs regular care, too. Only, rather than traipsing back and forth behind a mower, you sweep back and forth behind a stiff, dry broom.

Very regular sweeping is the key to decking maintenance. Brush the inevitable dust away to stop it from combining with grease from bare feet (yours and your pet's!) and everyday spills to become ground-in dirt.

The heat of summer causes wood to shrink, so for safety's sake, keep a look out for splinters or small shards of wood that break away.

Now and again, hose down the decking. If it's particularly dirty, you may want to use a proprietary decking cleaner. Garden centres have a good selection. Look for any moss in the grooves of the wood and get this out using gloved fingers and, if necessary, a water pressure-cleaner. If a bad outbreak has left the wood underneath looking ragged, lightly sand it down. Be aware, though, that you then have to re-stain or re-wax the wood.

Annually, keep the wood watertight with a coating of sealant, preferably one that contains wax. Wash and dry the decking before putting this on.

For speed, and so that you don't have to bend down, re-wax decking using a paint roller on an extension pole.

Laying it on the line to clean concrete and stonework

Strong, alkaline cleaners are right at home with the challenge of getting dirt from concrete slabs and individual shaped or coloured pieces of paving stone.

Soda crystals are an easy, cheap choice when you don't want to use bleach for risk of fading coloured paving. Make a mixture of 1 part crystals to 2 parts hot water. Sluice and go with a stiff outdoor broom. Don't rinse the solution off. The residue (sodium carbonate) acts as a mild moss killer and so helps keep your path weed free.

When you're ready to make a bigger job of it, using a power-washer is a great way to go and you don't need any soap or detergent – just lots and lots of water. In Chapter 9, I talk about using these handy machines to clean exterior walls, so turn there for advice. The results are terrific and your patio or drive looks every bit as stunning as if it were professionally cleaned.

Best off, power-washing a concrete slab is a job you need to do just once every two or three years.

Raking through gravel

Getting the grime from gravel is tricky. You'd have to be very bored indeed to want to take up sections of stones to give them a soapy soak and rinse. Instead, simply rake the stones around. First, look along the track where you park the car where there is sure to be significantly fewer stones as they get pushed to the outside. On wet days, you may feel as if you're walking into a major puddle. Take away any stones that have become discoloured through oil leaks. Now, working from the outside perimeter, simply rake the stones towards the centre so that the driveway is even once again.

Getting rid of persistent weeds

It's disheartening to clean off the drive if all your efforts are over-shadowed by the shabby sight of weeds poking through. Let me share a simple and permanent solution you can use around paving stones and gravel.

Around paving stones, pull out weeds that you can see, then use a strong weed killer in the same area. Don't wait to see whether it works, but go out a few hours later after the weed killer has had a chance to work. Plug gaps in the slabs by pouring in a mix of sand and cement. Add water to form a paste and when the mortar hardens, there won't be even a millimetre of room for new seeds to take root.

On gravel, regular weed killer is never enough. You have to prevent weed seeds from ever touching soil. Landscape fabric is essentially just a fancy name for solid plastic sheeting. Buy it on a roll and, whenever you've the inclination, shift off a small section of your gravel stones and lay the sheeting down. Don't wait until a weekend to do the lot – there is always something more pressing to do than this, and it's a back-breaking job. But working little and often means you stealthily creep up on those weeds.

Getting Garden Furniture Clean Enough to Eat Off

Eating outdoors is so often a spontaneous thing. But oh what a turn-off to arrive in the garden laden with a tray of delicious food only to find that the table is as dirty as garden boots. Exposure to the elements and, it must be said, what passing birds drop down on it, means cleaning garden furniture is a frequent task. Follow the tips in the following section, according to the surface of your tables and seating.

Protecting wood

Buying – and remembering to use – water-proof furniture covers for your wooden furniture keeps tables and chairs safe from their biggest danger – extreme wet. You're unlikely to want to shield them from their secondary attacker, however – the sun! On days that the sun's in full glory, you no doubt want to be out enjoying it. These tips help you to do just that for longer.

✔ Protect wood furniture at the start of each season with a sealant that's appropriate to its composition and style. For example, use teak-oil for hardwood chairs and preservative for a budget softwood bench.

Take care to avoid varnishing on top of screw fittings. The natural shrinkage and swelling of wood according to the weather mean you may have to regularly tighten these. If they're gummed up with varnish, it gets tricky.

✔ Avoid standing wood legs directly on grass. The moisture from the ground may rot untreated wood over time. If your garden is such that you truly can't avoid this, at least give wood legs some extra protection by standing table and chair legs in saucers of wood preservative for several hours, so that as much solution as possible gets soaked into the wood.

✔ In cleaning up wet spills, be sure to dry as well as wipe. Unless it's a real scorcher of a day, never assume that the sun will do it. The wood may take all day to dry out, and in that time, airborne dirt such as pollen may have formed an invisible yet sticky film on your table.

Every two weeks, wipe down tables and chairs with a cloth, wrung out from a solution of soapy wood cleaner. Use the cleaner neat on any particularly stubborn stains. Dry thoroughly, with a fresh cloth.

Get into the good habit of wiping tables and chairs with a dry cloth every time you go to use them. This gets off pollen or fine strands of grass that have found their way to your furniture and dried on rather than got blown away.

Treating plastic resin furniture well

Resin furniture doesn't cost much, so it often simply sits in the garden, taking all that the weather and the trees and bushes and the animals and insects throw and blow its way. But with just a little care, that plastic can outlive pricier wood furniture. Unlike wood, plastic doesn't rot or warp. Unlike metal, it doesn't rust.

Resin does, however, fade, and excessive heat can make some plastics become brittle. This brittleness can be accelerated by abrasive cleaners because tiny, gritty bits in the cleaner work against the plastic to turn it from a smooth to a slightly rough surface. To prevent this, wash down plastic tables and chairs with a mild all-purpose cleaner – the same one you use for vinyl floors indoors or for washing down walls.

When white plastic ages, it can yellow. If your furniture gets to this stage, you override the abrasives ban and use a mildly abrasive cleaner. An abrasive cleaner also helps to keep at bay the black grime that gets embedded in the rough edges of the plastic. Soaking such a stain in a strong bleach solution – 40 millilitres (ml) (2½ tablespoons) to 5 litres (1 gallon) of water – also helps whiten it but gives no guarantee of uniform results. If you can, position the chair so that the bleach solution covers an even area. Rinse the solution off after 30 minutes.

A last resort to restoring whiteness to discoloured garden furniture is spray paint. Look for a specialist paint to match the colour of your furniture. Test a small area first, then spray the entire front of the affected chair.

Pumping iron

Most metal furniture usually has a protective finish. So, essentially, you're simply washing a hard-wearing, synthetic top-coat, and all you need is to wash it with a cloth that's been dipped in and wrung out from a soapy washing-up liquid solution.

Problems start only when this coating begins to wear away, which should be a good few years according to the quality of the furniture. However, strong acids – in particular bird droppings – can eat through weak spots in the finish. So make a point of getting these off with a cleaning wipe whenever you spot them. If the coating has worn away, paint over it again, with a clear metal varnish.

Cast or wrought iron is mostly used for gates and rails, though you may come across benches made from this. Because water causes iron to rust, outdoor furniture is always painted with either an outdoor paint or a clear protective varnish.

At the start and end of summer, check the condition of the varnish carefully. If the coating has a bubbled appearance or rust damage is evident, get out sandpaper and sand the area carefully before re-applying paint or varnish. Then, regularly through the season, simply wipe down with a cloth wrung from a soapy solution of washing-up liquid and dry very thoroughly.

Cleaning Outdoor Accessories

People who spend as much of summer as they can outside often describe their garden as an extra room. Well, just like any lounge or sitting room that you spend time in your outdoor area has a host of items that need regular cleaning attention. Play equipment is the most demanding simply because it needs to be clean enough for your children to sit and possibly crawl all over. But fun elements such as the barbecue grill or patio lights and heaters also need your attention.

Degreasing barbecue grills

Cooking outside is fun and includes the not inconsiderable bonus that you can serve a garden full of guests hot food, yet keep your kitchen spotless. But you still have to do some clearing up. These sections tell you how.

To clean metal racks small enough to fit inside the dishwasher, put them in as soon as they're cool enough to handle. Otherwise, treat racks as you do blackened oven shelves and soak them in a strong dish-washing solution. Squirt a mild abrasive cleaner onto the rack and leave it to soak and soften the burnt-on food.

Clean tools and tongs at the same time as you clean racks. But remember not to put tools with wood handles into the dishwasher, as the glue binding the handle to the tool may melt.

If you plan to use the grill outside again soon, you may not want the hassle of cleaning the cooking grate. Instead, simply loosen bits of stuck-on food using a metal scouring pad. Use kitchen roll (paper towels) to wipe away grease.

Aluminium foil gets a cooked-on grate ready for another go in moments. Simply scrunch up a ball of foil and rub over both sides of the cooking grate. Wipe clean with kitchen roll.

Charcoal grills

Resist the temptation to throw a pan of cold water onto the coals after you finish cooking. There's no surer way to create a foul mess to clean up. If you need to put out a charcoal fire fast, use a fine mist of water from a trigger spray. Some manufacturers also suggest using sand to extinguish your barbecue. Or, you can leave it as is. In its dry state, charcoal isn't so bad and you may decide to grill again the next day.

Between big cleans, keep grease levels down by regularly removing fat from the barbecue body with a soft plastic or wooden scraper.

When you're ready for a full clean, always wait until you're certain the charcoals are cold.

If you want to save coals for re-use, salvaging is best done the next day when the coals are cold and dry. Use tongs to pick the big ones out. Next, put the ashen remains of the burnt charcoals into the rubbish. Depending on your barbecue this can be easy or infuriatingly tricky. Posh barbecues often have an ash drawer where all the debris collects. You empty the drawer and your barbecue is practically ash free. With some grills you can tip the ash right into the rubbish. But if you don't have a drawer and can't tip your grill, the simplest way to empty ash is to use a large spoon or garden trowel to scoop the bits out. What you want to avoid is ash flying out over your clothes or into your mouth and nose. If you're happier using a brush and dustpan, dampen the pan edge to help the ashes stick inside.

To clean the barbecue body, use hot soapy water and a non-scratch cloth. Quality barbecues may be up to stronger cleaning. A high-quality porcelain finish is usually thick enough to withstand even a spray-on type oven cleaner. Once a year, spray this on and all the accumulated grease will soften enough for you to wipe it away with paper towelling. Follow up with a squish of a mild washing-up liquid solution, a water rinse, and a thorough dry, and your barbecue will be the sparkling star of your next garden get-together.

Gas grills

With a gas barbecue you enjoy the pleasure of no soot or ash to deal with. The lava rock that lines the cooking base of gas barbecues needs no cleaning. Simply turning up the burners for a few minutes after you finish cooking gets rid of any food residues clinging to them.

Eventually, when lava bricks do get dirty, simply turn them over. When they are dirty once more, replace with fresh.

When you want to give the barbecue body a wash with hot, soapy water, be sure to remove the cooking surfaces and burners first, as these shouldn't be saturated. Unless you're an exceptionally keen griller, this is an annual task. At the same time, inspect the burners for blockages. Use a pipe cleaner to clear any obstructions such as a curious, now deceased, insect. Rub away any rust spots with a wire-brush.

Taking care of terracotta pots and stone ornaments

Cleaning pots helps halt the spread of plant diseases and leaves insects with no place left to hide. So at the end of autumn, swish a solution of household cleaner and hot water into all the empty containers that have held summer plants. Be sure to brush out the rims, where insects may hide. Take care not to have the water too hot with terracotta containers, as some may be prone to cracking. In spring, just before using, always soak clay pots in water, then let them dry out before filling with earth and plants.

To improve the cosmetic appearance of dirty stone pots and ornaments, spray on a solution of washing soda and leave it to soak overnight. Use a stiff brush to remove stubborn deposits. Stonework that has just dulled with dirt can be scrubbed with an abrasive cleaner. Be sure to thoroughly rinse. Conversely, if you like that aged effect for garden ornaments, you may want to accelerate the process with a mildly acidic cleaner. Simply add a few drops of lemon to water and wash down evenly.

Opening up table umbrellas and parasols

Use upholstery shampoo to carefully clean stained fabric table umbrellas. These umbrellas are easiest to clean whilst they're open. Shorten the pole to its lowest setting and work from above. Apply the spray shampoo sparingly. Rinse off, using a warm, damp sponge. For staining inside the umbrella work from underneath.

Swinging through outdoor toys

At the start of summer, give all your children's play equipment a thorough safety check as you clean. Check that nuts and bolts are still tight; look for fraying in ropes and rot in wooden seats and climbing frames. Pull on the bars of climbing frames (jungle gyms) to make sure that they are firm.

Use a disposable cleaning wipe to get off bird droppings. Make up a bucket of warm, soapy water using washing-up liquid and clean all metal, plastic, and wood surfaces. Use a sponge for large areas, but be ready to follow up with a bristle brush to get out ingrained dirt. Rinse, then dry thoroughly. Consider adding a light lubricant such as WD-40 to moving parts.

Plastic playhouses are likely to have suffered greatly, especially if left outside to weather the winter. Use a bleach solution – 30ml (2 tablespoons) to 5 litres (1 gallon) of water – to take away the griminess. Let the solution sit for 30 minutes then rinse off.

Each day, before your children get busy, you'll want to give play surfaces a quick check. Be ready with an old towel to mop up any water on trampolines and seats. You also need a cleaning wipe handy to remove bird droppings from areas children may sit on or hold onto.

Sandpits can't be cleaned once the sand is in! So always choose the type that has a lid that covers the sand and be vigilant about putting it on at the end of each session.

Giving Garden Tools Some Attention

Neglected tools don't just look sad. Forks and spades work less efficiently when their edges are blunt or their shafts are wobbly. More seriously, shears that stick cause accidents and a blocked-up electric lawn mower may blow a fuse. Happily, clean-ups are quick and simple. Sometimes, all that's needed is a drop of oil.

Making sure hand tools stay handy

Taking your tools out from the soil after you've finished using them does more than anything else to keep them clean and long-lived. After a good dig, the ideal is to stand the spade out to dry in the sun. If the weather won't oblige (and most serious digging is done on cold, damp days), wipe the handle dry and use an old butter knife to scrape mud from the prongs and shaft. Keep up the good work by storing tools in a dry shed or on hooks in the garage.

Oiling wood handles at the start and finish of each summer helps prevent splitting. Rub on linseed oil then wipe away any excess with a dry rag.

Keeping blades sharp

Get sap residue off the blades of any cutting tool by regularly spraying a light cleaner/lubricant (WD-40 for example) on the working parts. Wipe off excess with a cloth. For a more thorough oiling, liberally sprinkle oil on an old rag then use this to coat the blades. Be aware of your tool's sharpness at all times!

To oil with safety, sit down at a table. Partly open the shears and lay them flat in front of you. Then with one hand steadying the tool, use the other to move the rag over the blades.

Helping lawn mowers keep their cutting edge

You want a sit down and a long, cool drink after you mow that final stretch, but your machine actually needs a quick clean now, before the grass debris on the casing and blade dries hard. In particular, you want to brush grass away from the ventilation slots. Blockages here are an obvious cause of overheating and are rated a fire hazard.

Keep a soft brush and a thick cloth right where you store your lawn mower and you're more likely to make the effort to use them each time.

With hover mowers, you need to get grass out from under the hood. Some brands provide a tool with their machines. If your mower does not, buy a plastic kitchen spatula for scraping out grass. Many hovers also have rollers that lever out to aid cleaning.

Never use water or polishes to clean a lawnmower and always be aware of the blade. Always wear gloves to clean a lawn mower. Even a human-powered mower can inflict serious cuts. If your mower is electric, make sure that the plug is removed from the socket before cleaning any part of it. If it is petrol driven it's always a good idea to disconnect the spark plug.

Always thoroughly empty the grass box or bag. You save on mess if you give the box a final shake and sweep out wherever you leave your clippings.

To get at the blades of hand and electric lawn mowers, turn the machine onto one side. Some petrol mowers can't be turned on one side: so check the manual for advice. Mindful of the sharp blade, carefully remove compacted grass from hovers with a spatula or a smooth-edged plastic trowel kept for the purpose. For cylinders, a soft brush is a safer, speedier option.

A squirt of WD-40 on the blades of a traditional cylinder mower stops grass from sticking to them.

Now that most lawnmowers are made mostly of plastic, rust on anything other than the blades is rarely an issue. If yours is a metal exception to the rule, be scrupulous about wiping the box and body of your lawn mower dry before putting it away. Plastic mowers also enjoy a soft cloth wipe, but it's largely cosmetic.

Petrol mowers can be a problem to start in spring as the petrol left in the mower over winter can solidify in the jets of the carburettor. On your last cut of the season, allow the mower to run dry. This prevents 'gone off' petrol and it is safer to store the mower over the winter without petrol in it.

Cutting through hedge trimmers and strimmers

Whenever you replace the nylon cutting line of the strimmer (weed wacker or trimmer), take the opportunity to clean out the motor casing. Use a soft brush to remove dust and then lightly oil moving parts.

Hedge trimmers need to be wiped with an oily rag after each cut. Use a wire-brush to get off any dried-on grass clippings.

Shining Your Greenhouse

Most greenhouses start out a good size and slowly become too small as your love of non-hardy plants grows. Even so, when it comes to cleaning out your greenhouse pane by pane, you may be surprised to find how that structure of toughened glass isn't so small after all.

If you use your greenhouse all year, you need to clean it through the year, too. Plants need all the bright sunshine they can get, especially in winter, so regularly cleaning both sides of the greenhouse glass is a must.

In summer, keeping on top of your cleaning is the key to getting rid of tiny insects that would otherwise feed on your plants. If they bother you, knock out spiders' webs as well. Clearly, it's always less work to choose times when the greenhouse is emptier. So you might schedule a major clean in October then again in April and slotting in extra attention as needed. During very busy periods, even just hosing off the roof helps.

Choose a day when there is some breeze – it helps dry the greenhouse that bit faster. First, lift off any moss or algae that has taken root on the glass. Anything that won't scratch the glass is a good tool – plastic plant labels, which probably are already in the greenhouse, are perfect. Then, start washing. If you use anything but plain water, it's essential to protect your plants from getting a dose of chemicals. Take them outside if it's warm enough and you can do so without damaging leaves. In heated greenhouses, you also need to cover electrical sockets – using bits of plastic sheeting is fine.

A spray of liquid soda crystals is good for cleaning plastic frames but is *not* safe on aluminium. To be safe on any material, use a solution of washing-up liquid or, to cut the bubble factor, a mild all-purpose liquid cleaner that doesn't need rinsing. Key areas to tackle are the T-bars, where pests may set up home – red spider mites are a favourite. Use a firm brush or even steel wool to rub all traces away.

To clean the inside roof without drenching yourself, use a well-wrung kitchen mop.

Opening windows will help your cleaning to dry faster and when it does, be sure to give the hinges a quick squirt of WD-40 before you close them.

Don't forget the plant housing and the floor. If you use gravel, it's far quicker to replace with fresh, but stone floors can take disinfectant. Finally, inspect the plants. Now that their glass palace is so spick and span you need to treat or move out any plants that are diseased or carry pests.

Tidying the Rubbish

Your priority in cleaning your outdoors rubbish bins is the handles. Your aim is to avoid cross contamination whenever your hands lift the lid to deposit more rubbish. Using heavy-duty cleaning wipes is a fast solution. Keep a pack next to the bin liners and take one outside with you whenever you remember.

After the rubbish has been collected is the obvious time to clean the dustbin. Tip a bucket of diluted bleach into the bottom of metal and rigid plastic bins. Swish up the sides, using a long-handled outdoor brush, then tip down the drain. To dry, invert the bin, using the lid under one side, so that it tilts and doesn't form a seal on the concrete.

The size of large, wheeled bins makes this all far more of a challenge. Taking care to fill wheelie bins only with rubbish contained in tied sacks means you only need to clean them very occasionally. If the bin's size means that tipping it up is beyond you, simply wipe the insides with a kitchen cloth mop drenched in a bleach solution. Machine-wash the mop afterwards.

Of course the simplest way to keep your bin clean is to use it less! Recycling glass, cardboard, and textiles has become easier thanks to the door-to-door schemes now in many areas. Do them a favour by always washing out jars and tins first. The following also shouldn't go into your bin, but should be taken instead to the council waste (hazardous waste) disposal site:

- ✔ **Batteries:** Including car batteries and down to AAA size.

- ✔ **Bulky garden waste:** Unless your council runs a scheme that separately collects garden waste, an easier route is simply to start a compost bin in your garden.

- ✔ **Flammable substances:** Petrol (gasoline), paraffin, and highly flammable spirit oils such as white spirit (turpentine).

- ✔ **Gas cylinders:** The seller may take back the empty cylinder.

- ✔ **Gloss (oil-based) paint:** Paint can be highly toxic to the environment and needs to be disposed of properly.

- ✔ **Kitchen oil:** Grease and oil can clog your pipes and sewers, so never pour it directly down the drain. Instead, once the oil has cooled down a bit, pour it into an old can with a lid (coffee cans are great for this), pop on the lid, and throw the can in the bin.

Items that need extra attention or special disposal include:

- ✔ **Emulsion (latex) paint:** To prevent spills, including in your own driveway, leave off the lid for a few hours to allow the paint to solidify before putting it in the rubbish bin.

- ✔ **Medications:** Medicines thrown down the sink add to water contamination and those chucked in the rubbish may end up swallowed by a child. For safety, return to the chemist (pharmacist) or your general practitioner's surgery (office).

- ✔ **Mobile phones:** That old mobile phone can't safely go into the dustbin, because it uses a rechargeable battery. But instead of taking it to the council refuse (hazardous waste site), look out for a charity collection scheme. Handset manufacturers give several pounds for each returned phone and charity shops and even major supermarkets regularly have freepost envelopes that you can use to send off your phone for charity.

- ✔ **Sharp glass:** Always wrap broken glass securely in thick wads of newspaper before putting it in the rubbish.

- ✔ **Solidified fats from cooking:** These quickly start free-flowing again out in hot summer temperatures. So place grease in a lidded container, such as an empty margarine tub.

Chapter 12

Devoting Time to Your Vehicles

*T*his is a story repeated thousands of times each week. The car would not sell. People came to look at it, some even drove it, but nobody wanted to buy it. Then, some bright spark got busy with water, polish, wax, and effort. The car gleamed *buy me* and someone did – at the asking price.

No matter how dirty a car has become, a couple of hours spent vigorously going over it can get it looking good as new. As well as adding to its resale value and appeal, a scrupulously clean car is actually more fun to drive. This is especially true if you're part of a busy, cluttered household. In the car, you have a chance to control your environment and enjoy the clean calm of a clutter-free interior.

Going from grim to great also aids safety – and for bicycles and motorcycles, as well as cars. It's not just about being able to see out of the mirrors, clean bike pedals work better and unreadable number (license) plates break the law!

But maybe you're already a convert and recognise cleaning the car as a therapeutic way to wash away the stress of the work-week. In cleaning terms, it's a real humdinger of a job, bringing together a broad range of surfaces, each with specialised needs. So this chapter includes ways for even car/motorbike/

bicycle-cleaning veterans to get better results. Metallic, soft-top, brand new, or suffering with scratches, there are tips for every situation.

Cleaning Out the Car

On the face of it, car owners face a straight choice between cost (using the car wash) and effort (getting out the bucket yourself). But there's more to it than that, as each time you start to clean your car, you can decide whether to go for just the basics, or a full spruce-up. So here I cover washing both the interior and exterior of your car both at the car wash and on your drive.

Washing up at the automatic car wash

Great! A machine is going clean your car for you. But before that happens, you need to do a few preliminaries.

- ✔ Give the car a quick cloth wipe to remove grit.

- ✔ Retract or unscrew your aerial.

- ✔ Check that the windows are sealed tightly. Open each a little, then press the button or wind up as far as you can for total closure.

- ✔ Choose a programme. For a regular wash, pick a mid-price option that includes wheels and hubs and dries the car. On a wet day, skip the drying.

Badly maintained car wash bristles can result in pinprick scratches on your car. This is most noticeable in cars with metallic finishes. To avoid scratching, go only to car washes where you feel confident that brushes are replaced very regularly (the best way to find out how often brushes are changed is to ask the manager). You can also ask someone you know who cares about their car where they go.

Park up on the side of the forecourt immediately after the car wash and check the machine's work. If there are smears left on the window or bodywork, get them off now, with a soft cloth kept in the car for that purpose.

Car wash queues go crazy on Sunday mornings. You may wait 30 minutes for 3 minutes under the machine. If you can't go mid-week, consider the do-it-yourself power-jet wash. Probably because you have to do the watering yourself, there's rarely a queue. Yet, for a fraction of the price of the automated car wash, you can make your car look good for a lot less effort than you'd need at home.

Power jet is also a better choice for cars you're either very precious about or whose age and poor condition mean there is bodywork that might not withstand the force of a car wash brushing.

Washing up by hand

Filthy bodywork may have made you decide to clean the car right now, but according to professionals, including international car-cleaning experts Autoglym (www.autoglym.com), the painted part is nearly the last thing to clean. I recommend their washing order, which is:

1. **Wheels**

2. **Tyres and wheel arches**

3. **Engine bay**

4. **Interior**

5. **Bodywork**

6. **Windscreens (windows)**

Giving special care to soft tops

Vinyl-topped cars are hardier than their fabric cousins, but both need careful cleaning. To clean fabric tops, vacuum first then use a specialist cleaner, allowing a couple of hours for the detergent to fully work, before wiping it off with a soft cloth.

You can shampoo a vinyl convertible top now and again with an interior car shampoo. Use a brush to shift stubborn dirt and rinse and dry well.

A box, not a bucket, is the best way to get started. Take an empty one out to the car and fill it with everything that's accumulated inside. As well as any rubbish, empty the contents of the glove box, door bins, and foot wells. It's easier to prune back to essentials by replacing only what you need, rather than the alternative of taking out what you don't want. Take out the mats too and give them a shake against a post. With hatchbacks, remove the parcel shelf – it's easier to clean outside of the car.

If there's room on your drive, do the wet and dry jobs parked up in different spaces. You want to be like the professional car cleaners who always aim to do this so that they can hose away to their heart's content then move the car and have a safe, dry surface over which to run the leads of electrical equipment they use to vacuum the insides.

Washing wheels and tyres

Rubber tyres, which spin through mud and gunk as your car drives, clearly get extremely dirty. But it's the metal wheel arch – typically covered by an attractive metal wheel trim (hubcap) – that most car cleaners like to home in on. Especially if you paid out for a sporty wheel trim, it makes sense to keep up a shining appearance.

Work on one wheel at a time. If you're hugely keen, that can include the spare now and again. Hose off the mud. Lift off any mud that still won't move with a smooth piece of wood or a smooth plastic kitchen spatula. But take care: there could be sharp bits that could hurt your hands. Wearing rubber gloves, use a specialist cleaner along the metal areas. Follow up with a wheel cleaner, hosing this off before it gets too dry. To finish, a tyre-dressing product gives a mid-sheen finish.

Cleaning your car's engine

Serious enthusiasts may want the pleasure of knowing their car looks as good as it can. Everyone else may want to go to the trouble of cleaning the engine only before selling a car. As you'd expect, it's a messy job, because you pressure-spray a good deal of oil off your car.

Always wait until your engine is quite cold, then open up the bonnet (hood) and look for any components that need to be protected from water. Car alarms and distributor caps are unlikely to have watertight seals, so wrap them in cling film. If your car is older than 1980 or you can see recessed areas that are liable to trap water, you may want to seek advice before carrying on.

Otherwise, the aim is to get the specialist engine cleaner spray (on sale at car parts shops) everywhere that could do with degreasing. Be light but thorough, using a soft brush to work in the detergent. Hose thoroughly using your pressure sprayer, working up from the outside edge, then keep the bonnet up until everything is dry.

Valeting the inside of your car

However careful you are, you can't stop dirt from getting into your car. Most of it comes in through the feet of you and your passengers, but traffic fumes and airborne dirt also get in through the windows and air ventilation grills.

To get rid of the grime inside, use both the upholstery and the crevice tool to vacuum inside your car. Give the dashboard and shelving a vacuum. Also, remember to dip into the door wells and the parcel shelf, too.

Remember to stand an upright machine on a mat to protect its wheels and so that it doesn't suck up gravel from the drive as well!

Beating cloth seats with the back of a brush raises dust to the surface, making it easier to vacuum out.

Get right around all the buttons and dials on the dashboard with a soft paintbrush. For absolute fastidiousness, nothing beats a cotton bud (cotton swab) for getting into tight, dusty corners.

Don't forget to clean the front edge of the sunroof, which is its dirtiest part. Simply open it up a bit and give it a clean.

Treat leather as you do leather furniture in your home: Use only soft cloths and give it an annual feed with a leather-care product.

For a major clean, when you shampoo throughout the car, use a specialist spray product that's low on foaming and doesn't need to be rinsed off.

Dirty seats come cleaner if you use a brush, rather than a sponge, to work in the shampoo. Take care not to get the material too wet. Remember that the only means you have of drying your car is opening the doors.

Sitting in the back seat with the front seat pushed forward gives you access to practically all the roof. Using a sponge, work the cleaner into the fabric, using gentle, even pressure. Swap to a soft cloth to wipe off the dirt, rinsing and wringing out your cloth often.

Achieving perfectly clean paintwork

Your car's exterior is probably the most painstaking and satisfying aspect of washing your car. This section tells you how to get the best results.

Hosing beats buckets for wetting down and for rinsing off every time. If you don't have an outdoor tap for your gardening needs, being a car cleaner is reason enough to get a kit from a DIY (hardware) store and hook up an outdoor tap onto which you can clip your hose.

You do need buckets to hold your cleaning solution and clean sponge-rinsing water, however. Make sure to wash out the buckets before you start. Last week's grit can quickly become this week's scratches.

Some household cleaning products can harm car exteriors. Even the detergent of humble washing-up liquid can remove home-applied wax polish from your car. More seriously, repeated use of washing-up liquid flattens the natural gloss of car paintwork. Now, you probably know scores of people who've happily used washing-up liquid for years because it's cheap and does the job. But if you're serious about your car's appearance and long-term value, always choose specialist car cleaning products.

To get a sudsier cleaning solution, put the car-wash shampoo in first then watch the foam rise as you fill the bucket with warm water.

Give the car an initial all-over rinse with the hose, then work from the roof downwards applying shampoo solution with a large thick sponge. Take it one side at a time, so you can hose off the shampoo before it dries.

Adopt this good procedure: Dip the sponge into the sudsy bucket then onto the car; next wring out the sponge and put the sponge into the rinsing-water bucket to rinse off the suds from the car. This way, you remove dirt for good, rather than simply shift it onto different areas of the car.

 Watch out that cleaning doesn't make your car dirtier. Change the rinsing water frequently and if you drop your sponge on the ground, spray it with the hose to remove any gravel and grit before bringing it back into contact with your car. Tar splatters clean up in no time with a squirt of WD-40, but be sure to re-wax afterwards.

Clean bumpers and number (license) plates by rubbing on shampoo foam with a soft paintbrush before again rinsing off. Rub a lint-free cloth moistened with vinegar over your chrome for a sparkling shine.

After you wash everything, including the screens (windows) (see the next section), use the hose to rinse the entire vehicle. The big challenge now is drying the car without streaks on the screens or smears on the paintwork. Treating your car like one big window can help. Squeegee water away in long, steady strokes. Turn on the screen wiper to start you off. A specialist tool, such as Autoglym's Hydra Flexi Blade, helps the job go faster and rules out the danger of scratching your paintwork if the plastic side of the wiper ran against the car.

For final precision, open and slam both boot and doors to dislodge any standing water and run a cloth between the car and the bumper.

Drive round the block before you start polishing. This short drive blows away any standing water so that you can be confident that you car is absolutely dry before you begin polishing it.

Buffing with a soft, dry cloth brings shine to every part of your car. But brilliance calls for the intensive effort of wax polishing. Essentially, you need to coat all the paintwork with polish (applied via a cloth, never directly on the car). Take it by sections, and create ever decreasing circles to rub the polish in, before finishing off by layering the polish you can still see into straight, overlapping lines.

Leave it to dry whilst you go and have a drink and a biscuit. When you get back you'll be surprised to find that, providing you've chosen a quality car polish, buffing it off to a shine is a surprisingly easy task.

Wiping windscreens

It's hugely sensible to use a specialist glass cleaner. Household window cleaners that contain silicone can smear when wet, which isn't something you want to happen to your car windows. Typically you'll have already washed the exterior of your car by the time you get to scrutinise the windows. So I assume you have a surface that's been rinsed and also received a fair amount of soapy suds, too. So dirt isn't an issue. Wait for the windows to dry and you're ready to super-clean the glass. Apply your glass-cleaner liquid very sparingly onto a cloth, then rub into the windows, in the same way that you'd clean house windows. Switch to a second, dry clean cloth and polish to a shine. Don't forget to wash your wiper blades as well, or they can smear dirt across your clean windscreen.

Maintaining Motorcycles

A pressure washer will make light work of cleaning away the grease and everyday dirt from your motorcycle. Use the low-pressure setting and direct it first to the wheels, then move up the bodywork. For a precision clean, get busy with the buckets and sponge: follow the relevant sections in cleaning out your car that suit different surfaces such as tyres and metalwork.

Turning Out Your Bicycle

Bicycling enthusiasts know the usefulness of giving your bike a mini-clean after every ride. Washing off mud before it dries makes life a whole load easier and following up with a fast squirt of lubricant on the chains ensures smooth pedalling next time.

A good timetable for a proper clean is once a week if you cycle four or more days out of seven and fortnightly if you ride less often.

For a swift clean, simply wet down your bike with a hose, wash both frame and wheels using a car-shampoo solution, and rinse.

To get gunk off the chain and gears, use a degreaser, rinse then towel dry before re-lubricating both with a specialist bike oil. If you don't want to buy a specialist oil – perhaps your child is the only one with a bike – using a household oil is okay. WD-40, for example, is technically a solvent so it shifts grease on the chain, but because it's also good at displacing water, it provides some protection from rust, a key curse for kids' bikes that get left lying around in wet gardens.

Never be tempted to speed up washing with a power jet or pressure hose. The force of the water could get inside delicate bearings in the pedals, brackets, and so on and ruin the mechanism.

To undertake a more thorough clean, use these tips:

- ✔ Have two buckets of soapy solution and sponges, so you can clean the greasy bits – the wheels, chain, and pedals – separately from the frame, saddle, and handlebars.

- ✔ Take off the wheels so that you can tilt up each rim to brush wash it with precision.

- ✔ Use very fine steel wool to get out rust specks from the rims. Clean with a degreaser first, rinse and dry, then carefully rub with the steel pad.

- ✔ Get just the right amount of lubricant onto the chain. Degrease to remove the old stuff, then squirt on the fresh. Back-pedal to work the lube into the nooks and crannies where it's needed then wipe away the excess with a cloth.

Cheat by wrapping a thin soapy cloth around the chain then back-pedalling with the cloth in place. As the chain spins round, every part of it comes into contact with the cloth, yet your hands stay clean. Repeat with a clean cloth for rinsing then finish with a third rag coated with bike oil.

Part IV
Cleaning Special Items and in Special Situations

The 5th Wave   By Rich Tennant

GLEN REMEMBERED HOW THE LANDLORD TOLD HIM TO USE THE PLUNGER TO UNCLOG THINGS. ONE DAY, THE ELECTRICITY STOPPED FLOWING...

@RICHTENNANT

In This Part . . .

*N*ow we're getting to those little details about your
home and the way you choose to live in it that make
it unique. Okay, so everyone has basics, like the TV, the
telephone, and, increasingly, a computer too – all of which I
show you how to clean. But what about tennis racquets or
trombones? These chapters look at how to bring efficiency
and a shine to the items you treasure. I cover keeping
sports kit, musical instruments, and hobby equipment
clean, as well as dealing with delicate items like jewellery,
fine books, and other personal valuables.

I also take a look at who you're sharing all these good
things in life with: your children and pets, plus the family
and friends that you invite into your home. As well as the
everyday cleaning challenge of having a toddler, a teenager,
and an assortment of muddy paws as permanent residents,
I've included a section on parties and holidays that covers
how to host celebrations in your home with minimal
clean-ups. With just a little preparation, the party starts
here.

Chapter 13

Tuning In to Electrical Equipment

· ·

In This Chapter

▶ Cleaning the TV

▶ Taking care of PCs and other office equipment

▶ Caring for cameras

· ·

*E*lectric and electronic devices that fill our homes call for careful cleaning. Wiping with a soft dry cloth isn't really enough, but it's often all the care instructions you get. This chapter gives a somewhat fuller picture on how to clean the range of technology equipment most homes hold.

For specific advice on recent purchases, consumer help-lines come up trumps. Don't be embarrassed to call and ask how to get the dust out – keeping your appliance clean keeps it working. Also, technical support staff have had to deal with so much equipment that's broken due to poor cleaning that they'll know the tricks to keeping dust and dirt at bay. And, whenever anyone comes to install or fix anything at my home, I always ask what goes wrong most often with the product. Frequently, the answer helps me pinpoint where to concentrate my cleaning.

Showing the Full TV Picture

The magnetic fields within the TV mean that it attracts much more dust than a plain box of the same size so dust it weekly, or every time you clean the room. The screen needs a wipe with a dry cloth, although an anti-static wipe is a good idea if you're plagued by tiny shocks when you touch the screen.

Always pull out the plug, don't just turn off the power, before cleaning the back of your TV and *never* use water or a wet cloth to clean near the electrical connectors.

If you have young children or pets with an interest in touching or, worse, licking their favourite TV characters whenever they appear on screen, you'll be cleaning the TV daily. You won't find a TV manufacturer that agrees to this, but using glass cleaner is a quick solution to a smeary problem. Wipes are easiest to use – look for ones labelled *glass and modern surfaces,* which are the mildest.

Playing smart with the VCR

Treat your video player/recorder like part of the furniture and dust it with a dry soft cloth whenever you clean the room. Only if you have small children do you need to do more. Small, sticky fingerprints are very likely to be found around the slot for the tape. Unplug the machine and use a dampened microfibre cloth to get them off.

Dealing with the DVD

Some newer DVD players are now so thin that there's hardly room to hold a duster to them. However, you'll likely meet a dust-trap in the gap between the DVD and VCR if you stack them on top of each other. Cover a ruler with a thin, soft cloth and move it from side to side to get into the gap.

Dusting Off Office Equipment

You don't have to get in early or creep around once everyone's gone home like a professional office cleaner. Whether you work from home or have a roomful of computer equipment, you can choose your own time to clean it.

However, you do need to give your electrical equipment attention most days because the workroom is often the dustiest room in the house. The two culprits are the stacks of paper that line your desk and shelves (but which really should be clean and safe in cabinets) and your computer. Your PC comes with a built-in fan to keep the central unit cool. That whirr, along with accomplishing its vital cooling work, also stirs up dust. If you don't get round to shifting the dust, particles coat and perhaps get inside your computer, eventually shortening its useful life.

The following sections tell you how to keep everything from computers to telephones in clean working order.

Cleaning your computer the foolproof way

Before you start to clean your computer, switch it off at the plug! Simply not turning it on isn't enough: Your machine is still on standby, which means active electrical circuits.

For everyday cleaning, you may want simply to potter about with a dry cloth. You can get most grime off the housing using a cloth that's been lightly moistened with a mild detergent solution. Avoid any cleaners containing ammonia. Wipe dry.

Clean the monitor with a soft, dry cloth or use a specialised wipe for computer screens. If the screen is all you want to clean, it's fine simply to switch off the monitor and leave the computer plugged in.

The latest flat-screen monitors are more delicate than traditional glass monitors so take care when you touch them. If you're too heavy-handed, you may rip the soft-touch surface. When you're working and spot a smear, resist the temptation to give the screen a quick wipe with a tissue from the box sitting on the desk. Tissues may feel soft to your skin, but to a monitor screen, they're scratchy.

When the outer case of the computer starts looking a bit grimy, chances are that there is just as much dust inside. So every year, to do the full job, you have to peep about in the disk drives and unscrew the keyboard to dislodge the remains of a fair few of those desk-bound snacks. Get a cleaning kit for the CD-ROM and floppy disk drives from a computer shop and follow the instructions.

To clean a moderately dirty keyboard, turn it over and give it a shake out! If you've been eating near the keyboard, a gentle vacuum can help to suction up all those biscuit crumbs.

When the keyboard is really bad, reach for the screwdriver – but unplug your computer before you turn over the keyboard and undo the screws holding it together. Taking computers apart usually invalidates the warranty, so do this at your own risk. Most models unscrew to give you good cleaning access to the board. Where you can, use a microfibre cloth to get in between the keys and blow compressed air where you can't.

Go ten times as fast at keyboard cleaning without opening up the machine. Pop on soft cotton gloves and just touch your gloved fingers to a soapy sponge. Make circular movements with your finger on the keys. Remember that you only want to clean the key tops. You mustn't have enough water on your fingers that they drip. (It's never a good idea to have liquids near your computer, especially your keyboard. One little spill can cost you a whole new keyboard!) Cover the whole keyboard this way, in fewer steps than 108 key-cleans.

The first component to get dust seizure on a computer is the humble mouse, but getting it back to work is a 30-second job. All you do is rotate the disc at the bottom of the mouse, tip out the ball and roll it between clean hands to remove the dirt. Inside the hole that the ball came from are three small rollers that should be smooth and free from gunk. Pull away any lines of muck on the rollers with a pair of tweezers. A quick puff inside the empty mouse and it's sorted. A tiny trick, yes, but in cleaning so often it's this attention to detail that counts.

Troubleshooting tips for printers

When your computer won't believe that you just ran the *clean printer cartridge* operation, try this. Take out the print cartridge, and using a cotton bud (cotton swab) dipped in bottled or distilled water, carefully swab the *contacts* – the metal rectangles on the front of the cartridge. With ink able to flow smoothly from the cartridge, your printer should run smoothly once again.

Cleaning facts for your fax and copier

Fax machines and copiers are pretty low-maintenance and can get by on dusting every few weeks – but only if the paper you process through them is clean as well. Faxes and copiers get dirty inside when they process pages that are dusty or greasy. So check before you feed sheets through.

Keep your machines clean by not using stick-on notes. Detaching these immediately before making a copy or sending a fax results in fresh glue residue left behind on the paper, just waiting to transfer onto your machine. If you can't stop the sticky-notes habit, at least get into the new one of rolling the side of a pen over afterwards to collect up some of the tackiness that would otherwise dirty your machine.

Dirty glass on the copier screen slows down the machine's performance and, when it gets particularly grubby from fingerprints, smudges, and stray hairs, some features may not work correctly. So do a visual check now and again and when the glass needs a clean, turn the unit off at the plug and use a soft sponge slightly moistened with a non-abrasive glass cleaner. Dry with a lint-free cloth to prevent spotting.

Never spray cleaner directly onto the glass or get your cloth too wet. Liquid may seep under the glass and damage the unit. And, don't use a paper-based cleaning wipe – it may scratch the delicate backing.

You can clean faxes that take copier paper any old time you like. But *thermal faxes* – those that use rolls of paper rather than sheets – are best cleaned when you change the roll of paper. Simply brush inside with a soft, dry brush.

Getting tough with telephones

Like kitchen kettles, it's amazingly easy to avoid cleaning things you use all the time. You make a point of dusting ornaments and knick-knacks because that's probably the time you inspect and enjoy them most. No one notices the phone unless it's ringing, but that needs cleaning, too.

Clean with a just-damp cloth only after you unplug the phone from the socket. You'll feel more relaxed about rubbing each keypad in a circular motion if you know you're not going to accidentally call out the fire service.

Never use a completely dry cloth to clean a cordless telephone as this can cause a static shock.

Cordless and mobile phones get the dirtiest of the lot. They are not waterproof and mustn't get wet, but you can safely wipe them with a soft cloth dampened in a mild soap-and-water solution. Use a quality cotton bud (cotton swab) to shift dirt between keys. An on-the-move solution is glass wipes that state on the pack that they're suitable for electronic equipment.

To clean retro circular-dial telephones, use the blunt end of a pencil wrapped inside your cleaning cloth to get into each number space.

Pay special attention to telephones when someone in the house is ill. Sneezing over people or not washing your hands often enough are both factors that spread germs, and using a shared telephone handset puts you into close contact with both. When someone in your home has a cold or bug, it's prudent – not paranoid – to treat telephones with an antibacterial cleaner. Spray the cleanser on a cloth then wipe it over both the receiver and keypad.

Focusing on Cameras

You've probably smiled at this common advice to holiday-makers: Take only photographs, leave only footprints. Well, exposure to sand, sun, and rain means your camera picks up a good deal of dirt and dust too! To effectively clean a camera, you need:

- ✔ **A soft, absorbent cloth:** If you don't want to buy a specialist camera one, use a scrap of well-laundered white cotton, such as an old hankie.

- ✔ **A small, soft brush:** If you don't have a specialist camera brush, an *unused* make-up brush is fine.

- ✔ **A rubber squeeze-bulb, with or without a brush:** You can get a brush-on-a-bulb tool from a camera shop or use a rubber squeeze bulb – designed for shifting ear wax – from the chemist (drugstore).

- ✔ **A lens-cleaning pen:** Essentially just a tiny pad of smoothest leather, you can purchase one for around £6 at a camera shop. If you don't want a tool for just one thing, the cloth you use for cleaning your spectacles works well.

You can buy a complete camera-cleaning kit for under £6 from many camera retailers (such as Jessops at www.jessops.com).

You can prevent problems and forestall a lot of cleaning by protecting your camera with a case. And, whilst scratches on a metal camera casing are annoying, professionals focus their cleaning where dirt and dust affect the pictures they produce. Many feel that a weathered exterior is a badge of pride and proof that you work against the elements to get the best shot.

When the weather's blowing up dust big-time but you have to get that great shot, pop the entire camera into a clear plastic bag and take your picture, pressing the shutter through the plastic.

To keep your camera working cleanly, follow these steps:

1. **Clean the lens.**

   You may have to turn the camera on to get to the lens.

   A. **Use a clean, dry, soft brush to brush dirt off.**

   Look closely. Particles of dirt (and the most likely culprit – sand) can be carefully brushed away.

   B. **Add gentle air pressure if dust won't shift.**

   Whilst you can buy cans of compressed air from camera shops, these can send too much air for cheaper cameras. Use a rubber squeeze-bulb for a gentler touch.

   C. **Shift fingerprints and smudges with a lens-cleaning pen or cloth.**

   You can't brush oily dirt away, but leaving it on the lens can give your pictures an unwanted soft focus. Exert slow, even pressure. Don't rub back-and-forth as this could scratch off the protective coating.

2. **Clean the filters, using a camera cloth or lens cloth.**

   Filters get dirtier than lenses because they're handled so frequently. (By contrast, no one means to touch the lens.) If you use filters, keep a camera cloth in the filter box and use it every time.

3. **Clean the flash with a smooth cloth.**

   Getting dirt on the flash is like having a dusty light bulb. Give it a clean when you start to see less light.

4. Clean the inside of the camera with a soft brush.

Check inside a 35-millimetre camera each time you load film. This way, no dirt is hanging around ready to attach to what will become your negatives as they move across the back of the camera.

Bob Moore, director of the Jessops School of Photography, gives the inside of his camera a quick brush every time he loads new film.

Cleaning specialist cameras often means using the preceding steps, with some adjustments or additions, which are set out in the following list:

- ✔ **Camcorders:** These get significantly dirtier than cameras, and no wonder: Taking a still picture is a matter of seconds, but you use a camcorder for perhaps half-an-hour at a go, and it collects dust and dirt the whole time. Get into the habit of giving the lens a swift clean with a dry, smooth cloth before each filming session. (Keeping a cloth in your camcorder bag makes this simple.)

  Dust often gets into your camcorder through a dirty tape. Be scrupulous about storing tapes in their boxes. Now and again, run a cleaning tape in the camcorder.

- ✔ **Compact digital camcorders:** Some models use touch-screens rather than traditional buttons so the screens get greasy quickly. Clean the touch-screen with a specialist wipe. Look for individually wrapped ones that use isopropyl alcohol, a fast-drying grease cutter.

- ✔ **Digital cameras:** In addition to following Steps 1, 2, and 3, you need to wipe the viewing screen free of smudges quite frequently with a soft, dry cloth. A dirty screen doesn't affect the quality of the images taken, but it does affect how clearly you see what you're doing.

- ✔ **Digital single-lens and reflex cameras:** Some models allow you to take the lens right out, but take great care! Taking the lens out exposes magnetic surfaces, and dirt that gets into these inner recesses may – possibly expensively – need to be removed by a specialist camera cleaner.

Cameras, camcorders, binoculars, and so on are primarily pieces of working equipment. These days cutting-edge design means they look great too, but never jeopardise how a piece of machinery works for the sake of cosmetic perfection.

Chapter 14

Shining Sports and Hobby Equipment

· ·

In This Chapter

▶ Spinning the dust off discs

▶ Playing cleanly – in music and sports

▶ Buffing up books

· ·

*W*hether your hobby is playing or listening to music, you can enjoy it more if you're not distracted by smudges on your CDs or dents in your French horn. If you choose a more active pursuit, you want to keep your sports equipment in good playing order. You may prefer to read about any or all of these subjects, in which case, you need to know how to keep your books primed and ready. This chapter tells you how to take care of everything.

Keeping Your Music Collection Sound

Always start your cleaning where it counts most by cleaning your playing equipment. Cassettes in particular get damaged through being played on a dirty machine, and tape decks, CD players, and turntables can't help but attract dust.

Run a head-cleaning tape through cassette and video players regularly, including the car's tape player. It's in a dustier and dirtier environment than the players in your home and probably gets a lot more use. If you play vinyl records, check the needle and turntable for dust. The laser lens on CD players can also become dirty with time. Special CD lens cleaners that you play in your machine will help keep them clean.

When you have the equipment dust-free and in good working order, look to the tapes and discs that go in them – the following sections tell you how.

Cleaning CDs and DVDs

Blow off dust with a compressed-air spray and use a lint-free cloth to remove fingerprints. Use a straight sweeping motion from the centre out to the rim. The data is actually stored between a transparent layer of plastic and a reflective coating, so a surface scratch shouldn't affect the playing quality. The most susceptible surface is the non-shiny side. If this gets a deep scratch it will damage the reflective coating, and this is irreparable. It makes sense to handle these discs with the greatest care. Pick up discs using the edge and the centre hole only. Store CDs and DVDs in their boxes and set them on their edges, not on top of each other.

Caring for audio cassettes

You can't clean audio tapes so keep the dirt out by keeping them in their boxes. Also, keep cassettes away from extreme heat, direct sunlight, and strong magnets such as those inside speakers. In a parked car, temperatures can top 40 degrees Celsius (104 degrees Fahrenheit), when it's a moderate 25 degrees Celsius (77 degrees Fahrenheit) outside. So pare down your collection during summer and store any tapes you can't bear to be without in the boot (trunk), where it's shady.

Dusting off vinyl records

Clean using a soft, clean cloth following the grooves as you work from the edge to the centre. If the record is totally dirty, dip a cloth in soapy water, wring it out, then follow the grooves with the damp cloth.

Be sure to avoid the paper label of course, and afterwards, simply stand the records vertically to air dry. Do one side at a time, and you can lean the records against the wall.

Wiping up video tapes

A head-cleaning cassette can clean the video player, but for the tapes themselves you just concentrate on avoiding dust. Before you take a tape out from the machine, rewind or fast forward so that the tape is on one reel only. This stops dust hitting a section of tape that contains information. Store tapes in their boxes with their spines upright, like books.

Tuning Up Musical Instruments

It's a fact: The person who actually plays the instrument is the best person to clean it. And for one good reason: The player has mastered the art of holding their huge cello or heavy horn without dropping it on the floor.

Pianos aside, if you don't play the instrument, there's a very real danger that you may cause knocks and dents though poor handling. And, these knocks and dents aren't just cosmetic – they may affect the sound quality of the instrument. So, if you're new to playing (or your child's the player and you're the cleaner) be safe and sit on the floor alongside the instrument. For good measure, rest the instrument on a soft towel, which also protects the carpet from grease and oil.

Check out music shops for specialist cleaning equipment. Whilst you can get along nicely with a good, soft lint-free cloth for general dusting and buffing, you may need long brushes (similar to those used for cleaning baby bottles, only softer) in a variety of sizes to clean woodwinds and brasses. Be prepared to replace these very frequently, especially for flutes and clarinets.

Some tips to make cleaning musical instruments easier:

- ✔ Keep a soft, lint-free cloth in your instrument case, so you can give a quick wipe over before and after playing.
- ✔ Encourage children to build cleaning time into each practice session.
- ✔ Minimise the risk of spills on your instrument by drinking from a sports bottle during practice and playing sessions.
- ✔ Keep keyboards and fingerboards cleaner by washing and drying your hands before playing.

Laminate music sheets to make them last. When they get dirty, you can wipe away finger marks and other smudges with a damp cloth.

Polishing pianos

Dust the wood or synthetic case as you do other furniture of the same material. Using a just-damp cloth is fine for cleaning the body of a modern piano. The following tips tell you how best to clean the keys:

- ✔ Use a soft cloth.
- ✔ If needed, add a squish of washing-up liquid to the water that you dip your cloth into.
- ✔ Resist the temptation to bleach away stains on the white keys of older pianos. It may work temporarily, but staining will return and bleach may damage ivory keys.
- ✔ Wipe the keys from the inside to the outside.
- ✔ Dry scrupulously with a clean cloth.
- ✔ Don't polish. Polish just builds up residue that could stick and slow down your playing.

Clean inside the piano or keyboard at your own risk! A soft paint brush may lift the dust from wool or felt surfaces, but it's very easy to accidentally knock or loosen something else whilst you're dusting.

Blowing through woodwinds

Clarinets, bassoons, and oboes need cleaning every time you play. Before you start, use a specialist swab (from a music shop) to reach inside. At the end of play, wipe the keys with a dry cloth. Careful use of a silver-polishing cloth each week keeps keys shiny, but be sure to wipe off any polish residue with a dry cloth.

Never put a damp cloth or swab inside your case. It may cause the keys to discolour.

Flutes need to be cleaned with a flute rod and wiped with a lint-free cloth after each play. Never use metal polish to clean the outside. A specialist silver cloth is okay, but you need to take care not to catch it on the springs or rub it on the pads. To ensure that your flute is completely dry, put absorbent tissue paper under the keys and close them several times.

Burnishing brass instruments

Regularly polish the outside with a dry, lint-free cloth. Some players get more shine using a specialist cleaner, such as Brasso, now and again. Be sure to wipe off excess and keep the polish away from valves.

To get the insides clean, flush out the insides with warm (never hot) soapy water, rinse with cold water and then thoroughly dry with a soft cloth. If you're a casual player, doing this in the bathtub a couple of times a year is fine. Ask a music teacher or professional for advice on a more thorough cleaning programme.

With a horn, you have to remove felts, caps, and finger buttons from each valve. Lay every part on a towel beside the bath and use a _brass snake_ – a tube for cleaning that you can obtain from music shops – covered with a soft old T-shirt to help push dirt from the tubes. Go gently. You don't want to shift slide grease that's meant to be in the tubes out onto the valve openings.

Afterwards, dry as quickly as possible with a second, dry T-shirt. Finally, grease moving parts and add valve oil as you put the instrument back together.

If your brass is old and a bit battered, don't polish it. Bringing up a shine brings clearly into view dents and irregularities.

Clean your teeth before you play. It sounds a bit grim, but clearly any food particles left in your mouth are liable to be blown into your horn! So cleaning teeth dramatically cuts the number of times you need to clean your horn.

Plucking the strings

After playing a stringed instrument, wipe away perspiration and any dirt from both the strings and the body of the instrument with a soft cotton flannel. Use violin polish from time to time on all stringed instruments, keeping away from the bridge, where it may come into contact with the strings.

Using a soft, dry paintbrush is a quick way to clean the wood-work. To remove grubby spots from instruments in good condition and with their varnish intact, rub gently with a dampened cloth.

To clean inside your guitar, toss a handful of uncooked grains of rice inside, shake and then empty. Grease, moisture, and dust sticks to the grains.

Saying Goodbye to Dirty Books

Cleaning books is a big, once-a-year task. But hey, it's also a fun one, because the best way to keep books clean is to open them up and turn the pages! If you haven't the time to leaf through your entire collection every year, set aside a day once a year to clean out your bookcases.

If you can, enlist a helper so that whilst one person transfers a wedge of books onto a table to be cleaned, the other cleans the empty shelf. Incidentally, it's worth the extra work of cleaning your books away from the bookcase. That way you know the same dust you wipe off now won't just settle back on the books later.

Where dust has gathered on the top of books, take each one out individually. Be sure to keep the pages shut as you gather up dust with a cloth or, better still a soft paintbrush. If you have packed your bookshelf tightly, there won't be any dirt inside the pages. So the tops and sides are all that needs doing. If you feel there may be dirt inside, just hold a paper-back by its binding and give the pages a gentle shake. For hardbacks, open up the book, then fan through.

Bookworm isn't simply a term of endearment. Plenty of small, otherwise-harmless bugs love books. Sweep away any tiny specks you find in your books. To kill all traces, wrap affected books in plastic then pop them into the freezer overnight.

Vacuum the shelves of your bookcase with the crevice tool of your vacuum cleaner. If you're completely pressed for time leave the books where they are and just vacuum the fronts. Remember to do above the top shelf and also at floor level.

Old books need special care. Bits of binding can flake off and brittle pages can tear. Always consult an expert about cleaning if the books are also valuable.

Leather-bound books can crack if kept in rooms that are too dry. Store books away from radiators and add humidity to the room with a small saucer of water. (Keep this well away from the books of course, to prevent accidents). Annually apply a specialist polish to keep leather covers in good shape (you can use petroleum jelly on books that aren't that valuable).

Cotton wool (a cotton ball) moistened with milk cleans fabric vellum bindings. Leave to dry fully before returning to the shelf.

 Give a paperback that's falling apart at the seams a blast in the microwave for 10 to 15 seconds to give just enough heat to melt the glue so you can tweak the pages back into place.

You can also use heat – this time from a hairdryer on its coolest setting – to remove price labels from book jackets. If that fails, use a paste of flour and water. Coat the label with a teaspoon of the mix, then peel it away when it's almost dry. As you pick up the paste, the label comes up too.

Cleaning Up at Sports Matches

Play smart by using the tips here to keep your equipment in a winning condition.

Loving tennis racquets

Modern graphite racquets happily withstand rain. If you can hack playing through showers, so can they! (The balls tend to get a little soggy, however.) After a game, simply wipe with a cloth then put your racquet back into its protective cover.

Cleaning cricket bats

Wipe with a dry cloth when you remember, but resist the temptation to over-oil. New bats typically come already coated with linseed oil and won't need a second coat until the next season.

To revive a battered bat, peel off the plastic fascia then rub over the wood with fine sandpaper. Apply a thin coat of linseed oil and when it's totally absorbed, stick on a fresh plastic fascia.

Sweeping up hockey sticks

Mostly field hockey play is on artificial turf, so sticks now get more knocked than dirty. Use specialist putty such as Stick Fix to replace chunks that get knocked off the stick's head.

Buffing balls

Clean according to the surface of your sports ball. Plastic can take soapy water and a non-scratch kitchen scourer. With leather and vinyl, use a soft, wet sponge wrung from a bowl of washing-up liquid. Don't try to clean tennis balls, simply let mud dry and brush off.

Washing water wear

Eventually, chlorine rots the rubberised elastic that holds goggles tight and keeps your hair dry. Giving goggles a quick spritz under the shower before you put them away extends their life. Always wash out latex caps in cold water, then wipe dry. Occasionally, sprinkle the inside with talcum powder. Rinse swimming costumes promptly to remove the chlorine, then wash according to fabric care labels.

Getting squeaky-clean trainers

Many quality training shoes (sneakers) are machine-washable. However, if it doesn't specifically say so on the care label, don't lob your shoes into the machine: they'll probably shrink. Instead, use upholstery shampoo on the fabric parts of the shoe. Put the mousse (foam) onto a cloth first, then onto the shoe. Rinse off, using a damp sponge.

Leather trainers can take a cream-based polish. To be thorough, take the laces off whilst you polish. Clear polish gives a more natural look than white.

If it's odour rather than staining you're looking to fix, use a proprietary odour-banishing product. A homespun version is to sprinkle bicarbonate of soda (baking soda) inside your trainers. Let it dry – stick the shoes close by the radiator – then brush out.

Chapter 15

Treasuring Personal Valuables

A treasured book or photo, jewellery that once belonged to your great-grandmother or a vinyl record from the 1970s – everyone has things that cannot easily be replaced.

It doesn't matter if they're valuable, everything that's of value to you needs to be cleaned with care. Do it right, and you add to your enjoyment: gemstones gleam and cut glass shines. But always – take it steady! Whilst this chapter describes tested ways to clean jewellery, antiques, fine china, and art, it can't take into account the condition of any particular item. So you need to make your own judgment too. Sometimes, the dirt is so great it's worth risking quite a harsh, abrasive solution you wouldn't ordinarily consider. Other times, you may decide to leave well alone.

 Expect to be disturbed whilst you're cleaning. Plan ahead so that you have somewhere safe to drop your collection should the phone or doorbell suddenly ring.

One key to keeping valuables clean is to create good, expandable storage. Clearly, items in cupboards or behind glass doors are protected from dust. But getting dropped or scattered is an arguably larger hazard. So take extra care when moving things in and out of awkward spaces.

Putting Together a Basic Cleaning Kit

The unhurried cleaning of favourite possessions can provide an absorbing, relaxing way to spend a cosy afternoon at home. What you won't want is to spend an hour or so beforehand searching for equipment. So get the following together in a storage box and, when the mood takes, you'll be ready to go.

- ✔ **Adhesive:** With old objects, cleaning is often akin to repairs. You need a permanent resin epoxy for piecing together hard but porous surfaces such as china as well as standard household glue for tears in paper.

- ✔ **Blunt-edged toothpicks:** These are invaluable for picking out dirt from tiny places.

- ✔ **Compressed air:** Gets dust out without leaving smears.

- ✔ **Cotton buds (cotton swabs):** The top choice for precision cleaning. Use these to apply cleaning solutions and to absorb them from delicate items.

- ✔ **Distilled water:** Choose this when the impurities of tap water may be too much for very fragile items.

- ✔ **Metal polish:** Use to clean silver, brass, and other metals.

- ✔ **Old toothbrush:** It's the perfect mini-scrub brush for small surfaces.

- ✔ **A range of cloths:** A microfibre cloth, an old T-shirt, a scrap of silk, and ordinary rags make a good collection.

- ✔ **A small bottle-brush:** Those sold to clean the teats (nipples) of baby's bottles are perfect for getting scrubbing power to small places.

- ✔ **Soft brushes:** Get a combination of small paint and make-up brushes for dusting and brushing off dirt.

- ✔ **Washing-up liquid:** Soap for sensitive skin has a neutral pH – meaning it's neither alkaline nor acid. So it's gentle on your precious objects as well as your skin.

With this collection of implements to hand, you can give special attention to all your special objects.

Looking after Jewellery and Gemstones

Cleaning jewellery is one of those jolly jobs that's fun to do. As well as handling beautiful objects, you also get to remember the personal history behind each item. However, it's also a job that most of us rarely get around to doing. And that's a pity, because metals and stones that aren't cleaned lose their sparkle and shine. Even months of simply getting into the bath and under the shower coats rings and necklaces you wear most of the time with a film of soap scum.

Jewellery should be the last thing you put on and the first thing you take off, so experts insist. But, if you're like me, you have items you never take off at all. The 'last on, first off' rule is really designed to protect metals and stones from the tarnish and stains that the chemicals in perfumes and washing and moisturising lotions can cause. You'll go a good way to minimising the problem by finding alternative places to spray on perfume. Pulse points, the traditional choice for fragrance, also seem to be top choice for jewellery. But why not use the back of the hand on which you don't wear a watch, and target spray on the centre of your neck to avoid chains and earrings.

Making stone and metal sparkle

Stone jewellery benefits most from your attention. Most people know that diamonds are amongst the hardest of nature's rocks. Industrial ones get used as cutting blades, for goodness sake. Yet, many other precious and semi-precious stones don't share the diamond's hardness. Confusingly, they all look and feel hard to the touch, yet opals are soft enough for the glaze to get stained, whilst amber can fade in sunlight. It's no wonder, then, that one cleaning process doesn't fit all.

You can ask for ultrasonic cleaning at jewellery shops. If they have the equipment and consider your stone suitable, they put it into a container and ultrasonic waves remove the dirt.

One way to find out how much of a clean and polish your ring or necklace can take is to discover its position on the Mohs Hardness Scale, shown in Table 15-1. The Mohs scale ranks items according to how hard they are, usually by determining whether one material can scratch or be scratched by a second material. So the Mohs scale lets you know which stones can scratch others in your collection if their surfaces touch. For example, a sapphire brooch, with a high Mohs value, can easily scratch a coral necklace, with a low one. Basically any material – not just gemstones – at the same point or higher on the Mohs scale can scratch a surface made from a material with a lower Mohs value, which is why, when you're cleaning jewellery, you need to take care to keep items separate. Luckily, fingernails are only at 2.5 on the scale, so there's no problem touching everything.

Table 15-1 Mohs Scale Values for Common Gemstones

Rank	Stone or Metal	Washing Instructions
10	Diamond	Immerse in hot, soapy water and scrub with an old, soft toothbrush. Rinse and air dry.
9	Sapphire	Immerse in hot, soapy water and scrub with an old, soft toothbrush. Rinse and air dry.
8	Cubic zirconium	Immerse in hot, soapy water and scrub with an old, soft toothbrush. Rinse and air dry.
8	Topaz	Immerse in warm – not hot – soapy water. Topaz doesn't like rapid changes in temperature. Rinse and air-dry.
7.5	Emerald	Most emeralds are coated with a protective oil, which means you can't use ultrasonic cleaning. Use warm water only. Don't immerse, instead dip a soft cloth in plain warm water. Rinse and air-dry.
7	Ruby	Immerse in warm, soapy water. Rinse and air-dry.
7	Tourmaline	Use a soft cloth dipped in warm water. Avoid brushing the stone. Rinse and air-dry.
6	Marcasite (pyrite)	The stone cracks easily and cheaper marcasite is simply glued into place, so don't scrub, but simply rub carefully with a wet cloth.

Rank	Stone or Metal	Washing Instructions
5	Opal	Scratches don't show readily because of the stone's opaque qualities. Even so, avoid rubbing. Wet a silk cloth with warm water and gently wipe the stone. Dry thoroughly and store in a cloth bag – opals hate light.
4	Platinum	Soak in soapy water. Rinse and dry.
3.5	9-carat Gold	Soak in soapy water. Rinse and dry.
3.5	Coral	Wipe with a soft cloth.
3.3	Silver	Needs very regular cleaning. Immerse in warm, soapy water and scrub with a soft brush. Rinse and be scrupulous about drying.
3	Pearls, cultured and real	See the 'Building up to pearls' section.
2.5	22-carat Gold	Wash one item at a time in hot, soapy water
2.5	Jet	Wipe with a soft cloth.
2.5	Amber	Wipe with a soft cloth.

The weakest material may be the stone's setting. If the claws are out of line, get them fixed before scrubbing at the stone.

A stone down the plughole (drain) is no joke. So never wash rings in the basin. Few of us can guarantee that we'll never be distracted and it's just so easy to forget, tip out the water and find that a stone came adrift. Instead, make cleaning jewellery a sit-down task and use a small plastic bowl. Don't use glass – a softer stone could crack against it.

My great-aunts, and just about everyone else's, used to soak their rings overnight in glasses of gin every few months. It worked because alcohol is a cleaning solvent and a marvellous grease cutter. But so many other solutions are cheaper and better tailored to the job. If you must use spirits, vodka avoids any odour. Don't go the overnight route, though. Overnight immersion is a quick way to loosen jewellery adhesive, and besides, you don't need that long – your rings sparkle after just a few minutes.

At your own risk, try my favourite way to clean rings – a swift wash in the hot tub. Holding your ring-bedecked fingers towards a water jet very effectively shifts dirt that's become trapped in the setting. Diamonds start sparkling in seconds, without the need to take off the ring. Clearly, the high pressure may loosen a stone if the setting's insecure, so you need to judge whether your jewellery can take the pressure.

The biggest danger to jewellery is being scratched by other jewellery! Yet jewellery boxes are so small that it's inevitable that chains and stones get jumbled. Buck the trend and use boxes only for rings and earrings, putting those with butterfly clips into ring pads. *Jewellery wraps*, designed for storing necklaces for travelling, also make good long-term homes for chains. Pin bracelets onto velvet and store in an airtight box.

Building up to pearls

Cultured pearls are formed when a bead is inserted into an oyster shell. The oyster proceeds to give it a beautiful coat, or *nacre*. The oyster's response to a piece of grit produces a gorgeous pearl.

Compared to lumps of diamond, which may be millions of years old, this more recent coating is rather soft. Leave a string of pearls rattling in your handbag and they may scratch. Get them up against perfume or hairspray and pearls are porous enough to absorb and be damaged by the chemicals these products contain.

So your cleaning needs to be gentle. But – and here's the contradiction – pearls actually look better when they've been worn, rather than when they've just been cleaned. They lose their lustre if they get too clean, whereas the oils on your skin improve their sheen. So to get dull pearls looking their best pop them on for a few hours. Unfortunately, body oils don't do much for the silk used to thread cultured pearls. So afterwards, wipe the string with a soft damp cloth then put your pearls away, wrapped in tissue inside a box.

If you feel you must clean stained pearls, use no more than a drop of mild detergent in a bowl of just-warm water. Some people believe that real pearls are best washed in salty water – they come from the ocean, after all. Keep the cleaning session brief – you don't want to risk rotting the string. The most important bit is drying and polishing afterwards. Use a chamois leather, and buff gently to a shine. Fake pearls, of course, can be shined with a dry cloth as you would any hard, synthetic surface.

Gilding gold jewellery

Because gold is a soft metal, it's mixed with stronger metals, such as copper and zinc, before it's made into jewellery. The higher the carat, the higher the gold content, and the more care you have to take in cleaning it. Most gold sold today is either 9-carat, which is just over one-third gold, or 18-caret, which is three-quarters gold. Should you be lucky enough to have antique jewellery that's 22-carat gold, it's more than 90 percent gold and can be easily bent out of shape, so handle it with total care.

Polishing with a soft cloth is generally all the cleaning that gold jewellery needs or can handle. The soft cloth you use for cleaning your glasses makes a good gold-polisher. Use necklace wraps in your jewellery box to keep chains apart from each other and stones.

Use an old, soft toothbrush to get into the crevices of gold charms and initials. On chain-link watches, bend up each link and use a blunt-edged toothpick to get at dirt that collects in the hinges.

Make cleaning an opportunity to look for signs of wear. Do up the clasps of necklaces and bracelets. Inspect charms for snags.

Shining silver jewellery

Clean silver jewellery last because it's likely to be the dirtiest. Whilst chains come clean in soapy water, you may prefer to use a silver cloth to shine thick bangles or brooches.

Tarnish – a black coating – happens to all silver that's exposed to the air. It's actually far worse today because the atmosphere of our modern world now contains lots of sulphur. Low levels of pollution before the Industrial Revolution meant silver rarely needed polishing. Luckily, tarnish need not damage the metal, because it comes off easily. Add half a cup of soda crystals to half a litre (1 pint) of water, drop in your silver jewellery, and after ten minutes all the tarnish should be gone without the need to rub. A silver cloth makes a quick alternative, if you've just the odd piece to do, though it's not very good for intricate designs.

A liquid silver cleaner (applied to a cloth, not to the jewellery) gets into crevices. Toothpaste is also an effective silver cleaner, and to keep it simple, you can use an old toothbrush to apply it. Afterwards, rinse well and dry.

Plated silver needs extra attention. If the coating is wearing away, you're effectively washing a base metal (typically nickel) that will rust if any wetness remains. To guard against this (and also to protect sensitive skin) paint suspect areas with a coat of clear varnish.

To slow down tarnishing, wrap silver items in tissue paper before they go into the jewellery box or – best of all – put items into individual sealable plastic bags. Although this doesn't look very nice, and perhaps you feel it's inappropriate to store valued and precious items in cheap plastic bags, your silver will appreciate being in an airtight home and thank you by not needing to be cleaned when you take it out.

Taking Care of Antiques

If it's old, it may be delicate. Cleaning may actually decrease the value of the item. Some collectors prefer to see an antique in its original glory rather than cleaned. If you are certain that the article can be cleaned, as a first step, determine how to clean anything else made of the same materials. Then, before you go ahead, check out the condition of your item.

Look for wear on varnishes and finishes. If the underlying material is exposed, you have to modify your cleaning method. For example, if varnish has worn off a wood table, you're essentially dealing with untreated wood, which is quite vulnerable. You need to re-varnish as quickly as possible to protect it. Alternatively, you may decide to get a professional re-finish.

Always dry-dust first. A soft brush sweeps away dry deposits whilst light rubbing with a dry cloth picks up surface grease. This may be all that's needed.

Cleaning tips for collectors

Special items need special care. The following list tells you how to clean a few collectibles.

✔ Silk flowers are real dust magnets, yet they're destroyed by water. So blow the problem away using the cool setting of a hairdryer. This method works for dried and plastic flowers too (although you can wet-wash plastic).

✔ Fountain pens that clog need to be taken apart and the pieces soaked in a dilute white vinegar solution. Flush through with water, dry the pen casing, then refill with ink.

Be aware that dirt can hide scratches and dents in wood pieces. In the interest of overall appearance, you may decide to tolerate the deeper dirt and simply sweep up surface dust.

Bear in mind that wetting most things – especially fabric and wood – makes them more vulnerable. If that Edwardian quilt or nineteenth-century table is just hanging on, wet cleaning may finish it off. Hold fabrics up to the light to check for thin areas that may fray when wet.

Avoid polishes that contain silicone. The shine they produce can look unnaturally modern on antique wood.

Handling Fine Breakables

Cleaning fine china, crystal, and cut glass you keep on display is mostly a dust issue. Don't let fear of breakages mean you put off cleaning them. With just a little care, your collection can really sparkle.

Caring for china

Perhaps unexpectedly, the very finest looking china may be the hardiest. Bone china does indeed include bone material, and is also fired at exceptionally high temperature. Both facts add to its durability.

Plates with a thick glaze can be scratched by metal knives and forks, and also by metal pan scourers should you resort to this as a cleaner for burnt-on food. Dishwashers speed up the ageing process in plates. Over time you see the pattern fade, but you don't see that the strength of the plate is also taking a regular pounding.

Use your thumb and index finger to give bone china and porcelain a gentle ping. If a dull sound comes back, there's a crack that you need to find before you go any further. Glue may be all that's holding the item together and cleaning could wash this away.

Be sensible and use both hands to move china objects and ornaments. Work at a table after giving it a soft surface by laying a bath-towel on top. If you've already checked against cracks and other vulnerable areas and are feeling brave enough to immerse your ornament in water, use a plastic bowl to eliminate risk of banging against the sides.

To clean antique china ornaments, use cotton buds dipped in a mild soapy solution to dab away at dirt. Thoroughly air-dry in a non-dusty place.

To ensure that your quality china has a long life, stack and store it with care. Check for grit between plates before stacking and stick to small piles – certainly no more than eight.

Washing crystal and cut glass

Line the sink with a tea towel so that glass won't smash against a solid sink.

Somehow, accidents always happen when you're rushed and a favourite disaster is banging a glass on the tap. So move the spout to one side after you fill the sink.

Using soapy water, wash each item with care. A handled scrubbing brush gives more precision than a sponge or dish-cloth. After you remove all the dirt and dust, rinse in very hot water, taking care not to crowd the sink. Heat makes the glass dry faster, which minimises the time for streaks to appear, so wear gloves to protect your hands.

A neat trick to give sparkle to party glasses that are clean but have been in the cupboard some time is to dunk them in a basin of hot water to which a teaspoon of washing soda or a tablespoon of white vinegar per half litre (one pint) of water has been added. This works for cut-glass wine carafes, too.

When you're ready to put away the glasses always store them on their rims and never stack.

Tending to vases and decanters

Narrow necks can make it tricky to get down to the bottom with your cleaning cloth. If even a bottle-brush won't get there, fizz a soluble aspirin tablet or denture-cleaning tablet into the bottom of a mucky flower vase. Leave overnight and rinse clean for a spotless vase.

Pour a handful of uncooked rice grains into an empty decanter and swill the grains around to remove port and brandy stains. If your decanter can't safely stand on its head, turn a large saucepan into a drying rack. Simply crumple a tea towel into the base of the saucepan and rest the decanter against the side of the pan.

Protecting Artwork, Prints, and Paintings

Frame everything that you value and you'll go a good way to knocking out a few of paper's many enemies. Under a glass or clear plastic frame, art is protected from dust and tears. The frame also shields prints and artwork from two of their biggest attackers – smoke and sunlight.

Especially if you live in the countryside, gaps between the picture and the frame won't prevent tiny paper-loving insects. Black thunderbugs and larger, lighter silverfish feed on the paper and the glues used in frames. With clipped frames, simply undo and sweep carcasses away with a soft make-up brush. From time to time, you may have to unseal professionally framed pictures.

Use microfibre cloths to dust plastic and glass frames and use glass cleaner only as a last resort. It's difficult to clean the glass without also getting residue onto the frame. To check you've got all the smears from a picture, look at the frame sideways, rather than straight on.

Oil and acrylic pictures can't be framed under glass. The texture that is so much a part of the painting would be crushed and colour tones lost under glass. Clearly, only professionals should touch paintings of value. Home cleaning has irreparably damaged many a masterpiece worth thousands. But if yours is a modest or homespun creation, do what you can to keep dust at bay by lightly going over the picture with a soft paintbrush.

You may decide to protect your own creation with a coat of varnish. Artists' shops also sell cleaning solutions for dirty oil paintings. But if you're unsure, ask a picture-framer for advice.

Bread, in particular the soft, doughy filling of an uncut loaf, is an unusual but often effective paint-cleaning tool. Basically, it mops up grease (think how it soaks up butter and margarine, effortlessly adding so many calories to that sandwich). On an oil painting, spotting bread over the surface (absolutely *not* rubbing!) can pick up dirt and soil. Afterwards, gently shake the picture to remove crumbs.

Stop cleaning if flecks of paint stick to your brush or bread! It's better to enjoy a duller version of a painting you love than one with a bare patch. It is near impossible for amateurs to retouch paintings. If it's too fragile to clean, try improving the lighting on your picture instead.

Polishing the Silver

You can't prevent tarnish on cutlery. Just eating eggs, mayonnaise, and onions ups the chances that your knife and fork get a light coating. What you can do is remove tarnish regularly to ensure that corrosion patterns don't form permanently.

If you wait until the dishwasher gets full before you run it, be sure to rinse off cutlery after meals.

Very light tarnish rubs away with just a cloth and perhaps a spot of dilute washing-up liquid. But now and again, perhaps because you've let food residues sit awhile, your silver may need specialist attention.

You could reach for the silver polish to clean tarnished silver, but that's a slow, item-by-item process. Instead, speed things up with the all-in-one approach. Follow these steps:

1. **Line a large bowl with aluminium foil.**

2. **Fill the bowl with a solution of soda crystals dissolved in very hot water.**

    Use one cup of soda crystals or powdered water softener per half litre (one pint) of water.

3. **Soak silver for 5 to 15 minutes.**

    The tarnish simply melts away.

4. **Rinse then buff gently with a soft cloth.**

Clean up very dirty knives and forks by boiling them on the hob in an old saucepan filled with water and a scrunched up bundle of aluminium foil. After 20 minutes, drain and dry.

Sports cups and silver display ware are best cleaned with a proprietary silver cleaner.

Use a blunt toothpick to get out trapped dirt in salt and pepper pots.

Whether you go for silver polish as liquid, cream, or impregnated wipes is a personal choice. But whatever you use, open a window as you work and wear gloves to protect your hands. Polish works best on a dust-free surface. So wipe over surfaces before putting on the polish. Purists suggest rubbing in straight lines, not the circular movements most of us do without thinking when we clean.

Most polishes suggest that you start rubbing the polish off before it sets dry. Take care not to over rub because doing so takes some of the silver coating away as well.

Resist the temptation to squeeze life back into old, dried-up liquid polish. The active ingredients become very concentrated and may damage your silver.

Looking after things you love

You can't prevent everyday dirt, but you can guard against accidents that cause permanent damage to the possessions you treasure. When you're around things in your home that are precious to you:

✔ Don't eat or drink.

✔ Avoid cigarettes. Over time smoke can damage paper, video tapes, and photographs.

✔ Shield items from strong heat. Radiators and the sun can both cause damage.

✔ Wash your hands! Natural oils and grease effortlessly transfer to everything you touch.

Silver dips are the final choice if your silver is particularly stained. They are strongly acidic so where there are two surfaces, take care not to get the polish onto the second: it can strip the finish from wood handles and pit stainless steel.

Chapter 16

Facing Family Cleaning Challenges

● ●

In This Chapter

▶ Keeping children's rooms in order

▶ Adding extra hygiene for babies

▶ Making peace with teenagers!

▶ Providing for pets

● ●

*A*fter bringing my twin girls home from hospital, I was stunned at how two such small bundles could result in so much chaos and mess. And then when the cat had five kittens in our bedroom . . . well, you get the picture.

In part, the cleaning pressures that children and animals bring are exaggerated by the fact that you now have a baby to burp or a dog to walk and a whole load less time to do your automatic clean-ups. So, as well as having extra washloads of baby clothes, the time that you used to spend catching up with a TV soap whilst you ironed the week's work shirts is now spent watching it with a feeding baby on your lap.

Relaxing high cleaning standards is the best route to enjoying calm and happiness in a home shared with children and/or animals. That doesn't mean bowing to rooms that are like pigsties or redecorating to match the fur-coloured carpets. Rather, it means finding a workable middle ground. It's fine to accept that you're going to spend that bit longer on cleaning than during your pre-child, pre-pet days. But it defeats the object to try for a home so pin neat it looks as if the kids and animals don't live there. So if you only let one toy out at a time and give it a wipe afterwards or restrict Pongo to the utility room, you've gone too far.

Cleaning Up after Children

Like bumblebees with pollen, children are busy creatures who spread clutter to every room and surface they breeze past. A great deal of the cleaning challenge that is children is about tidiness rather than dirt. (Their clothes of course are another matter and are dealt with fully in Chapter 18. Remedies for the stains they create are listed in the Appendix.)

 When you can't fit it all in, prioritise. Go for good hygiene first (fresh towels and vacuumed floors) then safety (moving toys that could cause trip-ups). Everything else can wait.

Tidying the bedroom

From around age three, most children can take some responsibility for their room. That's not to say that they can wield the vacuum or duster – although actually, it's usually the tiny ones who are the most enthusiastic. But simple routines, such as tidying away toys into the toy box each night, can drastically cut your work. From age five, you can also ask them to put each day's worn clothes into a linen basket (clothes hamper). You may want to start a stars chart. Each day that the room is tidy give one star and when your children earn ten stars, give them a treat.

Ask your children simply to throw back the sheets as they get up. When you make your rounds later, the beds are already aired and ready to make up.

Having a place for everything – and not too much in one place – makes tidying up easier for both you and your children. Allocate a corner for shoes, school bag, and sports gear. Keep only the clothes your children are wearing right now in their room. Clothes from overly full wardrobes always hit the floor. So, during the holidays, store away their school uniforms and pack away cotton trousers in winter.

Provide two small rubbish bins in their room. Stand one by the desk for paper and put the second by the door so that they can drop rubbish into it as they are coming or going. Because its contents may be so unpredictable, you may want to empty at least this bin on days when you haven't time to go right in and tidy the room. Keep the place a bedroom. Don't let them turn it into a dining-room by bringing in snacks and drinks.

Let them know in advance when you're going to clean. They probably have treasures they don't want you to touch. If they put these away before you get there, that's less work for you.

Position the bed so that it is against a wall rather than in the middle of the room. Most children's rooms are small, and it speeds up the vacuuming if you have to vacuum on only two sides of the bed. Also, sheets stay in place better. You don't need to walk around a single bed to change it.

Picking up the playroom

Children lucky enough to have a room in the house given over solely to toys also get the benefit of having to tidy everything away less often. If you can shut the door on it all each evening, chances are you'll be more relaxed about leaving a train set on the floor or an unfinished jigsaw on the table. This is great for everyone, but can cause huge shocks when you decide it's time for a clean-up. To keep everyone happy, follow these steps:

1. **Choose a time when the children are out.**

2. **Open the windows fully.**

   Due to safety concerns, playrooms tend to be among the least ventilated. Remember to close and child-lock the windows when you finish.

3. **Wear an apron with pockets.**

   Dumping tiny items you come across while working into a pocket to sort later is a huge timesaver.

4. **Get two boxes.**

   As you pick up toys off the floor, take the opportunity to inspect them for damage. Put everything that needs a repair or cleaning into one box to deal with later and fill the second box with toys ready for next playtime.

5. **Dust the shelves and use a spray cleaner to disinfect hard surfaces.**

   Pay attention to light switches and the wall areas around them, which may be exceptionally grubby.

6. Vacuum with care.

If you're concerned that small bricks or doll shoes will be sucked into the machine and lost forever, do a quick sweep with a soft bristle broom first.

Rotating toys – a month in the playroom, a month in the garage, then back out to the playroom – makes playtime fresher for a child, and also stops the room from disappearing under clutter. Be ruthless and sell or give away any that they are now too old for.

Storing well

It doesn't take long before the average child has more personal possessions than the parents. We're talking a mini mountain of plastic, soft fabric, and paper. And, unless you provide sufficient shelving and boxing, the floor is the only home these toys have.

Fortunately, effective storage doesn't have to be expensive. Here's what you need.

✔ **A basic shelving system:** Untreated wood is cheapest, but metal is stronger. It makes sense to go from floor to ceiling (whilst they are small, there's the bonus that you can store stuff out of reach). You can find simple, self-assembly units at DIY (hardware) stores.

For safety's sake, always screw shelving units to the wall. Drill through the shelving near the top and near the bottom on each side and fix with extra-long screws. You don't want a shelf filled with toys to topple onto your child.

✔ **Boxes and crates to stand on the shelves:** Look for rigid-plastic boxes with detachable lids. Big may seem best, given the colossal toy volume. But if you want to encourage your child to put toys away, buy small boxes, so that your child can lift them up onto the shelves.

If you're on a budget, shoeboxes make for great storage. Check with a local shoe store; the staff are likely to be delighted when you ask for spare boxes as it saves them the bother of dismantling them.

✔ **Hooks:** Use these to hold onto painting aprons, playtime shopping bags, sports racquets, and dress-up clothes and hats. With very young children, instead of traditional metal hooks, choose rounded wooden pegs.

✔ **Large plastic storage bucket with rope handles:** There are always occasions when you need to do an emergency tidy-up – unexpected visitors, for example. Choose a container large enough to handle everything that may be on the floor. You can toss everything into this temporary container without spending an age putting plastic blocks into their box or tidying track into the railway crate, and so on.

✔ **A lidded desk or a table with built-in drawers:** Built-in storage provides a natural place to store pencils and crayons as well as paper and other art supplies.

Taking care of toys

As well as cleaning up marks on toys, your job is also to wipe away germs. A child who plays with toys that were recently handled by another child who has a virus frequently picks up *rotavirus,* the most common infant tummy bug in the world. Regularly disinfecting hard plastic toys can go some way to preventing this. In developed countries, rotavirus isn't serious; it's just an unpleasant few days as your child fights a fever and has foul-smelling, watery bowel movements.

The fastest way to kill germs is with a specialist spray cleaner. Look in the supermarket for an antibacterial cleaner. There are several brands that particularly target hygiene in the nursery. However, good old bleach also does the trick. Clean with 30 millilitres (ml) (2 tablespoons) of bleach in 5 litres (1 gallon) of water, then rinse and dry.

Greasy, sticky fingers mean that toys get dirty fast. How often you need to clean them depends on the age and stage of the children playing with them.

During potty training, you need to be particularly alert to hygiene issues. Nowhere is this truer than if you have a mini-pool filled with balls, an inflatable castle, or the like. Your child may forget or be too embarrassed to tell you that he peed in the pool, so to speak. You may also need to pay the same attention to the sandpit (sandbox). Fill a watering-can with a solution of 30 ml (2 tablespoons) of bleach and 5 litres (1 gallon) of water and spray it onto the affected area to disinfect it. Keep your child off the sand for a day whilst it dries out.

Handling hard toys

Scrub wooden toys with a wet brush that's been dipped in your cleaning solution of choice; just don't soak them in water lest they swell and crack or lose their adhesive. Use sandpaper to smooth away any nicks or splinters. If you can't eliminate the risk of a splinter, throw the toy out.

Small rigid-plastic toys are likely to be dishwasher-safe. Make your own judgment by comparing the plastic to beakers (cups) that you already put into the dishwasher. Using the dishwasher (use the top rack only) has the added benefit of disinfecting toys by subjecting them to very hot water. If the plastic isn't dishwasher-safe, hand wash in hot soapy water.

Brushing out fur and soft-fabric toys

Unless it says *machine* or *hand wash* on the label, you can assume that surface sponging is as far as you should go with your child's most precious fur and soft-fabric toys. Use the foam from a bowl of soapy washing-up liquid and scoop this onto a thick sponge. Dab gently all over the toy; following up with a dry cloth to blot up the wet.

If this isn't enough, make your own decision about whether you can safely machine-wash the toy. I confess that I've washed loads of lambs, rabbits, beanies, and fabric baby dolls and suffered just two disasters. So do a risk assessment based on how much your child loves that particular toy and whether it can be replaced. Your main concern may be shrinkage. This is likely to be a problem if the toy has long fur, which may mat, or if the toy is made from a combination of different fabrics that shrink at different rates, giving a puckered finish.

Sometimes, washing toys presents a colourfast problem. Snipping off dolly's red bows (to sew on again afterwards) may solve the problem.

If you do go with the machine option, remember that tatty (raggedy) toys are also delicate toys. Check and mend any tears first and wash toys inside a pillowcase, so there is no risk of them getting caught on a zip or button that's also in the wash. Naturally, you want to use a delicate programme (cycle) and non-bio washing detergent.

As well as grease and dirt, soft and fur fabric toys attract dust mites. This is especially true for the ones that share your child's bed. All machine-washing kills live mites, but the water temperature needs to be 60 degrees Celsius (140 degrees Fahrenheit) to kill their eggs, which is more than most toys can bear. An easy alternative is to zap the wee beasts in the freezer. Pop the toy, in a sealed plastic bag, into the freezer for 48 hours. If you've a child who is wheezy or asthmatic, make this freeze-and-clean a monthly routine.

Speed cleaning action figures and dolls

Use an old toothbrush dipped in undiluted washing-up liquid to scrub off dirt and pen and crayon marks on your children's dolls. Sticky hair is easy – simply shampoo. Follow up with a wash-out conditioner (yes, really!), and your daughter can have more fun playing with a doll whose hair isn't in scraggy tangles every time she takes out some plaits (braids).

Cleaning Up Baby

Providing a baby with sufficient protection against germs is a challenge. Because the hand-to-mouth reflex is so strong, every surface that your newborn touches needs to be as clean as you can make it. Fortunately for both sanity and cleaning time, your young baby can't move about. So you can concentrate your efforts on three areas:

- ✔ **Where baby sleeps:** Cot, sheets, blankets, pram (stroller), and car seat.

- ✔ **Where baby eats:** If you breastfeed, there's no work needed. Otherwise, bottles, beakers, bowls, spoons, and highchair.

- ✔ **Where baby plays:** Activity mats, baby gyms, bath, towels, bouncy chair.

A new baby in the home is the time to take up every offer of household help that you get. Make sure that it's the right sort of help by giving precise instructions. If a friend offers to run the vacuum around, it's not bossy to say that you'd rather she put on a load of washing or did the dishes. Friends and family will be pleased that their efforts are going into the right place.

Cleaning bedding

Expect to change your baby's sheet several times a day. Inspect it closely whenever you take your baby out of the cot (crib). If you can see staining, whip the sheet right off for a hot-water machine-wash. Buy around six bottom sheets – choose ones with fitted corners for fast changes.

Babies need waffle-weave blankets, never duvets under which they could get too hot. Hot machine-wash blankets frequently.

Mattresses are often washable on one side. Follow label instructions to sponge them clean. Dry scrupulously. If your baby wets or soils on the non-washable side, avoid unnecessary wetness as you clean up. Scrape solids with a knife, and then blot up the worst onto an old towel or several thicknesses of paper towel. Use the foam from a bowl of soapy water to sponge clean the fabric, then rinse with a clean sponge. Only bring your baby back to the mattress when it is thoroughly dry.

Sterilising bottles and beakers

Old milk, and the bacteria it contains, is exceptionally bad news for babies. Their developing immune systems lack the ability to fight off infection. So even the few bad bacteria that could be in a speck of old milk could result in an upset stomach or worse. So, bottles and beakers (cups) need to be cleaned scrupulously to remove all traces of infant formula or breast milk. Heat-steaming or using a non-toxic chemical cleaner kills bacteria. A third line of defence – very careful handling – ensures that germs from your hands never touch surfaces your baby's mouth also touches.

As a mum of twins, I know how busy life with small babies can be, but this is one area where no shortcuts will do. Make a point of choosing a time each day to spend the 15 or so minutes it takes to clean and refill your baby's bottles. Some time after breakfast, before you go out for the day, is ideal.

To clean baby bottles, follow these steps:

1. **Wash your hands.**

2. **Gather up all used bottles and empty any remaining contents.**

3. **Wash the bottles and the plastic tongs you use to help re-assemble the bottles in hot, soapy water.**

   Use a bottle-brush and a tiny teat (nipple) brush that gets right into the drinking teat to scrub away any milk deposits.

4. **Scrub in plain water, paying extra attention to the teat.**

   Now you're ready to sterilise.

5. **Sterilise the bottles, teats, and lids.**

   A. The fastest method uses the microwave and a microwave steriliser.

   In essence, a *microwave steriliser* is just a lidded bowl with racks on which to stand bottles, lids, and teats. It converts to a steamer when correctly filled with water and heated in the microwave. Follow the manufacturer's instructions on the amount of water to use and the steaming time – around eight minutes is typical – then take care when removing the hot bowl.

   The sanitary effects of steam sterilisation don't last. If you get too busy to actually fill the sterilised bottles, you need to put them through the microwave again after two hours. Don't attempt to make your own microwave steriliser using plastic lidded bowls. A microwave oven super-heats water and if handled incorrectly can erupt from containers.

   B. An alternative to the microwave is an electrical steamer.

   These are bulky, taking up almost the same work-top space as a microwave, and expensive. Buying a budget microwave is a better route – and of course you can cook your own dinner, too. For time-pressed parents, microwave-ready meals are much appreciated!

   C. Cold sterilisation – the method your mum and gran probably used – is a third option.

Buy sterilising tablets or liquid at a chemist or baby store, and you need a lidded container large enough to hold fully immersed bottles. Scrupulously wash bottles, as described in Steps 1 though 4. Immerse the clean bottles, lids, and teats into the sterilising solution for 30 minutes.

There's no need to wash off the sterilising solution before filling the bottles – doing so utterly defeats the sanitation purpose. The solution has no taint or aftertaste. Left in the container with the solution, bottles keep sterilised for 24 hours.

Always use clean plastic tongs to move and help fill the bottles. Never touch the teat that your baby's mouth is also going to touch with your fingers.

Washing down prams, buggies, car seats, and baby gyms

Depending on where you live, there are any number of names for the various methods to transport young children. In the UK, a *pram* is a device on wheels in which an infant can lay flat. A *buggy,* on the other hand, is more portable and more like a seat, albeit one that the infant or toddler can lie right down in also. Both versions are called *strollers* in the US.

Most lie-flat prams for newborns have lift-out mattresses. So clean these and the sheet, as you do cots.

Buggies, unfortunately, can be tricky to wash just when your older baby or toddler starts to eat all manner of sticky things. Most fabric you can only sponge off. However, you can also try vacuuming up dirt with the upholstery tool.

To clean the wheels, shift dried mud and other deposits with a stiff brush. If this fails, lower the front two wheels into a large bowl of soapy water – an outgrown baby bath is ideal. Let the water soften the dirt, then rub away whilst the wheels are still submerged, and air-dry on an old towel.

Car seats typically have machine-washable, detachable covers, which is just as well as they get dirty quickly. It's fine to sponge down the hard plastic part of the seat with mild soapy water. But don't use detergent on or around the buckle or integral seat belt – repeated washing may make the buckles not work as well as they should.

Baby gyms made of plastic are simple to clean. Just spray disinfectant and wipe. Fabric gyms, which get dirty faster than plastic ones, need sponge cleaning. Dip the sponge into warm soapy water, then work systematically over the fabric mat and arch. Hanging toys that don't have battery cells inside them are generally safe to go into the delicate cycle of the washing-machine. If in doubt, simply sponge.

Tidying Tips for Teenagers

Mess and dirt in your older child's room is rarely an act of rebellion or an attitude statement about you and how you keep the rest of the house. It's simply the healthy sign that your youngster has found plenty of things to do rather than tidy up or take the long, dull trek to the dirty-laundry basket.

As long as bedclothes get changed regularly, fresh air is let into the room now and again, and the place checked for old food and unwashed clothes, there's no health hazard – the visual assault is another matter! Take your pick from these ways to handle the situation.

- ✔ Accept the extra work of keeping your teen's room to the same standard as the rest of the house as cheerfully as you can. We're all young once. Don't expect or care that your tidying up produces no change in behaviour.

- ✔ Enlist your teen's help. Decide on three areas that really bother you – maybe dirty socks on the floor, an unmade bed, and scrunched-up computer paper strewn on the floor – and enforce cleanliness in these areas. Turn a blind eye to everything else. Provide a linen basket and rubbish bin in the room and stack a fresh sheet and duvet cover on the bed each week. You may want to negotiate cleanliness by offering a treat as incentive.

- ✔ Hand over the vacuum and duster and insist that your teen perform one major clean during each school holiday. Provide sacks for clothes and hobby items that have fallen from favour and can be given to charity and set out a large bin for old paperwork and magazines to recycle.

Dealing with Blue Tack

You don't want walls pitted with drawing pin holes, so you tell your kids to use adhesive putty, such as Blue Tack, to attach their posters and paintings. But you still get a mess when they move everything around.

What's gone wrong? Most likely, you have one of two problems: The poster was yanked off the wall or the wall surface isn't totally smooth or is semi-porous. Wallpaper, fresh paint, and textured paint are poor surfaces for using adhesive putty. Lifting off the putty can also lift off a top layer of your wall covering. Gloss paint, metal, wood, and plastic are generally fine. Use a light-coloured adhesive on light-coloured walls as a darker putty may stain the paint.

To avoid marks when you're taking down a poster, use your fingernail to get right under the putty and ease it out and away from the wall, so that it comes away still attached to the poster. To get off any small pieces still on the wall, rub a fresh piece of putty over the stragglers in a gentle, circular motion.

The same rubbing approach works for getting off old tack stuck onto the back of posters. However, if it has been there a considerable while and grown hard, you're best off leaving it where it is or you risk tearing the paper.

Your teenager's efforts are likely to be greatest if someone other than just parents are going to see them. So choose a day just before friends are coming round. (This approach works better with girls or with boys who are inviting girls round.)

✔ Decorate the room so your teenager will be determined to keep it nice. Talk paint charts together and buy furniture and flooring that reflect your teen's idea of cool.

Tending to Pets

If you lay down a few ground rules, sharing your home with an animal needn't mean too much extra work. Don't worry that you might not be able to train your animal well enough to follow house rules – the rules are for you, not your pet!

✔ Decide which parts of the house you want to share with your pet and be consistent about enforcement.

- ✔ Restrict your pet to its own bed – not yours!

- ✔ Carry out regular grooming. Fur caught on the cat comb is fur that isn't lining your carpet.

- ✔ Give your pet sufficient exercise and spend quality time together. It's bored dogs, cats, and rabbits that get scratching and chewing.

Determining how much work keeping an animal means

Always do research before you get a pet. Animal charities, such as The Royal Society for the Prevention of Cruelty to Animals (RSPCA), are a good source of information. The RSPCA's Web site at www.rspca.org.uk gives you basic details on caring for different types of animal. After you know whether it's going to be a dog, cat, or insect, talk to breeders, rescue workers, and other owners about just how much clearing up this animal entails.

Before getting a dog, most people find out how much exercise a breed needs but overlook grooming and cleaning needs. A larger dog creates more dirt and fur about your house. Also, if you're thinking of getting more than one pet, remember that there are no economies of scale to cleaning. Two pets always mean twice the amount of shed fur and toileting clear-ups. Finally, be honest about what might upset you. The wear and tear on a house of four frequently dirty paws isn't for everyone. You may feel happier with a small, caged pet.

No matter what type of animal you decide on, you need to give daily cleaning attention to its feeding and sleeping areas.

Avoiding health hazards

Animals carry diseases that they can pass onto you through saliva, as dogs lick your hands and cats, rabbits, hamsters, and reptiles give a quick bite. Bacteria and viruses can also be spread through direct or indirect contact with your pet's excrement, or that from other animals that may have found its way onto your dog's paw. Snakes can spread salmonella. The dead skin, or *dander,* that cats shed contains airborne particles that can produce an allergic reaction in susceptible people.

Dealing with animal waste

Dog mess on the pavement and grass verges in the road where my children go to school has me seething. One of my children steps into this every few weeks, so I now carry plastic bags and a pack of large-size wet cloth wipes in the car, ready for a fast clean up. Baby-wipes are ideal. Use wipes to lift up as much matter as you can, then seal in a bag and bin.

If the accident happens on the homeward journey or you have spare shoes, put the dirty shoe into the other plastic bag, to finish later. Wash the sole under the hot tap, using a scrub brush. Spray with antibacterial spray and air-dry.

Each type of pet has its own catalogue of animal-to-human health risks, and it's common sense to find these out from your vet as you start to keep a new pet. But an awareness of potential risks shouldn't stop you from keeping a pet. More than 6 million cats and 5 million dogs live happily within homes in the United Kingdom, and the vast majority give their owners no health concerns. However, if you keep a pet, good health and hygiene practice says you should:

- ✔ Keep pets away from areas where you sleep, eat, and prepare food.
- ✔ Wash your hands after touching your pet.
- ✔ Take an animal that appears sick to the vet promptly. Regularly worm and protect your pets from fleas.

Maintaining a clean environment for your pet

Table 16-1 lists various types of pets, how much room they need, and how to clean and care for them. For complete care and feeding advice on your pet, look for the appropriate For Dummies book on your specific animal.

Table 16-1 Popular Pets and Their Cleaning Needs

Animal	Boundaries	Cleaning and Care	Special tips
Cats	Roam freely over your home, high surfaces are no bar! Provide a flap if you want your cat to go outdoors.	Attend to litter tray daily; clean cat bed fortnightly.	Fleas are inevitable unless you take action. See the vet for specialist sprays and tablets. Use a flea collar and change it every three months.
Dogs	With training, can be restricted to certain rooms in the house. Consider restricting to downstairs only or not allowing the dog in the kitchen or lounge.	Shake out bedding weekly; thoroughly clean it at least monthly.	Keep a towel by the door to rub down your dog and clean off muddy paws before it comes into the house.
Fish	Small coldwater fish in a goldfish bowl; larger and warm water fish in tanks.	Replace 20 per cent of the water each week using a siphon. Monthly, scrub away algae using a specialist scrubber on a handle.	Never be tempted to put your fish into a temporary bowl with water straight from the tap for a few moments whilst you do a complete water change on a tank. The shock of so much fresh water could kill them.
Gerbils	Indoors in a lidded tank.	A gerbil can make a big mess simply burrowing about, so check that its bedding (white kitchen paper) is still in one place each day. Scoop out soiled wood shavings regularly, and top up.	Every three months do a major clear-up. Take everything out the cage and disinfect. (Put your gerbil into a secure ventilated container while you do this.) Dry very thoroughly.

(continued)

Table 16-1 *(continued)*

Animal	Boundaries	Cleaning and Care	Special tips
Guinea pigs	Outdoors in a weatherproof home. Bring into the shed or porch when the temperature drops below 10 degrees Celsius (50 degrees Fahrenheit).	Each day, take up soiled wood shavings and replace with fresh. Change soft hay bedding weekly.	Prone to mites. Get treatment from your vet and wear gloves when replacing bedding.
Hamsters	Indoors in a large clear plastic cage that's somewhere warm, but not in direct sunlight.	Each week replace sawdust on the floor and put out fresh bedding – soft kitchen paper is okay.	*Never* use cotton wool for bedding. The fibres could choke your hamster. Try to clean the cage in the morning or evening. Your nocturnal hamster likes a long daytime sleep.
Rabbits	Outdoors, in a large weatherproofed hutch.	Clean out soiled wood shavings daily. Change hay or shredded-paper bedding weekly.	Don't slacken with the daily cleaning. Rabbits in dirty conditions can fall prey to *flystrike* – basically an infestation of maggots – which can be fatal.
Reptiles	Keep snakes and lizards indoors in a totally secure cage; keep tortoises outdoors, with access to a dry, secure hutch.	Snakes and lizards need specialist care, so much so that many animal charities don't recommend them as pets.	For detailed advice see *Reptiles & Amphibians For Dummies* by Patricia Bartlett or *Turtles & Tortoises For Dummies* by Liz Palika, both published by Wiley.

Changing the goldfish bowl

Cold-water fish such as goldfish are way more sensitive than you may imagine. Moving them into water that's a different temperature, or that's come straight from the tap and so has a high chlorine content, can make them die of shock. So never rush the fortnightly chore of washing your cold-water fish's bowl.

Begin by organising a temporary home. Any small, clean bowl that you can fill with water from his main bowl will do. Your fish lives in here for a day, whilst the fresh water that you put into his main bowl comes up to room temperature. Use a net to pop your fish in safely.

Now – get cleaning. Empty out rocks and use hot water and a commercial cleaner specially designed for your fish to soak away dirt and germs. Rinse with cold water, pop the rocks back, and refill the bowl. After 24 hours, it's ready for your fish.

If a fish dies, scrupulously clean out the bowl before putting another fish into it. Ask at the pet shop for a chemical cleaner and follow instructions.

Feeding your cat and dog cleanly

Consider an outer room, if space allows, such as a utility area to feed your pet. A utility area often has a sink so you can wash your pet's dishes and any knives or spoons you use to dish out the food away from your own. Store your pet's food here too – only opened cans need the fridge.

To clean food and water dishes, use hot water and dishwashing liquid, then rinse bowls thoroughly before drying with a paper towel.

Stand food and water bowls inside a large plastic tray and you protect the floor from spills and can also keep the tray clean by washing it in a solution of bleach and hot water each week.

Avoid feeding your pet on carpet, which is a chore to wash. Remember, cats don't have to be fed on the floor. A worktop (but not, of course, a kitchen worktop!) may be suitable.

Limit feeding times. How often you feed your pet is probably dictated by your working day, as much as its needs. But for good hygiene, you need to get those bowls cleared up promptly, especially in hot weather. So teach your animal to eat right away so you can wash up his food bowl before you go to work. (Leave the water out of course and, if you're out all day, some dry food.)

Winning the war against animal fur

A quality vacuum cleaner is an essential tool in your campaign to lift pet hair from your home. If anyone in the household is asthmatic or prone to allergies, get a vacuum with a high-grade filter. The filter helps keep the microscopic allergens sucked up by the vacuum safely inside the machine.

Use the upholstery tool on your cleaner to suction hairs off sofas and curtains. But don't bother with those gadgets that use an adhesive roller to lift up hairs. You'll be there all day, just cleaning one armchair. To rid your clothing of pet hair, wrap a circle of wide adhesive tape around your fingers, sticky side out, and dash up and down your clothes, pressing the tape smartly against the fabric. Pay attention to the bottom of your legs where your pet may have brushed against you. The fur sticks to the tape, leaving your clothes smart again.

For chairs, beds, and blankets (or anywhere your pet sits), brush the area wearing a wet rubber glove. Use your fingers to get right into the corners of cushions. Afterwards, simply rinse the gloves under the tap to remove fur. (Remember to scoop this out of the plughole [drain] and drop it into the bin.)

Groom your cat and dog outdoors, to minimise airborne skin particles that contribute to allergies. Get loose fur off a moulting cat or dog by rubbing over its body whilst wearing damp rubber gloves. Metal flea combs make good grooming brushes for cats. They're quicker to use and clean than traditional wood and soft-bristle brushes.

Rub off mud and dirt from your dog using a damp towel. If it's cold, follow up with a rubdown with a warm one, straight from the tumble dryer or a radiator.

Go with the flow. If you've a Dalmatian, buy cream or beige carpets, and avoid dark floor coverings and seating. Black Labrador owners should do the reverse.

Vetting the bedding

Quilted fabric pet baskets look cute. Probably they're snug and cosy too. Unfortunately, in cleaning terms, they're hopeless. A bed for your cat or dog has to be one that you can clean out and disinfect regularly. Failure to do so means that your pet's bed is likely to become home to mites and fleas that live to bite your pet, making that basket not so cosy after all.

Wicker is a better choice because you can wash down the basket. Take it outside to clean. Shake out loose dirt then use a small stiff brush or the crevice tool on your vacuum cleaner to get out the rest. After vacuuming, always change the bag with care or empty the cylinder, as adult fleas may now be in your cleaner. Repeated wetting can weaken wicker, so only give the basket a thorough hose down occasionally. Choose a dry, sunny day so that it can air-dry quickly and thoroughly. The rest of the time content yourself with spray cleaner.

TipKing (www.tipking.com) recommends removing odours by sprinkling bicarbonate of soda in the smelly dog or cat's bed. It won't harm your pet, and freshens him as well as the bedding.

Avoid cleaning out your cat or dog's bed altogether – a cardboard box lined with old T-shirts makes for a super disposable bed. Each week, take it outside for a thorough shake and air. Each month, throw everything out (straight into the rubbish, sealed in a plastic sack) and begin again.

Taking care of toilet hygiene

People have moved house to get away from persistent indoor fouling by their cats and dogs. It really can be that bad. Don't let this happen to you! Accidents and behaviour problems leading to fouling happen. But failing to clear up the mess completely leads to repeat performances. Unless you clear up very thoroughly, your pet will recognise its own smell and see the inappropriate patch as its rightful place to perform!

Once urine has penetrated into floorboards and been left to sit for a long time, the potential for smell is always there. The damp atmosphere from a rainy day or an innocent water spill on the spot wakes up that pungent ammonia smell. There is no short cut: you simply have to go on cleaning and then cleaning again until you get up all the stain and smell. I run through exactly what needs to be done to remove tough stains in the Appendix at the back of the book.

If you keep a pet, be prepared to deal with waste products by having at hand an old spoon, disposable gloves, and a protective-breathing mask to block out the smell. Clearing up is an unpleasant and sometimes lengthy task that you are more likely to stick to if you're suitably equipped.

Keeping your dog on the spot

Think about how to present your garden or back yard to your pet. Just as a puppy gets quickly trained to go outside in the first place, it's relatively easy to teach your pet to confine itself to one section of the garden. Grim though it may sound, choosing a small earth bed for this purpose is best. Your task at picking up solid matter afterwards is easier – and you and guests can tread with safety over the rest of the garden. You can also buy commercial products from pet stores that are designed to break down your dog's excrement sooner, which may help combat fly problems in summer.

A woman who shows large dogs, and therefore has many, has the novel solution of an outside flush toilet. This means she can clean up her concrete yard in moments. But it's an excessive approach if you've only a dog or two.

If your outdoors is mainly concrete or lawn, the only solution may be putting waste material out with the rubbish. Keep a scooped trowel only for this purpose and a small lined dustbin, with a weather-tight lid, alongside the bed. On the day when your rubbish is collected, simply seal up the bag and discard it with everything else.

Staying on top of litter trays

Indoor cats, of course, need litter trays. But even if your pet goes outside, providing a tray in the house so that your pet doesn't use the lawn makes your garden a safer place to play for children and a nicer place to be for everyone.

Pregnant women should not clean the litter tray. *Toxoplasmosis* is an illness caused by organisms found in some raw meat and hence may also be present in cat faeces. If a mother catches toxoplasmosis during certain stages of pregnancy, the disease can affect the baby's development. If you're pregnant but absolutely have to be the one changing the cat tray, wear disposable gloves and take great care not to come into contact with faeces.

You can buy litter trays, liners, and litter at pet stores and supermarkets. You can also use just about any old large, deep, quality plastic tray. An old paint or garden seed tray is fine if it's a minimum of 30 centimetres (12 inches) long. (Two cats need a larger tray.) If your male cat has a habit of spraying rather than squatting consider buying a litter tray with a cover that he can go inside. Initially, start with the cheapest cat litter that you can find, moving up to a more expensive brand only if your cat won't use it.

To get the tray ready, put on the plastic liner, if you're using one, then lay down several thickness of newspaper. Pour out enough litter so that there's a depth of 5 centimetres (2 inches) in the tray.

Economy cat litter does the job, in that it absorbs wet, but it lacks the scent-retarding properties of pricier litters. Sprinkle a little bicarbonate of soda on the litter to mask bad smells.

Where you put the litter tray is crucial. It needs to be in a quiet place for your cat to want to use it and away from food preparation and eating areas. Naturally, you also won't want the tray in your bedroom or lounge! In many homes, this leaves only the utility room, if you have one, or a bathroom. The latter is a popular choice – especially a downstairs loo because you can simply pick out solid matter (with a gloved finger and special tongs) and flush it down the toilet. However it's no good if you've a big family or like to keep the door shut all day. Your cat may not wait!

When you're thinking on where to put the tray, remember that cats have no problem getting through small gaps or climbing. So look above the floor. Especially if you have toddlers or young children, it may be far safer to put the tray up on a shelf or even inside an open cupboard in the garage.

Dealing with cats that scratch the furniture

Cats adore hunting and sharpening their claws, and, clever creatures that they are, they don't need the natural recourses of live mice or tree bark to do these things. They're quite happy to use your carpet, curtains, and furniture instead.

Until you've lived with a wilful cat, you can't over-estimate the amount of damage one determined feline can do with its claws. One home I moved into had embossed wallpaper on the lounge. Within weeks, my cats were standing on the chairs, shelves, and even curtain-rails to plunge their claws into its satisfying depths and pull it off the wall shred by shred.

Your focus may be on damage limitation. If your cat is a scratcher, unless there is a good reason not to, you'll save a great deal of angst and money by letting her go outside. To protect your furnishings, you may also want to:

✔ Cover divan bed frames with a valance.

✔ Make use of smells that cats hate. Use a lavender-scented furniture polish; add small trims of orange peel into a pot-pourri.

✔ Secure delicate ornaments onto shelves with a dot of adhesive putty so that they won't fall and break if kitty jumps up.

✔ Go without net curtains. If privacy is an issue, consider light fabric blinds.

✔ Choose short-pile carpets. Steer away from Berbers. The weave in these is such that if one thread is caught, a whole row quickly becomes pulled out.

✔ Consider buying a scratching post, available at pet shops. (Once you have seen one in the shop you may decide to make your own.)

✔ Avoid embossed wallpapers.

Let your eyes and nose tell you when to change the tray – every day is ideal. Go outside, if you can, to change the tray. That way, you keep airborne particles that get raked up as you clear up outside your home.

Keep a plant sprayer ready with a mix of five parts water and one part white vinegar. Spray it regularly onto an area your pet mistakes for a bathroom as a deterrent.

Chapter 17

Cleaning for Special Occasions

• •

In This Chapter

▶ Getting your home ready for friends, family, and other important guests

▶ Keeping it all good clean fun at children's parties and sleepovers

• •

*O*pening up your home to friends and family is one of life's pleasures. And, believe me, entertaining at home can actually end up being less work than checking out an outside venue ahead of time, transporting yourself and possibly your family and guests to and from the place, and picking up the bill for the whole party as well as masterminding overnight hotels. How much easier is it to simply open your door on the day?

Whether you plan an intimate dinner or a major celebration, if you party at home, you can tailor the food, drink, and general ambiance exactly to suit the people you're spending time with. And if you really like them, you can simply let them stay over, perhaps all weekend. No wonder that staying in is the new going out!

Preparing Your Home for Visitors

Set aside extra time for cleaning in the days before you expect guests so that you can present your home at its best. Whilst it may seem that you're doing a whole load more cleaning because someone special is due, you're actually doing the same cleaning you always do. You're just cramming in big jobs, such as shampooing the carpets perhaps, that you might otherwise have spread over the next month or so. After the guests leave, you can relax and enjoy a spruced-up home for the next fortnight or so. I talk about timing and techniques for a major clean in Chapter 3, so check there for the particulars and pay special attention to these tips:

- ✔ Concentrate on shifting clutter. More people about the place definitely means less space. Scoop paperwork, magazines, and items you don't have time to put away properly into a lidded crate and hide it away.

- ✔ Free up tabletops so that your guests have somewhere to stand that welcoming drink. Put out extra mats and drinks coasters to protect furniture from ring marks. Position plenty of ashtrays if you permit smoking indoors.

- ✔ Pay good attention to the hall. If it looks clean and inviting, your guests are likely to see the rest of the house in the same light, even if other rooms aren't so sparkling.

- ✔ Dust mirrors, pictures, and any other notables, such as unusual ornaments or collections. Guests always check these out.

- ✔ Assess the damage potential of your guests. A score of teenagers romping through the lounge may mean clearing all breakables and protecting upholstery with washable throw covers. But it's good sense to put away anything irreplaceable anytime you host a large or lively event.

Hosting Parties at Home

The secret to successful entertaining lies in setting a few limits. Cut your preparation and after-the-event clearing up substantially by setting restrictions in these key areas:

- ✔ **The number of rooms open to your guests:** Close the door on unnecessary work by shutting off out-of-the-way rooms. For a supper for friends, for example, you might concentrate your time and cleaning efforts on the room where you'll eat, the lounge, and the bathroom.

✔ **The variety of food and drink that you offer:**
Restaurants offer a full menu because they have plenty of
staff and an amazingly well-stocked freezer. But as the
home entertainer, you know your guests and can find out
whether a guest prefers a veggie or low-carb option.

✔ **A time limit to the occasion:** It's not just children's parties that benefit from having start and finish times.
Letting guests know what's expected of them allows you
as host to allocate to yourself sufficient time to get ready
for your guests and clear the decks after they have left.

The people you invite to your home come to see you and to
enjoy your company. If they wanted to see spotless floors and
immaculate furnishings, they could tour a show home or
traipse through a furniture store.

Getting ready for a party

Make it easy on yourself by getting out everything you need
ahead of time. In particular, organise the glasses. If you
haven't used them in a while, restore a clean gleam by washing in soapy water, rinsing in hot water to which a tablespoon
of white vinegar has been added, and drying with a linen
cloth. Polish away any scratches by rubbing over them with a
toothbrush topped with a pea-sized dab of white, non-gel
toothpaste.

Whether you let guests help themselves to drinks or tend bar
yourself, leave a clear-up kit of cloths and kitchen roll (paper
towels) by the bottles. (I cover spills remedies in Chapter 19.)

Be creative with lighting on evening occasions. Turning down
the dimmer switch or placing lamp stands with upturned
lighting in the main room very effectively hides the state of
your carpet or the marks where the cat clawed the chair.

Bracing for a children's party

A party at home lets your child have the unique joy of playing
mini host at the place she loves best. Prepare ahead of time
by moving furniture to the sides of the room, and turning
sofas around so that they can't be sat on. Now, there's just
the floor to fret over. Choose non-mess sweets, such as hard
candies – never chocolate! – for treats and you'll be fine.

Plan to serve finger foods such as sandwiches and one-bite cakes. The ultimate in no-mess eating is to provide individual cardboard lunchboxes. Fill them in advance with sandwiches and treats. Avoid any food that may leave permanent stains. Don't torture yourself with the prospect of blackcurrant juice on a cream carpet when children enjoy lemonade just as much.

Forget using a tablecloth for the party table. Tablecloths with cartoon characters look cute, but it only takes one child to give a tug and send the whole spread onto the floor. Go for large plastic mats instead. Don't even go to the table with pre-schoolers. Lay down old sheets on the floor and get everyone to sit in a circle for a party picnic.

Keep plates and cups plastic to avoid breakages, and use bowls rather than plates for under-eights. Steer clear of disposable cups and bowls, which aren't very child-friendly. The cups crack and the plates aren't rigid enough to hold with one tiny hand. Durable plastic is tougher, gets dropped less, and is really very little hassle to wash up afterwards. Look for plastic picnic sets at sale time and, after you've used it for a few parties, you'll save money too.

Get together an accident kit, because it's an odds-on certainty that you'll need it. I'm not talking plasters (bandages) here, although of course you should have a first-aid set handy. Rather, an accident kit is your first defence against spills. I always have the following to hand:

- A blunt knife and spoon for scraping solid residues.
- Paper kitchen roll (paper towels).
- A lidded plastic container to safely and very quickly contain any glass or sharp splinter breakables.
- Spray stain-remover for carpet.
- Thick tea towels for spills.
- A spare T-shirt. I like to prepare for the children themselves and always have a spare T-shirt handy. Girls especially can fly to hysterics if they drop spills on their special party top. I guess the final preparation is an empty washing machine so that you pop the party poppet into the spare T-shirt whilst you run dirty clothing through the

quick wash cycle. Sometimes it's the only way to mop up a tiny guest's tears.

Holding the party in the garden – even if the weather is poor – may be the best way to safeguard your home from the perils of a children's party. Clear out the playhouse or your shed, then fit up a plastic or canvas extension using garden gazebos.

Follow these tips to cut the mess during the party:

- Ask children to take off their shoes – but not their socks – if the room is carpeted. Hard floors are too slippery for stockinged feet.

- Keep everyone busy. Bored children are the ones who grind toffees into the carpet, so plan stacks of games or pay for a professional child entertainer if this isn't your strength.

- Limit food and drink to one room. This can be tricky, because children can feel thirsty almost as soon as they arrive. Get in a supply of small drink cartons or have water available in plastic cups.

- Mop up spills promptly. I run through cleaning up everything a children's party is likely to throw your way in the Appendix.

Firing up the grill

You escape most of the mess in your home if you host a barbecue party. But you have to make some preparations. In Chapter 11, I discuss cleaning charcoal and gas grills. You also need to wipe seating, sweep patios and decks, and move container plants away from the barbecue.

Before you set up the barbecue, hold up a wet thumb to check the wind direction. Position your grill so that the smoke blows away from your home and guests. Practically everything you grill means a greasy plate, so cut the mess by cooking food on disposable wood skewers that guests can simply hold.

Never empty your barbecue's drip tray down an outside drain. It could start a blockage. Let the fats solidify then put them into a sealed plastic bag and put out with the rubbish.

Managing a major celebration

Don't be scared by big numbers. Yes, there is more work to do if you have 100 rather than 10 guests. But it's very unlikely that you're doing it single-handed. In fact, you may find that your role becomes that of organiser, so much so that you don't get your hands dirty at all.

Cut out cooking for the family on the night before party day. Eat cold or get in a takeaway meal. You don't want to be dipping into the cutlery and plates you already sorted for the party. Making the kitchen a no-go zone means that once you're cleaned up, you stay ready.

Make ready a sturdy box for empty bottles that you can take to the recycling depot later. Stand it on a worktop, not the floor. Smashed bottles are hard to deal with.

You simply won't have time to wash used cutlery and plates as you go along. Scrape food leftovers promptly into the bin then stack dishes carefully into lidded plastic storage boxes. You can get the dishwasher going tomorrow.

Cheap rubbish sacks are the ultimate false economy. Party rubbish is likely to contain half-full beverages and uneaten food. Avoid the revolting clear-up job that a split sack means by choosing heavy-duty rubbish sacks. The garden refuse kind hold up best to wet rubbish.

Welcoming Overnight Guests

Most of the preparations that you do before people stay over in your home are to do with welcoming, rather than cleaning. So take yourself into the room where your guests are going to sleep. Sit on the bed and try to think what extras would make you feel at home in this room.

You probably only need to do minimal cleaning. Vacuum and make up the bed with fresh bedding. Many people like two pillows and as well as the duvet, leave an extra blanket in case your guests keep their central heating higher than you do. Don't forget to leave fresh hand-towels on the bed.

For a children's sleepover party, there's no need to do the preparations you might with conventional overnight guests, such as clearing out wardrobe space. Ask the children to bring their sleeping bags. Limit numbers so that your child and her friends can all sleep in the same room, even if this means taking out the desk and chest of drawers.

Unlike daytime events, where you can police what your children do, eat, and drink, sleepovers tend to mean a freer rein. Staying up too late and snacking into the night are the name of this game. So you'll need to backtrack on cleaning and tidying away, too. This is also one event where you will have time to do it all in the morning: it's unlikely that your young guests will surface early.

Part V
Removing Stains

The 5th Wave By Rich Tennant

"You know, you're never going to get that dog to do its business in your remote control dump truck."

In This Part . . .

Clean is good, but staying spotless is even better. Yet accidents do happen, so this part looks at what to do to prevent spills from turning into permanent stains. First, there's a thorough spin through how to correctly wash, dry, and iron your clothes and home laundry. Then, it's on to troubleshooting. Many quite different stains behave similarly when they hit fabric or carpets, so I run through how to tackle these groups of stains. Some of the bad guys may already be familiar to you – for example, if you run a car, you've probably encountered oil-based stains, and if you run a household full of kids, you've dealt with ink-based marks in all likelihood.

In this part, I tell you what to do the instant an accident happens. Or maybe you already have a hard-to-shift mark on something in your home, such as pet soil on a carpet or grease on your favourite shoes. Chapter 20 on treating problems around the home aims to help you lift and shift the impossible! Finally, I give solutions for scratches and rips. If your dog has chewed the sofa or clawed into a wood floor, Chapter 21 is for you.

Chapter 18

Caring for Your Clothes

· ·

In This Chapter

▶ Understanding care labels

▶ Choosing between the washing-machine and hand washes

▶ Explaining detergents and fabric conditioners

▶ Ironing tips

▶ Folding and storing clothes

· ·

Cleaning your clothing is one area in which it's easy to do passably well without much effort: Simply stuff everything into the washing-machine, wait through its rinses and spins, pop the clothes into the drier, and possibly iron a few of them. Barring a washday disaster now and again, you get by with a minimum of fuss.

However, if you do the washing with that bit more care – giving your clothes and home laundry the attention they deserve – the rewards are huge. As well as getting the whole wash load as clean as can be, you have items that feel fresh, keep their shape and colour, and look new for longer. You also realise big-money savings because correctly washed clothes, bedding, and towels last years longer.

Looking after Fabrics

Before you clean anything, you must first discover what materials it's made from. Ideally, check when you're in the shop, before you buy, not standing in your home in front of the washing machine! There's no shame in knowing that you'll never bother to hand wash delicate silk and begrudge the money to take it regularly to a dry cleaners. But it's a major waste to buy a silk shirt then leave it in the wardrobe because you can't hack the attention it needs.

Modern technology means that the clothes and textiles in your home are made from scores of combinations of natural and synthetic fibres. It's not enough anymore to know how to wash cotton, polyester, and wool. You also need to know whether your item can withstand the heat and tumbling of the drier and whether to fold it or hang it in the wardrobe (closet).

Fortunately, this isn't knowledge you need to learn by heart. Thanks to care labels attached to clothes and household textiles, the basic care instructions are written down for you as symbols. Each gives the maximum water temperature and the degree of spin speed – fast, medium, slow – that can be safely used.

In the UK the law states that all fabric items must have care instructions. So look for the label when you buy. Formulated by an international panel, these symbols should be the same no matter where the clothing is made or sold. So these symbols hold good for items you pick up on holiday on the Continent, in the US, or in Asia. Table 18-1 lists the various symbols and their meanings.

Table 18-1		Understanding Care Labels	
Action	*Symbol*	*Description*	*Meaning*
Washing		A wash tub without a bar underneath suitable for cottons	Normal (maximum), washing conditions, including full spin, at the temperature written inside the washtub.
		The single bar underneath the washtub suitable for synthetics	Reduced (medium) wash conditions at the temperature shown on the care label. This is likely to mean a lower spin speed.
		A broken bar beneath the wash tub means suitable for washable wool	Much reduced (minimum) machine wash conditions. Choose the *wool or delicate* programme.

Action	Symbol	Description	Meaning
		Hand wash Only	Do not put into the machine! Wash by hand, keeping to any temperature shown.
Caution: Do Not		St Andrew's Cross	This sign superimposed over any washing symbol means that you cannot do that particular process. If it is seen on a wash tub, it means that you cannot wash that item at all, either in the machine or by hand.
Bleaching		Triangle, with letters *CL*	Chlorine bleach may be used.
		Crossed triangle	No chlorine bleach to be used.
Drying		Square with inset circle	May be tumble dried.
		Square with inset circle and two dots	May tumble dry on a high heat setting.
		Square with inset circle and one dot	May tumble dry on a low heat setting.
		Square with inset circle, crossed through	Do not tumble dry.
		Square with vertical lines	Drip-drying is recommended. So do not squeeze or wring. Hang whilst still dripping wet.
		Square with half-circle, inset like a washing (clothes) line	Hang out to dry having first removed excess water, through gentle wringing.
		Square with horizontal line	Dry flat.

(continued)

Table 18-1 *(continued)*

Action	Symbol	Description	Meaning
Ironing	An iron with three dots inside	An iron with three dots inside	Hot iron. Use the hot/maximum setting on your iron.
	An iron with two dots inside	An iron with two dots inside (many irons use the same dot system, so you don't need to estimate warm)	Warm iron. Use a warm temperature.
	An iron with one dot inside	An iron with one dot inside	Cool iron. Use the minimum setting.
	An iron crossed through	An iron crossed through	Do not iron.
Dry Cleaning	Circle (P)	Circle	The letter inside shows the type of solvent the dry cleaner can use. However, unless you see the words *professional dry clean only,* you are free to use the dry-cleaning machine at a launderette machine, matching the solvent letter to the solvent the machine uses.

Courtesy of the Home Laundering Consultative Council

Because standard (non-biological) detergents work best in hot temperatures and clothes that have been very thoroughly wrung out take less time to dry afterwards, high temperature/fast spin conditions are the ideal – but only if your clothes and bedding can take them.

Wool causes an enormous number of washday problems, because once it has shrunk, it cannot be stretched back to shape. Only wool marked *Pure New Wool – washable, pre-shrunk* can be washed in a machine, using the wool programme. All other types of wool or wool-rich garments must be hand washed or dry-cleaned.

Looking after your clothes requires more than simply washing them correctly. How you treat them whilst in storage, in drawers and wardrobes, and how you behave when you wear them is important too. For example, a just-cleaned fleece jacket won't stay looking good if it gets dropped onto the floor or scrunched into a drawer at home – fleece benefits from airing out on a hanger. Identify with the three stages of clothes care – washing, storing, and wearing – and you'll enjoy being clean and smartly dressed with less effort and expense.

New clothes and household textiles have labels that detail the fabrics they're made of. But you may have older clothes, curtains, and material for dressmaking that carry no identification. This is hard to get around. As a first step to identifying the type of fabric, compare it with known items. Take the item along to a dry-cleaners or a fabric store to get an expert opinion. But if you'd rather get going at home, you may like to try a couple of tests:

- **See how the fabric reacts with water.** Wet a small, inconspicuous area using a wet sponge. Let it –air-dry. If the fabric is washable, there should be no change. If instead you spot shrinkage or the material appears weaker or puckered, the fabric is dry-clean only.

- **Test for colourfastness.** This simple laundry test takes just a few moments, yet can save so much disaster and distress! Follow these steps every time you buy a new, coloured item:

    1. **Find an inconspicuous area of your garment.**

        You're looking for a spot where, if the colour does fade, it won't be a worry. Inside a seam allowance is perfect.

    2. **Make up a small solution of water and washing-detergent.**

        A teaspoon of powder in 100 millilitres (ml) (¼ pint) of warm water is fine.

    3. **Use a sponge to dampen your test area with the solution.**

        Let it sit for a few moments.

    4. **Blot up with a dry, white cloth.**

5. Check for colour on your cloth.

Any colour transfer means that your garment is *not* colourfast.

Repeat the test with hotter water if you plan a hot water wash, or try again with cold water if the fabric wasn't colourfast with the warm water solution.

Do this sneaky colourfast test when you're short on time: Simply get out the iron and steam press an inconspicuous area of fabric between two layers of white linen, such as an old tea towel. If there's no dye on the towel, your item is colourfast.

Wash coloured items separately the first time, even if the care label doesn't tell you to take this caution.

Knowing Your Washing-Machine

Two things sell washing-machines: a high spin speed and a large selection of wash programmes. But once back home, research shows that practically everyone ignores most of the options available on their new machines and sticks instead with two: one programme for everyday washing and a hot-wash option for linens and heavily stained items.

Yet this is all such a waste. Selecting the correct wash cycle saves energy, saves water, and saves unnecessary wear and tear on your clothes. If you're simply freshening clothes that haven't been worn in a season, why subject them to an hour of agitation and hot water? Similarly, you're wasting your time and the machine's life to use the standard cycle if a dust mite allergy means you need to rid all trace of the pests from bedding. Only a hot wash at 60 degrees Celsius (140 degrees Fahrenheit) destroys all mite eggs.

Washing machines imitate extremely vigorous hand-washing. With a hand-wash, physical strength to wring out wet items and a limit to how hot you can tolerate the water put a ceiling on how roughly you can treat your clothes. But with a machine, your only limit is the maximum temperature, maximum wring, or spin programme! All you need to do is match this up with the range of programmes your machine offers. Here's how:

1. **Select a wash temperature that's as close as possible to the maximum wash temperature on the care label.**

   If you need that shirt this evening, you may need to select the quick wash programme (cycle), even if you know your garment could have got cleaner still on a full-length cycle.

   Many people fail to realise that you have to take in two bits of information on wash labels: the temperature of the water _and_ the type of wash programme the item can safely withstand. These are not one and the same. So when you see the cotton symbol, you can't assume that the fabric can take the top temperature. Ditto when you spot a high temperature number on the label; it could be that the material still needs a gentle wash cycle and carries the wool wash sign. A maximum, fast wash could pull your item to shreds.

2. **Choose the proper spin programme.**

   Clothes going in the tumble drier can take a long or extra spin. But if you're washing nylons and synthetics that you plan to hang out, choose a lighter spin, so that the clothes don't pick up creases in a long spin.

3. **Put detergent in the machine.**

   Add tablets, powder, or liquid to the dispenser. If you use liquid capsules, put them in before the clothes. However, powder tablets contained in the manufacturer's net bag need to sit on top of the washing, so add the bag _after_ you add the clothes.

4. **Put the dirty items in the machine.**

   Don't overload the machine. If you pack it too tightly, there's less room for the machine to agitate the dirt out of your washing. The best way to get a correct load is to weigh it to fit in with your machine's capacity (check out the upcoming 'Weighing your washing' section for more weight advice). As a very rough guide, if you have more than 15 items, you've put in too much. I realise that this is hard advice to stick to. It's always so tempting to add just that one more thing, but restraining yourself gives you much better washing results.

Make these important checks before every wash:

- ✔ Empty out pockets. One tissue can leave fluff on an entire wash load.

- ✔ Do up zips. Left undone, they may snag other clothes.

- ✔ Take out items that need sewing attention. A small rip is likely to become larger through washing and a small, loose button could disappear.

- ✔ Turn T-shirts with a pattern inside out.

- ✔ Put small delicate items, such as sheer tights (nylons), into a mesh wash bag to protect them from snagging.

- ✔ Load the drum (basket) loosely, alternating big and small items.

- ✔ Follow instructions for the most delicate part of an item with two or more materials. It may make sense to separate the two materials. For example, you may want to detach a delicate lining from strong but dirty curtains or remove a non-washable ribbon from a child's outfit.

- ✔ Be on the lookout for stains. Some may need pre-treating. This is especially important for blood, emulsion (latex) paint, ink, rust, and grass, which becomes harder to shift if it sits in hot water. See Chapter 19 and the Appendix for extensive advice on removing stains.

- ✔ Think about colour. Ideally, divide your washing into separate loads for whites, coloureds, and darks/blacks. This means you can use a detergent with brightening agents for whites, and a separate detergent for colours.

 Wash red fabrics you suspect may bleed colour separately. Put an old white hanky in the wash load. If it emerges white, you know that the colour run on these items has finally stopped.

Use your judgment. Items that are old or worn may not react as typical for their fabric type. You may want to pretend that they're made of something more delicate.

Weighing your washing

Question: How many items fill a washing machine? Answer: A whole load less than you think!

Get out the bathroom scale and scoop on all the clothes and bedding you'd normally push into one wash load. Now throw off items until you get down to 5 kilograms (kg) (11 pounds [lb])...then down some more to 2.5kg (5 lb). Unless you have a large capacity machine, these weights represent the maximum weight load of a typical washing machine at full and half capacity – but only if you're doing a general wash of cottons and linens. Switch to man-made or wool fibres, and you can load in even less – synthetics and delicates max out at 2 kg (4.5lb) and woollens get just 1kg (2.2 lb).

These lower weights are because synthetics and delicates are washed at lower temperatures, and so need more agitation and washing detergent to get clean. Synthetics are also more prone to creasing if overloaded. However, wool needs more room because it swells in water. For all fabrics, overloading the machine means clothes aren't washed as well as they could be. Some stains may remain because they didn't have room to get agitated away.

Table 18-2 lists the weight of various items you may put in the washer in grams (g) and in pounds (lb) and ounces (oz) in parentheses.

Table 18-2	Weight of Selected Fabrics	
Article	*Material*	*Weight*
Clothing		
Anorak, adult	Cotton mix	750g (1lb 10oz)
Anorak, child's	Cotton mix	450g (1lb 1oz)
Briefs	Cotton mix	40g (1½oz)
Dress	Cotton	150g (5oz)
	Synthetic	350g (12oz)
Jeans	Cotton	700g (1lb 6oz)
Jumper	Wool	450g (1lb 1oz)
	Synthetic	350g (12oz)
Shirt	Cotton	300g (1lb 6oz)

(continued)

Table 18-2 *(continued)*

Article	Material	Weight
	Synthetic	200g (7oz)
Socks	Cotton mix	50g (2oz)
T-shirt	Cotton	125g (4½oz)
Household Items		
Bath sheet	Towelling	1,000g (2lb 3oz)
Bath-towel	Towelling	700g (1lb 8oz)
Double duvet cover	Cotton	1,500g (3lb 5oz)
	Other	1,000g (2lb 3oz)
Double sheet	Cotton	800g (1lb 12oz)
Hand-towel	Towelling	350g (12oz)
Pillow-case	Cotton	200g (7oz)
Single sheet	Cotton	350g (12oz)
Tea towel	Cotton	100g (3½oz)

Choosing detergents

Personal preference is a huge issue in deciding on what brand and form of laundry detergent to use. But in truth, powder detergent best suits some wash loads, whilst liquids or capsules give top results in other situations. I give you the pros and cons of various forms of detergent in Table 18-3.

Table 18-3 **Comparing Types of Detergent**

Detergent Style	Advantages	Cautions
Washing powder	Measure out how much you need	Easy to spill
	Dissolves fairly quickly for short washes	Bulky to store

Detergent Style	Advantages	Cautions
	Economical	Can clump in damp cupboard
Washing tablets	Speedy. Pop into the dispenser or back of the drum and you're ready to go!	Don't do as well on quick washes as tablets take some time to dissolve
	No mess; compact storage	No good for hand-soaking
Liquid detergent	Great for short, low temperature washes as no need to dissolve	Can get messy to store
	Use as spot treatment: dab liquid onto cuffs and collars then machine-wash at once for concentrated cleaning	Can't hold liquids for both pre- and main wash. After the pre-wash has finished, you have to return to pour in more liquid
Liquid capsules	No measuring, just sit capsule inside the wash drum	Can't use as spot treatment
		Messy when capsules split, and liquid is also a big skin irritant

After you decide on a form of detergent, there's the issue of whether to use bio or non-bio detergent and whether to use all those extras, from pre-wash boosters to clever fabric conditioners that cut down on ironing time. Strip away the hype, and it doesn't have to be complicated. Check the following 'Touching on fabric conditioner' section for information on conditioners, and here's my take on the wash-programme questions:

✔ **Pre-wash treatment:** Adds a concentrated squirt of detergent before clothes go into the wash. A good idea if you want to target particularly dirty areas like shirt cuffs. But a quality detergent probably doesn't need them.

A little lateral thinking goes a long way in the laundry. If dirty shirt collars are a regular problem, the best cleaner may be hair shampoo. Simply rub into the spot, then machine wash as normal.

✔ **Wash booster:** Adds cleaning agents, often including oxygen bleach, to your wash. Fill with detergent, then pour the wash booster in only when you hear the water running. It's too strong to land undiluted onto your clothes.

✔ **Detergent:** Dissolves grease and loosens dirt, including surface stains. It's not unlike washing-up liquid in that it's a chemical mix. However, washing-powder detergent is more concentrated and low lathering. You can choose from several types of detergent:

   • **Biological:** Contains enzymes, which improve stain shifting. So choose this type if your laundry is dirtier than average or has hard-to-shift stains. Quality brands work even at low temperatures. However, they can irritate delicate skin.

   • **Non-biological:** A detergent that has no enzymes. Those specifically aimed at people with sensitive skins may also be fragrance free.

   • **Colour-care:** Contains no bleach. This type gives the full wash power of bio without colour fade.

Touching on fabric conditioner

Fabric conditioner (softener) works the same way as the conditioner you choose for your hair. The conditioner coats individual strands – in this case fabric strands – to give a smooth, soft final texture. For clothes, this invisible layer also provides some protection from wear and tear. Fabric-conditioned clothes last longer. The drawback is reduced absorbency. So if you accept that a good bath-towel needs to be absorbent rather than smooth, ditch the conditioner on towel wash loads. A handy alternative is to add a cup of white vinegar to the rinse. This adds softness without compromising absorbency.

Fabric softener, or conditioner, usually goes into a set compartment in the washing-machine dispenser, ready to be released during the final rinse.

Always choose concentrated conditioner. It cuts storage space and is cheaper as long as you follow the correct dosage exactly.

Troubleshooting washing-machines and wash loads

Especially when you're up against time, it can sometimes seem that there is so much that can go wrong with this area of domestic life! Your washing-machine is subject to water problems, detergent and conditioner build-up, and other problems that make it function with decreasing efficiency. Likewise, your wash loads may come out smaller or a different colour than you intended. In the following sections, I offer help and solutions to a variety of machine and wash-load problems.

Taking care of your machine

Sixty per cent of the UK, as well as some areas in the US, has hard water. As well as meaning that you have to use more detergent to create effective suds, there's the risk that limescale deposits may build up on water pipes. Over time, the limescale clogs up the pipes until there's hardly room for water and suds to travel along the pipe as well. If you notice that your pipes are slow to drain, use a limescale shifter. White vinegar is another option. Simply pour around 500 millilitres (2 cups) into the wash-powder dispenser, and run an empty cycle on hot.

If your washer has a filter, clean it after every wash. In a front-loading machine, look for the door at the base of the machine and before you open it place a shallow bowl underneath, ready to catch any drips. Unscrew the filter, then give it a quick clean under a tap before putting it back.

Fabric conditioner can quickly clog the dispenser. Simply pull out the drawer if you can and wash in the sink. If you can't detach the dispenser, leave it where it is and pour in neat (undiluted) white vinegar and run an empty machine cycle.

Don't forget the drawer recess. Every few months use an old toothbrush to clean out detergent residue.

Use neat (undiluted) white vinegar to shift partially dissolved powder tablets in the dispenser. To avoid this, lay tablets flat, rather than as a stack.

When it's below freezing outside, don't run a washing-machine located on the outside wall of an unheated utility room. If you suspect water pipes are already frozen, turn off the water taps and run a wash programme for a few seconds only. Unscrew the inlet hoses and position the rear drain hose so that it drips into a bowl. Run the rinse or drain programme to run water through the frozen hoses and shift the ice.

Running the hottest wash programme (cycle) with a generous amount of detergent but no clothes easily shifts stains inside the drum.

Prevent stagnant water smells inside the drum by emptying clothes promptly. Between washes, leave the door ajar or lid open. This also helps the door seal last longer.

Trapped wire from underwired bras is a popular reason to call for the washing-machine engineer (repairperson). So hand wash wire bras.

Turn down the volume on noisy washers by standing the machine on a rigid support base, such as thick chipboard. Machines standing on carpet or sprung wood floors will get a whole load quieter. Make sure the base is a few centimetres (inches) larger than the machine, so that it won't fall off during a violent spin cycle.

Correcting washing disasters

Sometimes your wash may pick up colours they shouldn't have; sometimes they lose colours they should. I tell you how to deal with some common problems in the following list:

- ✔ **Grey or dull whites:** Wash in the machine again using biological detergent. Choose the maximum/heavy soiling amount and a programme that's as hot as your clothes can take. Line-dry for light bleaching from sunlight.

- ✔ **Pink shirts:** Make them manly again by using a colour corrector. The easiest to use are in-machine liquids. Alternatively, if your item is bleach-safe, hand soak overnight in a solution of 10 millilitres (ml) (2 teaspoons) of bleach per 5 litres (1 gallon) of water.

- ✔ **Stretched out sweater cuffs:** A fast spin can stretch cuffs and ribbing out of shape. To restore them, dip the cuff in water, then dry with a hot hairdryer.

✔ **Shrinkage:** Whilst still wet, pull the garment gently back to shape, paying special attention to shoulders. You'll have more success with acrylics than with woollen items.

Try gently re-washing shrunken woollens in a mild hair shampoo. Just as it softens your hair, so shampoo can add sufficient softness to animal wool to allow you to stretch your garment back to shape.

✔ **Bobbles (pills):** This method works especially on acrylics. Cover affected areas in sticky tape, then pull up sharply to catch the bobbles.

✔ **Faded patches:** Infuriatingly these can be caused by splashes of concentrated detergent in the drum. Your aim is to put colour back onto the faded patch, which can be tricky as usually you're trying to remove dirt and so on from fabrics. Rewash with other items of the same colour, including any you know aren't fully colourfast.

✔ **Stiff-dry clothes:** If you left clothes too long in the tumble drier or on the line and they're now stiff and creased, the simple solution is to wash them again. With cottons, you can struggle to iron instead. But synthetics need to be washed to get rid of creasing. Add fabric conditioner to the final wash.

Peg (hang on the line) carefully to avoid creasing. Avoid pegging the shoulders. Instead, peg at the underarm seam. Turn brightly coloured clothes inside out, so that they don't fade in the sun.

Washing by Hand

Hand-washing is simplicity itself. Just follow these steps:

1. **Dissolve 2 teaspoons of soap flakes or powder in 10 litres (2½ gallons) of hot water or 45 millilitres (ml) (3½ tablespoons) of hand-washing detergent into the same amount of warm water.**

   Wait until the water drops to the temperature shown on your item's care label. If you're unsure, go with tepid.

2. **Immerse the fabric in the soapy water.**

3. **Wash clothes by gently squeezing the suds through them.**

Don't rub or wring.

4. **Rinse in warm or cool water.**

5. **Rinse again, adding 10 millilitres (ml) (2 teaspoons) of fabric conditioner to the water.**

    Agitate clothes with care and remove after three minutes.

6. **Take out the excess water.**

    How you do this depends on what you're washing. If there's no danger of stretching, then hand wring tightly and tumble or line-dry according to care label. But you cannot wring woollens or net and voile materials. Place non-wringable items between two dry towels to blot off the excess water. Smaller items can be rolled up inside one towel.

    Always dry woollens flat on a drying rack. Never hang them out on the line. Net curtains can be folded vertically then line-dried until just damp, at which point take them in and hang them again.

Hand-washing isn't a license to do as you please. Choosing to wash by hand is a way of limiting the rough-and-tumble that clothes get put through when they're wrung and spun through a washing-machine. So don't undo this good work by forgetting to give hand-wash clothes the lower temperature they also need. Especially if you wear rubber gloves, you may happily withstand a water temperature of 40 degrees Celsius (104 degrees Fahrenheit), but your delicate items may not! So use a thermometer – a drop-in children's bath temperature measure is ideal – to keep the temperature within the maximum on the care label.

Turning to Your Tumble Drier

An average drier holds between 5 to 6 kilograms (kg) (10 to 13 pounds [lb]) of dry cotton or woollen items. Synthetic fabric needs more space to tumble without creasing, so the maximum weight drops to 3kg (6.6 lb). Provided you don't overload your washing-machine – see the ' Weighing your washing' section for the weights of everyday wash items – you can simply transfer washing between the two machines. Exceptions are the few things that you can't tumble dry for fire safety reasons.

The high, dry temperature inside the tumble drier is suited only to items that have been washed in water. It isn't safe to tumble items that have been dry-cleaned. They may contain traces of flammable dry-cleaning solvents. In addition, you can't tumble:

- Foam rubber or rubber-like materials
- Plastic-backed film, as found on children's waterproof sheeting and PVC rainwear
- Large bulky items such as continental quilts, sleeping bags, pillows, double duvets

Don't tumble dry bulky quilts, even if you can fit them into the machine. A dry quilt is bigger than a wet one. So, as your bedding expands during drying, it could block airflow through the drier and create a fire hazard.

Tumble driers use heat to dry clothes. As the hot air tumbles through the wet washing, it converts to steam. In an air-vented machine, this steam goes through the outlet hose to the great outdoors. Condenser driers cool or condense this steam back to water, which sits in a tray at the bottom of the machine, ready to be emptied after each load. Although more expensive, condenser driers win on noise, lack of steam, and drying accuracy.

The most likely reason for a tumble drier fire to start is when a spark from the drier's heat source ignites a pile of the lint that hasn't been cleared away. Always empty the lint filter after each wash. Run your finger along vents too, to pick up any fluff that collects there.

Unless you're on a tight budget, there's no need to let fear of cost stop you from using your drier to the full. On high heat, electricity costs around 15 pence (p) per hour; around 8p per hour on low. And if you're really counting the pennies, tumbled clothes need less, and sometimes no, ironing. So there's an electricity saver there.

Tips for better tumble drying

- Cut your work on items that you know are hard to iron by giving them more room in the tumble drier and taking them out when they are slightly damp.

- Cut static by using fabric conditioner on clothes you plan to tumble.

- Take out and shake bulky items such as anoraks and fleece jackets every 15 minutes or so.

- Reduce the drying time when you're drying synthetics. A full wash load of synthetic fibres takes around 80 minutes to dry, compared with 120 minutes for a cotton load.

- Follow drying times on your machine, but take care not to over dry as this makes clothes feel hard and rough.

Many hand-wash items can be tumbled – just look on the care label. But don't take them dripping into the drier. Wring them if the material can handle it or wrap items between two towels and press out water.

Freshen unworn, dry clothes by popping them in the drier on a low setting with a fabric conditioner sheet for five minutes.

Pressing Your Clothes

Ironing is a job you either love or hate. So, I'll share a secret: Some weeks, I don't iron. Modern appliances and modern fabrics mean that you can do as I do yet still look smart. So to avoid or minimise ironing:

- Shop for clothes made from no-iron fabrics. Previously, this used to mean synthetics. But today, you can buy natural fibres, too. The 100 per cent cotton, no-iron shirt is a chain-store best seller.

- Stop line-drying. Along with fresh air, you can't help but blow in creases.

- Tumble dry on the low setting if possible. Remove garments promptly, and whilst still just damp.

- Put just-damp clothes onto non-wire hangers. Use the laundry basket only for undies and bedding.

- Remove light creasing by hanging your work clothes in the bathroom whilst you shower. The steamy heat loosens minor folds.

Ironing with a plan

For those items for which only perfect pressing will do, here's how to whip through the ironing that bit more quickly:

1. **Get your equipment sorted.**

   The equipment you need includes:

   - **Ironing board:** An ironing board with a large surface lets you work more quickly and easily.

     Most people keep the board down too low. Adjust it so that your arm is at a comfortable right-angle as it holds the iron over the board. Remember, too, to soften your shoulders as you iron, to cut the backache. Resist the temptation to hunch over!

   - **Iron:** It's the smooth, metal sole plate of an iron that, once heated, presses clothes flat. The steam function improves on this by adding fine sprays of steam onto your clothes. This dampens the fabric, making folds and scrunched material easier to press flat.

     Tap water eventually causes scale to form on the inside of the iron. You may want to buy distilled water, which is sometimes sold with a scent as ironing water. There's no need for this if you have a condenser tumble drier: the water that collects in the drier reservoir is already distilled. So pour it into your iron and go.

     Traditional irons have an onboard reservoir for water. But if you iron large loads regularly, buy a steam generator iron. These have a large separate water-tank that sits on the board, whilst you lift up the iron. This makes the iron light and easy to move and also means no waiting for re-heating.

   - **Water or distilled water:** For steam ironing.

   - **Wooden or fabric-covered hangers:** For just-pressed clothes.

   - **An old cloth:** For protecting delicate items.

2. Sort the laundry into ironing order:

- First iron silk, polyester, nylon, acrylic, and other synthetics that need the low heat setting. Start with small, fiddly items whilst you're freshest.

- Next come cotton and wool blends and polycottons that need medium heat.

- Lastly are linen and 100 per cent cotton, which you iron on the high setting.

3. Make sure the laundry is in prime ironing condition.

Ideally, the laundry is just damp. If the washing has stayed on the line too long and is very creased, you may need to dampen it with a fine mist spray before ironing.

4. Make sure the iron is ready.

Don't begin to press until the iron indicator shows it's at the right temperature and the water for steam has heated. Going too soon may make the soleplate leak water over your clothes.

5. Start ironing.

Use the whole board as you iron, arranging clothes so that you need to move them around as little as possible. Fold sheets into quarters before you start. Straighten trousers so that you can do a complete leg in one go.

As you work, move the iron gently across the board. It's tempting to dig down in an effort to knock out creases. But irons don't need pressure to work at their best. Go for a glide instead.

An iron that's too hot can pucker or discolour fabric in seconds. So never leave your iron stationary on fabric. If you are concerned that it may be too hot, test the temperature of your iron on an inconspicuous area of each fresh garment.

When in doubt, go inside out. Ironing on the wrong side protects the right side of the garment from the full heat. It also keeps distinct pile intact. So use this technique for ironing velvet and cord.

To prevent wool from developing a flattened shine, lay a damp cloth on top of the wool, then press gently.

6. **Hang ironed items.**

Have hangers ready and waiting for your clothes. That popular standby, the back of a chair, doesn't just lead to creases, but wood stain could come off onto any still-damp clothes!

Cleaning your iron

A dirty soleplate can transfer marks onto clothes as you iron, so if you notice grime, take action at once.

Whilst the iron is still warm (but not hot!) clean it with a nylon pan scourer and a non-scratch cream cleanser. Rinse afterwards using a dampened cloth.

Follow your iron's care instructions about descaling, using a kit which you can buy at any appliance or department store. The more you choose distilled water over tap, the less you need to do this. Indeed, some of the most expensive irons now never need descaling. If just the steam holes are clogged, when the iron is cold and unplugged, use a toothpick to get the bits out.

TIP

The quickest way to iron a cotton shirt

Pop the shirt across onto the board, and with the iron on the hot cotton setting, go round the collar, taking time on the points. Then do the cuffs, opening up double ones. Next up are sleeves: do the backs of the sleeves first, which keeps the front the smartest. Now fit the shirt along the ironing board so that you can iron from shoulder to tail in single strokes. Start with the left front, do the back, and then the right front, going around in a circle.

Folding and Storing Clothes

Do the final step in the washing chain correctly and whenever you open your wardrobe and drawers, you'll always have smart, clean clothes ready to greet you.

Less is more! Give the clothes that you like the hanging and folding space they deserve by regularly shifting those you don't wear. In the wardrobe, give enough distance so that items don't touch each other.

Develop a wardrobe system that works for you. Popular ideas are:

✔ **Colour coding:** Clothes run from black, navy, down to cream and white.

✔ **Like with like:** All skirts together, all trousers together, and so on.

✔ **By occasion:** Formalwear together, workday clothing together, and casual clothing together.

Keep clothes in shape by hanging up with buttons and zips fastened.

Fold jumpers (sweaters) across, not down. Gravity makes horizontal creases drop out more easily when you wear them.

Rotate bedding and towels by always putting just washed items onto the bottom of the pile in the airing cupboard.

More synthetic clothes mean fewer clothes-moths about. So unless you've had a problem, it's over-the-top to get out mothballs. A lavender sachet in the wardrobe is a gentler, more pleasant deterrent.

Chapter 19

Understanding Basic Stain Types

*T*here's a science to understanding stains, but don't worry, it isn't tricky. Simply take one porous item – your best shirt perhaps or the lounge carpet. Then bring it into direct contact with a liquid or part liquid – a glass of wine or stepped-on chocolate bar. As the two meet, particles from the wine and chocolate coat the fibres of your shirt or carpet. Result – a visible stain that needs to be shifted.

In a great many cases, getting the stain out is no problem at all. In fact, you probably do dozens of easy-peasy clear-ups each week, without paying any attention. Examples are bath water spilling over onto your clothes, shampoo or toothpaste on your top, and a digestive biscuit crumbled into the carpet. Solving these problems is as simple as waiting for your clothes to dry, spot-washing your top, and getting out the dustpan and brush. Because the liquids involved dissolve easily in water, and the plain biscuit is totally dry and solid, taking care of these problems is no problem. So it sits solidly on top of the fabric and can be picked up, or brushed off, without leaving a mark.

In this chapter, I give you the basics about stains and how to deal with them.

Discovering What Makes a Stain Take Hold

Stain problems start when liquids aren't readily water-soluble or there's a colour transfer between a spill and your clothes or carpet. The staining substance visibly coats individual fibres on the stained material.

Some substances – ink, for example – stain instantly and you have to use some sort of solvent – methylated spirits (rubbing alcohol) in this case – to shift them. Some substances, such as egg on clothing, you merely have to rinse thoroughly in cold water and toss in the washing-machine.

Depending on the substance, you may want to wait for it to dry, you may want to freeze it or dilute it with water, but the one thing you almost always don't want to do is to heat it. Heat from the drier is probably the number one culprit when it comes to setting stains permanently. If you're treating a stain by washing the stained material, *always* check to see that the stain is gone before you put the fabric in the drier.

Sometimes the staining substance penetrates and then changes the structure of the fabric or surface forever and becomes impossible to shift. But all is still not lost. You may be able to get the same stain-free look by deliberately altering the fabric again. If your red cotton shirt suffers a bleach spill and develops pink patches, just dye the shirt.

Spotting the Basic Stain Types

Identify the problem ingredient or ingredients in a food or drink spill and you're on your way to getting the problem sorted. In beetroot, it's a straightforward, if vibrant, colour dye. A vegetable curry can combine oil from the sauce with the colour transfer from a great many different spices. So small wonder that in surveys of UK dry cleaners, curry rates as the stain seen the most often.

Essentially, applying a solvent to a stain is like putting a car into reverse. Your aim is to find the solvent that rubs out the mark.

Often, finding that solvent involves nothing more than using your common sense. Poster-paint, that you have to mix with water before applying it to paper washes away with yet more water. If you need to clean brushes used to paint doors and windows with white spirit, you need to use white spirit to remove any paint splashes on the carpet or on your clothes.

Personal experience turns all of us into smart stain-shifters. Whenever you get a good result in stain treatment, you'll remember what you did, and when a similar accident happens, you'll be ready to act.

In the Appendix, I give an A-to-Z list of how to shift the most likely stains. So if you have a particular stain problem, you can turn directly to this now. If, however, there is no current emergency, it is worth spending a little time looking at how many different stains actually need similar treatment. This approach is also invaluable if you're not sure exactly what's been spilt. As I see it, you can divide most spills into just five categories, which I put into Table 19-1.

Table 19-1   Identifying and Treating Types of Stains

Stain Base	Examples	Characteristics	Treatment
Water	Ink from washable felt-tip pens, emulsion (latex) paint, potatoes	May look bright and alarming; may have distinct texture and appear solid.	Flush with running water; where possible treat the stain from behind. So turn clothes inside out, before holding under the tap. Use cold water, unless you know specifically to do otherwise.

(continued)

Table 19-1 *(continued)*

Stain Base	Examples	Characteristics	Treatment
Grease and oil	Butter, mayonnaise, curry, gravy, engine oil	Leaves a shine rather than a colour problem. Initially, things may not look too bad: but the grease residue becomes a magnet for passing dirt. Untreated grease stains, especially on carpets and pale clothes, can look worse over time.	Lift up the excess using a high-absorbency powder or substance such as salt, bicarbonate of soda, or cat-litter granules. Then dissolve the stain using biological laundry detergent. Rubbing neat liquid directly into the stain or pre-soaking may improve effectiveness.
Protein	Egg, blood, perspiration	These are deceptive because they look just like any other food and drink stain. However, using hot water on a protein stain sets it in the fabric.	Always soak in cold water before washing with detergent. Ideally soaking removes the entire stain, but machine-washing generally removes any residue.
Fruit and acid	Blackcurrant juice, lemon, bleach	A strong colour stain.	Hold stained fabric inside-out under the cold tap. Sponge with solution of bicarbonate of soda to neutralise the acid. Machine-wash. Use methylated spirits (rubbing alcohol) to remove any remaining colour residue, especially on carpet and non-washables.

Stain Base	Examples	Characteristics	Treatment
Chemical	Ink from ballpoint pens, hair dye, nail polish	Does not dissolve in water and is likely to bond with hard surfaces. Ink and hair dye may stain wood, enamel, and plastics and other surfaces from which protein- and fruit-based stains can be wiped away.	Find the correct solvent, which may be a trial-and-error proposition. Whilst some ink can be removed with acetone, the ink from other pens dissolves only in white spirit (turpentine) or hairspray. Before each attempt, it is essential to remove traces of the previous chemical.

Choosing the Best Approach for Every Surface

Clothes, carpets, and curtains are without a doubt the three key areas in stain removal. But there are stains waiting to happen to wood furniture, plastic toys, and floors too. In short, almost any surface is vulnerable to staining.

Always be aware of the limitations of your stained surface before applying a solvent. Practically any fabric can handle diluted washing-up liquid, but a bio detergent may be too much. Likewise, most materials tolerate cold water but hot water can make a wool carpet shrink.

Read the care label before you treat a stain. You must abide by the same maximums set for washing. Delicate fabrics and non-washables may have limited treatment options.

Whether you can physically pick up a stained surface and take it to the basin or get at both sides of the surface affects treatment along with the size, weight, and location of the stained surface.

Working on carpets

Stains on carpets lock into the pile and, if very wet, can penetrate down to the base.

Unlike fabric, you can't get underneath the stain on a fitted carpet in order to work at it. The next best thing is to use an oxygen-based cleaning product, or a regular cleaning mousse that lifts the stain up out of the carpet fibre. Your cleaning job is then to blot up the stain as it surfaces.

Finally, you need to rinse and then dry. Most carpets are at least partly synthetic and so cannot withstand hot water or bleach. Laying a colourfast towel on a clean dry carpet, then stepping on top, is kinder to the carpet fibres than bringing over a hairdryer.

Tending to upholstery

Excepting sofas and chairs with removable covers, the clear-up job means working on the spot and being careful not to wet the wood or metal interior. Do that and your sofa could rot before it dries out. So cleaning up here mostly means sponging. That's not to say it has to be just water. When the stain needs detergent to shift it, simply mix up bowl of soapy water, then use the foam only. Apply this via a sponge and you bringing cleaning power without excess water.

Most upholstery is best dried using the lowest setting on your hairdryer. Use a diffuser attachment to spread the heat. On velvets and piled fabric, use your hands to brush the wet patch so that it lies in the same direction as the rest of the seat.

Caring for clothes

When you're home, stain shifting couldn't be simpler. A quick change and you're ready to spot-clean, soak, or machine-wash as best suits the individual stain.

Make use of having access to both sides of the fabric. For standard washable stains, rinse the fabric under the tap inside-out. When a solvent is called for, put the stained side face down on a cotton pad. Then drip the solution from the back, so that the dissolving stain gets absorbed into the pad.

One caution: don't be too quick to tumble dry. The intense heat of the tumble drier can set a stain as it dries. You will find it much harder to get out a stain that has been through the tumble drier. After machine-washing, do a careful check to see that the stain is gone. If not, wash again, then consider trying a different stain-shifting technique, as detailed in the Appendix. If at any stage you want to get on with wearing the item as it is, even though there is still some staining, then peg it outside to dry using the sun's gentle bleaching power.

Fussing with furniture and other home surfaces

See Chapter 4 for advice on cleaning floors, walls, and ceilings as well as information on the maximum treatment various surfaces can take.

Always make sure that getting rid of the stain doesn't cause more problems than you started with. For example, there's no point getting a stain off a prized wood table if you warp the surface or cause ring marks.

On painted surfaces, a limited repaint can work out quicker than a complicated stain treatment.

Protecting Carpets and Clothes against Stains

Taking that bit extra care as you eat, drink, and carry out everyday work and leisure activities is the obvious first line of defence against stains. But there's no need to slow yourself down to a snail's pace – there's plenty you can do to protect your clothes and home surfaces yet still race happily about daily life!

Taking three small steps can make a big difference:

1. **Buy furnishings, furniture, and work surfaces for your home that are durable and washable.**

2. **Avoid whites, cream, and large blocks of pale colour with no pattern.**

   This holds just as good for clothes as sofas and walls.

3. **Think prevention.**

   This involves everything from using a serviette (napkin) when you eat soup to laying down an old cover over the bathroom floor before you do a home hair dye at the sink.

When you next choose carpets and sofas, ask about stain protection. You can get fabric that has an invisible layer on top of the material that traps stains. Stains simply can't penetrate through to cause permanent damage. Instead, spills sit on top of the material ready to be sponged off.

You can add stain protection to carpets you already own with a top-of-the range home carpet cleaner.

Some simple tips for avoiding everyday stains follow:

- ✔ Wear a kitchen apron whenever you cook with flour or make jams or pickles. Certainly wear one when you make anything at all helped by small children! A man's button-up shirt makes a super apron for children as you can wash it clean afterwards.

- ✔ Get the toddler dressed after breakfast. You'll save his smart day clothes from stains.

- ✔ Sit at a table to put on make-up and, if you're to wear a special party outfit, get your face on before you dress. Standing in front of a mirror is a recipe for dropping foundation powder onto the floor.

- ✔ Always protect floors and furniture before you undertake DIY projects. Flicks of paint spread further than you'd imagine.

- ✔ Ban non-washable pens and paint from the house whilst the children are small. Biros that have a built-in eraser are no good: The eraser works on paper but leaves a white mark everywhere else.

✔ Go into the garden to do messy jobs if you can. As a bonus, it's less of a chore to polish the silver or groom the cat if you can do it in the sunshine.

✔ Avoid putting down newspaper to protect surfaces. Wet newsprint can leave permanent staining and the paper sticks, too. Old sheets are much better.

✔ Stand jugs and bowls in the sink or on a draining-board when you fill them with liquid from saucepans. Serve soup at the table, using a spouted jug.

✔ Get to know which foods the kids especially can't handle neatly, and insist on serviettes tucked in at the neck for these times. Foods on our home's hit-list include spaghetti, soup, and ice-cream sundaes.

✔ Don't practise home juggling! Whenever you carry more than two glasses, plates, or food items, get a tray. Trays with in-built handles are the steadiest.

✔ Close the gap between your chair and the table. In the lounge, don't lounge to eat! Most coffee-tables are around the same height as the sofa or chair. So sit forward and use a side table or slip your legs sideways so that the table and food can get closer.

Get together a set of messy clothes and wear these whenever you paint or do heavy, dirty cleaning jobs. Machine-washable jog trousers and a long-sleeved T-shirt are ideal.

Chapter 20

Treating Everyday Stains

*O*nce, writing a feature for *Prima* magazine, I had to create the dirtiest jacket ever. On went a dollop of curry. Whoosh – I sprinkled blackcurrant juice onto the front. Kiss – I smudged lipstick along a lapel, and dipped a cuff generously into gravy. Finally, I got the cat to sleep on it. Now you might think that taking this little lot into the dry-cleaners would elicit disbelief. Yet, at four different chains of dry-cleaners everyone believed my explanation of a toddler gone mad in the kitchen, with my cream linen jacket the victim. More incredibly still, two managed to get the lot out . . . and the one that did it the best admitted that they actually washed it *three times*.

Dry-cleaning is good, but on fabrics that can take it, wet washing can shift more. In short, the sort of attention you can give at home is enough to clear up practically any mess. But you do have to be persistent. One lady at a dry-cleaning shop admitted she'd taken on my cream linen jacket as a challenge, and spent a great deal of time on it. Not in one go, because stain removal works best in short bursts. But whenever she had a moment, she tried something new: a range of stain-busting solutions, soaking, drip-wetting, cold, and heat. Eventually, she got there – and so will you. When a stain seems impossible to shift, but it's on an item that you really like, give it just a few more tries. So often, it's patience and persistence that win through. In this chapter, I walk you through all the techniques you can try.

Putting Together a Stain-Shifting Kit

Keep these items together, so that you can take them at once to wherever you need them in your home. A plastic tool caddy with a handle is ideal.

General items to collect include:

- ✔ **Bar soap:** Use it to cut through dirt- and grease-based stains. It's especially good for delicate fabrics.

- ✔ **Carbonated water (club soda):** A soda siphon if you have one is super. But sparkling mineral water is also good. This is an essential for carpet spills. The oxygenated bubbles help lift semi-solids and liquids out from the fibres.

- ✔ **Disposable gloves:** Some stain jobs are just so yucky that you don't want to have to wash out gloves afterwards.

- ✔ **Plastic spray bottle:** Ideal if you can't take your stain to the basin. Also, having one of these handy bottles about means that you can regulate the amount of water or diluted solvent you apply to your stain.

- ✔ **Protective facemask:** Use to protect your nose and mouth from chemicals as you work. Also, you'll stick at an unpleasant clear-up longer if your sense of smell is masked.

- ✔ **A roll of white paper towels:** Practically everything that you can spill can be blotted up with a few sheets of this. For sheer convenience, paper towels win out over old rags.

- ✔ **Small stiff brush:** Careful brushing can lift up dry particles before they get the chance to do damage. A brush is also perfect for loosening dried mud and grease stains that you've treated with an absorbing solvent.

- ✔ **Sponge:** You need this to deal with carpet and upholstery spills. Because you can't take the floor or the furniture to the sink, a thick sponge acts as your go-between. You use it to introduce soapy solutions to the stain, then to rinse the suds out.

✔ **White cloths or rags:** Save money by switching from paper towels to these when you've a major-league mess to sort out. Treat as disposable, and don't be tempted to launder them afterwards. There's a risk you could pass the stain to the rest of the load.

✔ **Blunt knife or spoon:** Great for scooping up solids before tackling the stain.

Add to your collection a variety of stain-fighting solvents, which I talk about in the next section.

Other household items that you may also call on include:

✔ **Biological detergent liquid (detergent with enzymes):** Use diluted to soak stained fabric. Can be applied neat to spot-treat cottons before they go into the wash.

✔ **Bleach:** Visibly fades stains on a variety of fabric and hard surfaces around the home. Great for mould stains on fabric and yellow perspiration stains on white shirts.

✔ **Denture cleaning tablets:** These are quite versatile with concentrated cleaning power. In the same way that they stop false teeth from yellowing whilst also removing everyday food stains, they also take out yellowing from stored cotton bedding, remove tea rings from mugs, and get scum stains out of vases.

✔ **Pre-wash stain remover or wash booster:** Give your regular detergent a helping hand whenever you load the washing-machine with highly stained items.

✔ **Shaving foam:** Good at lifting grease-based stains out of carpets. The mousse (foam) sits on the surface encouraging the stain to get up out of the carpet and join it. As it's in the bathroom anyhow, it may be the first thing you have to hand to clear up spilt cosmetics and body lotion or that creamy coffee in bed.

✔ **White vinegar:** You can do so much with this humble wonder. You use it most often as a final treatment, to remove all traces of smell from a stained area. But vinegar also has bleaching qualities, which means it can lighten colour stains such as ketchup.

Choosing Cleaners and Solvents That Work

A *cleaning solvent* is any substance that helps loosen or lift a stain. It doesn't have to be a chemical or be picked up in the supermarket's cleaning aisle. Solvents range from plain tap water to dry-cleaning solution. You just have to match the solvent to the stain and to the stained surface. I tell you how to do that in this section.

Like detergents, opened bottles of spot treatment lose their strength over time. So you don't want to keep a whole cupboard full of cleaners. A better plan is to use trial and error to find three basic multi-stain treatments that you like: one for washable fabrics; one for dry-clean-only fabrics; and one for carpet and upholstery. Then get in the following generic products (many of these cost less than £1 per standard bottle). Table 20-1 lists the uses and cautions of common solvents.

Table 20-1	Common Cleaning Solvents	
Solvent and Source	*Uses*	*Cautions*
Acetone. Get over the counter at the pharmacist (drugstore). Sold as non-oily nail polish remover for a premium on the beauty shelf.	Removes paint-based products, including nail varnish and ballpoint pen and correction fluid.	Do not use on acetate materials, as it will dissolve them.
Bicarbonate of soda (baking soda). Get at the supermarket.	A mild alkali that can neutralise acid stains and stop them from causing colour damage to fabric. The absorbing qualities of bicarb also make it useful for grease stains: Sprinkle the powder to mop up and lift grease and oils from fabric and wood surfaces.	

Solvent and Source	Uses	Cautions
Dry-clean stain remover. Look for it in the cleaning aisle at the supermarket.	Gets stains out of non-washable fabrics. If you've exhausted other ideas, can also be used with some success on washable materials. Best at grease-based stains.	Flammable. If used heavily on fabric, do not then tumble dry.
Glycerine. Sold as a cake-icing or soap-making ingredient at the supermarkets and craft stores. Can also be bought over the counter at the chemist (drugstore) where it is sold for use as a cough relief treatment and to soothe dry, sore skin.	Use to pre-treat tough, dried-in stains so that a second solvent can get to work on shifting them.	
Hydrogen peroxide. Sold as a mouthwash and disinfectant at the chemist (drugstore).	A non-smelling mild bleaching agent useful for getting dairy and protein food and drink stains out of carpets and clothes. Not a first line of attack, but worth trying if original solvent or a machine wash fails.	Rinse away all trace of previous solvent before applying hydrogen peroxide to avoid chemical reactions. Can remove the colour from fabric.
Methylated spirits (rubbing alcohol). Sold at the DIY (hardware) store and chemist (drugstore).	Good for removing colour stains, especially fruit-based. Apply neat, using a cloth or cotton bud (cotton swab) for extra control.	Harmful if inhaled; skin and eye irritant. Work in ventilated area.
Lubricant. You can pick up a light oil, such as WD-40, in DIY (hardware) and car-parts stores.	It gets under dirt to lift grease and oil off hard surfaces. Removes residue from sticky labels and wax crayons from walls.	Flammable. Work in a ventilated area.

(continued)

Table 20-1 *(continued)*

Solvent and Source	Uses	Cautions
White spirit (turpentine). Find at a DIY or paint store.	Traditionally used to clean paintbrushes, but also useful to thin down (and eventually shift) grease stains.	Harmful if swallowed; skin and eye irritant. Work in ventilated area.

Personal preference may lead you to proprietary stain removers. I like the cling that comes with mousse (foam), especially for carpet stains. For clothes, I want the precision that comes with a pump-spray cleaner.

Always read the cautions before opening any solvent. Not just your clothes and household surfaces are in danger! Your health is at risk too if you work incorrectly and particularly if you do so in poor ventilation. Methylated spirits (rubbing alcohol) and white spirit (turpentine) can cause irreversible lung damage if inhaled in quantity. Many stain removers, including acetone and those that mimic dry cleaning, are highly flammable, and that quality can persist. Therefore, never tumble dry clothes that have been heavily spot-treated.

Test for colourfastness before using any solvent. On a hidden area, dab on a little of the solvent. Blot off some with a cotton bud (cotton swab) – no colour should come off on the bud. Then wait until the solvent has dried to check that the final colour of the fabric or carpet remains unchanged.

Getting Rid of Stains

People like to act fast with stains because experience shows that a liquid that sets is harder to get out. But if you change just one thing about how you treat stains, my advice is to slow right down. I don't mean that you can think, 'oh, I'll clear that little lot up tomorrow' whenever a foreign substance hits your clothes or furnishings. But springing into action at an amazing speed is not the answer. First up, you'll probably spread the stain more by dashing about. Second, you need a few moments to decide on the best course of action.

Doing the wrong thing to a stain can be worse than doing nothing at all. Water that is too hot can set some stains, making them impossible to get out later. Any water at all on a fabric that is dry-clean-only can permanently ruin the material. Or even if it does no permanent harm water can make your stain shifting take much longer. Just compare sweeping up a spot of dry ash from the hearth to getting wet soot from the carpet. So with stains, as well as treatment, you have to be aware of damage limitation.

However often life throws stains at you, it's still hard to keep in your mind exactly how to treat them all. Of course, keeping a copy of *Cleaning & Stain Removal For Dummies* to hand takes away the need for memory or guesswork. But carrying it with you on holiday or to every restaurant meal is going a tad too far – so there will always be occasions when you have to wing it. At these times, aim to keep just five things in mind:

- ✔ **Keep it dry.** Reach for the soft brush before the wet cloth. Never add water to stains formed from totally dry powders. This is especially true for things dropped onto the carpet.

- ✔ **Keep it calm.** There is more time than you think before a wet spill turns into a set stain. In normal temperatures and situations, liquids give you more than a few seconds of thinking time.

- ✔ **Keep it white.** Blot up spills using white cloths only. A colourful napkin can create a second stain problem.

- ✔ **Keep it cool.** When you decide to try washing your wet stain away, always go to the cold tap, unless you specifically know otherwise.

- ✔ **Keep it simple.** Modern biological detergents are great. Once you get home, these will shift practically everything. So don't let what's bound to be a temporary stain ruin your fun.

Taking six steps to treat every fresh stain

Whenever you're able to react right away to an accident, there's a very high chance that you'll succeed at removing all trace. So think action, not crisis. Whatever you spill, this handy step-by-step process will work for you.

1. **Limit the damage.**

   Take a plain white – not coloured – paper or cloth towel to a liquid spill and, with care, blot from the centre of the spill to minimise spreading.

2. **Lift off solids, using a spoon and a blunt knife.**

3. **Stop and think! Identify the stain and its stain group – water-based, grease-based, and so on.**

   Read the care label, if there is one, so that you know what this fabric can happily withstand.

4. **Unlock the stain by turning it into a liquid.**

   To do this, you use a solvent. Look up the individual stain in the Appendix at the back of the book.

   Water, the simplest solvent, works more often than you might think. But don't guess on this; you also need to get the temperature right, because getting it wrong (as in too hot) can make the stain permanent.

5. **Work from the inside out if you can.**

   It's far simpler to push the liquid back out the way it came, and doing so stops the stain from going right through the fabric on its journey out. (Clearly you can't do this with fitted carpets.)

6. **Be ready to repeat everything, perhaps several times.**

Treating older stains

If you can soften or totally wet your old, but previously untreated stain, you can relax because it won't seem old to the stain solvent.

Liquid glycerine can successfully soften most food-based stains. Apply it neat or, on delicates, mix it with an equal part of water, then leave it an hour to soften. Rinse off, and begin stain treating.

The hardest stains to shift are those that have been set by heat. A stain that has been through the drier is unlikely to come out. Of course, there are exceptions as well as new ways to look at an old problem. For example, if a hot drier has set a bloodstain, you may want to consider bleaching it away. At this stage, it's also worth buying a proprietary stain remover especially for your stain type, though this is an expensive way of doing things.

Today, bio-detergents are so good that they get at stains like chocolate, wine, coffee, ice cream, and grease that needed a specialist remover 20 years ago. To give the detergent its best shot, remember not to overload the machine and choose the hottest programme safe for your item.

If you've already had a good go at removing a stain, it takes persistence to keep coming back to it. But do go to the Appendix at the back of the book and check for ideas that are new to you.

Taking emergency action when you're out

Embarrassment isn't a valid reason to delay attending to a food or drink stain at dinner. But personal modesty may mean you have to treat stains differently. Here's what to do when the sauce hits your shirt.

✔ Don't reach for the serviette (napkin): If it's a coloured tissue one, the dye could come off on your shirt.

✔ Excuse yourself from the table and go to the cloakroom. Before thinking about wetting the stain, check to see that there's a facility to dry it off afterwards. If there's no hot-air drier, you will be far more self-conscious walking back into the restaurant with a large wet patch on your shirt than with a small gravy stain.

✔ Wet the stain from underneath, by holding it directly under the *cold* tap. Your aim is to push the stain back out through the fabric. If you aren't able or don't feel comfortable doing this, do not be tempted to get a wet tissue and rub at the stain instead. You'll simply spread the problem.

✔ Blot the fabric dry. If you're certain that the stain has gone, go ahead and dry with the heater. If some staining remains, do not use heat as it can set the rest of the stain.

Carry a sachet of spot-stain treatment in your bag or in the car. Add a small roll of sticky tape to pick up dry and powder stains and you have the perfect on-the-go stain-shooting kit.

Fighting impossible stains: What to do when nothing seems to work

Defeat isn't a word I like to associate with a stain. But let's be realistic – every now and again, you meet with a mark that you just can't shift even though you've tried everything you can think of and everything I suggest. When you reach that point, try these tips:

- ✔ **Seek expert advice:** Take the item along to a dry-cleaner, even if it is washable. They may have met with a similar problem and found a unique or unconventional approach that worked.

- ✔ **Take more risk:** If you cannot bear to use the item as it is, it's not such a big deal to risk destroying it altogether by using too harsh a stain treatment. So decide to ignore the care label and wash at a hotter temperature than is recommended. Or wash a non-washable. Remember you're doing this only as a last resort and that you could ruin the item completely.

- ✔ **Cut the stain out:** On carpet, hold small scissors as horizontal as you can to cut away damaged pile. On laminate or wood floor, refit a new panel.

- ✔ **Mask the damage:** Choose from the following options or try your own:
  - Add a floor rug.
  - Only wear the shirt under jumpers.
  - Adjust curtain pleats at the top to hide a stain within a fold of fabric.
  - Turn up shirt cuffs and skirt and trouser hems if possible.
  - Add trimmings, badges, or bows to cushions, children's clothes, or tableware.

- ✔ **Bleach out the stain:** On whites, this is generally a good idea. But it's a last resort for coloureds, as you'll remove colour throughout.

- ✔ **Dye the fabric:** Including towels, bedding and shoes. Go dark to cover over the stain as well.

- ✔ **Paint over hard surfaces:** With specialist paint, you can cover plastics, enamel, ceramic, and metal as well as wood. Doing so also paints out your stain problem.

Don't knock learning to live with the stain. Like that old saying – don't throw the baby out with the bath-water – there's no sense in throwing out the bathroom suite (fixtures) for the sake of one hair-dye stain on the sink.

Chapter 21

Tackling Scratches, Scuffs, and Rips

··

··

*E*veryday wear and tear is the classic clause that gets quoted when companies don't want to pay up against your complaint that this season's shoes have already fallen apart at the seams or your five-year-old sofa has developed a split. When the shop won't take it back and the insurance company doesn't want to know (or you'd rather hang on to a no-claims discount), it pays to get fixing. This chapter tells you how.

Dealing with Simple Furniture Problems

Call in a professional wood or furniture restorer when a valuable item gets a scratch or dent. But for everyday pieces, you can do a very acceptable cover-up job yourself.

Making quick work of scratches

There are two ways to tackle a scratch on wood or other hard surfaces: Either sand the surrounding area down to the level of the scratch so that the surface is smooth once again, or colour in the damage, which means that you can still feel the scratch indent but you can't see it.

The first method needs fine sandpaper and loads of patience. The sanding itself isn't a big job; you simply rub with care over the length of the scratch, moving in line with the wood grain. The time-consuming part is that you need to re-varnish, paint, or wax the area to get back to a uniform colour.

So, for everyday wood and wood-effect furniture, you may want to take a short cut and simply cover up the scratch. Ideally, use wood stain or a coloured polish that matches your furniture. Apply the solution to a soft cloth, and then work it into the wood. If you can't get a colour match, use a wax crayon. Most children's ranges have a tremendous variety of browns – and these duller shades always kick about in pencil cases after the snazzy reds have long gone.

To fix scratches in leather, again use wax crayons. This is effective for both bags and shoes, and can work as a last resort for coats. Polish afterwards with a soft cloth to remove loose wax.

Scratches in plastic are less easy. It is worth trying a light oil such as WD-40 on white appliance scratches, such as fridges and washing machines. However, on white plastics that have a natural matte finish, doing nothing brings a solution of some sort. Scratching shows up most obviously on surfaces that are highly polished. As your items ages, scratches blend in.

Repaint over scratches in paint. Simply paint over the scratch and then, just before the paint has dried, take a damp cloth and blend the edges of the new paint in with the original paint to avoid any tell-tale lines.

Dealing with dents

It's a paradox: Metal and wood can be strong enough to sit on yet dent with a simple blow from a hard object. Here's how to fight back.

Bang out dents in thin metal, such as a patio tabletop, using a hammer. Work with care from the other side – you don't want to create more dents.

Careful use of water can get a dent out of wood. But be aware that you're treading a fine line. Water can stain and warp wood, so don't try this on an irreplaceable item. Put a small amount of liquid over the dent. The wood swells as it absorbs the liquid, thus filling the dent. Dry thoroughly.

Use filler to repair dents in painted walls. Smooth the filler, or a basic bonding paste (spackle), onto the dent making it even with the rest of the wall. When dry, rub down with sandpaper and repaint.

Wiping away watermarks

If you catch that water ring whilst it's still wet, you can simply wipe it away. Once the stain is dry, you need to use more drastic measures.

Go over the surface with great care using very fine steel wool. Work in the direction of the grain, not the circle of the ring. Next, wipe over the mark with a cloth that has a few drops of olive oil on it, then leave to sit for as long as possible – ideally overnight. Next day, polish up with a dry cloth. Try mayonnaise on really bad marking. Bizarre, yet it often works. Don't despair if it doesn't work instantly. Repeated applications can make a big difference.

Don't re-wax or apply polish to the wood until you are certain the mark is gone. Otherwise, you're simply sealing it in.

Repairing Rips

Taking care of tears in either wallpaper or fabric in involves making patches, as these sections advise.

Patching wallpaper

It's a surprisingly simple job to hide a tear in the wallpaper or cover a stain that you haven't been able to shift. Just use the following method. (But do see Chapter 20 on treating everyday stains and the Appendix first.)

1. **Locate a piece of leftover wallpaper.**

   You need a piece big enough to cover the tear or stain completely.

   You have to match up any pattern, so choose your patch piece with care.

2. **Tear, rather than cut out your patch.**

   Rough edges look more natural up on the wall.

3. **Coat the back of your torn piece with border adhesive, or any glue suitable for sticking paper to paper.**

4. **Position your piece over the tear or stain and carefully smooth it into place by rubbing over it with a dry cloth.**

   Carefully mop away any adhesive that spills over the edge. It leaves a permanent mark if allowed to dry and then you have another stain to patch!

Mending upholstery

Make a patch from a fabric armrest or, if there's nothing else, a piece of material cut from the underside of a cushion (and then replaced with plain fabric). Your patch needs to be significantly bigger than the tear. Hem the patch, then lay it over the tear, so that it exactly matches up with the pattern of the sofa underneath. Use a strong thread and a small, slanting hemstitch to sew.

Fixing Problems in Carpets and Floors

Heavy table and chair legs can cause dents in the carpet. Get the pile back up to normal by dissolving an ice cube over the dent. As your carpet slowly absorbs the water, the fibres straighten up.

Rub over small cigarette burns with fine sandpaper to smooth down the remaining carpet fibres. However, a burn that's gone through the carpet calls for a patch. Cut a square to fit over the mark. Then, place the patch over the burnt area and cut right through the carpet using a craft (utility) knife. Lift out the burned piece. Apply double-sided tape to the back of the carpet piece and stick the patch directly onto the underlay.

Use a light lubricant to get scuff marks made by shoes off wood and laminate floors. Squirt a little WD-40 onto a dry cloth, then rub over the marks.

Part VI
The Part of Tens

The 5th Wave   By Rich Tennant

In This Part . . .

To anyone who says cleaning is dull or routine, read on for the perfect antidote! In this part, you find advice for occasions that are anything but ordinary or regular. When friends drop by unannounced or your partner arrives home with her boss, read how to transform the social rooms in your home from tip to tidy in moments. It can be done, if you're willing to be a bit unconventional now and again.

I give you advice, too, on how to prepare if you have 24 hours' notice for a landlord inspection, whilst the chapter on being clean in other people's homes calls for brainpower rather than broom skills. Finally – because you can take cleaning just too seriously – I take a wry look at putting ordinary objects to extraordinary uses. You won't believe what a humble hockey stick and a roll of sticky tape can do for your home!

Chapter 22

Fast Fixes for Unexpected Guests

. . . .

In This Chapter

▶ Creating a welcoming feel

▶ Using clever cheats to make your place look perfect

▶ Hiding dirt and clutter

. . . .

Spending time with family, friends, and neighbours is one of life's pleasures. Don't let worrying about the state of your home spoil the fun.

A totally unexpected guest turning up on your doorstep is actually fairly rare. Usually people phone up to say they're passing and ask whether they can drop by. So you can expect five to ten minutes' notice. If you experience that rare situation of getting no warning at all, you can create three minutes waiting for the kettle boil.

Looking Pleased to See Your Visitors!

Guests feel awkward if they think they're interrupting something important or personal. So turn off the TV, save the computer file you were working on, throw on a smart jumper, and swap slippers for shoes.

Closing the Door on Problem Areas

Greet your guests with a warm smile, then, as you guide them to the room you choose to entertain them in, close the door on any rooms you'd rather weren't on view. It's your home, so you can dictate whether you provide coffee in the kitchen or drinks in the lounge (living-room). If appropriate, take coats and bags to hang up to prevent your guests taking in areas that aren't tidy.

Taking Emergency Action When Your Entire Home Is a Problem Area

Go to the door with your keys in hand and tell your visitors that you're on your way out. In appropriate weather – and if you like your guests – ask them to join you on a walk. In summer, if you have a side entrance, appear from here when the doorbell rings. Tell friends you're out in the garden, and suggest they come right on round.

Clearing Away Food and Drink

Guests may feel embarrassed to catch you eating, so drop mugs into the sink and cold snacks into the fridge. If you're eating a hot meal, stick it back into the oven on the lowest heat – serving dishes, cutlery, and all. This is quick and far more discreet than covering up food at the table and closing the kitchen door. Plus, this way if your guests only stay briefly, you can carry on.

Disposing of Everyday Clutter

It takes less than a minute to scoop up newspapers, the day's post, and any shoes, bags and shopping lying around. You will doubtless invite your guests to sit down, so you need to clear the chairs. The trick is to have somewhere fast to drop the clutter into. A seat with a lift-up lid is perfect. But you can also temporarily take over the toy box, or slip the post and magazines under the seat cushions on the sofa (don't do this with newspapers, though: the print could transfer). If it's dark, the quickest hiding place is on the windowsill behind drawn curtains

Hiding Personal Stuff

However close you are to family, friends, and neighbours, there may be parts of how you live that you don't want them to see. It may be harmless stuff, such as the economy brand of teabags you buy, or the CDs you play air-guitar along with. If it matters to you, drop the evidence into a drawer before you move on to quick clean-ups. Knowing the bathroom isn't perfect won't affect anyone's enjoyment of the visit. But it'll be no fun for you if you're on edge about what your guests may spot.

The fastest way to keep your schedule secret is to cover your events calendar. Turn over a wall calendar or put it in a drawer temporarily.

Getting Cleaner in an Instant

Your hall, a reception room, and a bathroom are the minimum areas you can restrict a guest to. So clean and tidy only those rooms. Follow these tips:

- ✔ Open the windows. Even just five minutes brings freshness into your home.

- ✔ Empty any ashtrays and take the rubbish bin out of the lounge. Emptying it is too involved, so simply hide it in a closed room.

- ✔ Check the bathroom and soap/towel/tissue paper supplies. Add toilet freshener, then flush. Wipe the sink with a cleaning wipe.

- ✔ Plump the cushions on the sofa and push chairs into a conversational grouping.

- ✔ Take up rugs if you don't have time to vacuum. It brings a cleaner look to the room.

✔ Free up coat pegs in the hall, ready for guests. By using coat hangers on hooks, you can get more onto less space.

✔ Fill the kitchen sink with warm, soapy water. You can drop any dirty dishes and cups you collect into the sink and thus hide them.

Adding Welcoming Touches

Think five senses and cater to each:

✔ **Hearing:** Put soothing music in the CD player at low volume.

✔ **Sight:** Add instant colour by moving flowers to a vantage point in the living room. If you don't have flowers, fruit is an acceptable substitute. A bright, mixed bowl makes your home look a healthy one, too.

✔ **Smell:** I have a coffee-scented room spray that adds a nice ambient touch. But steer clear of artificial flowers or meadow breezes. You don't want your home smelling like a just-cleaned bathroom. In the kitchen, get up a welcoming aroma by putting a bread roll in the microwave for 30 seconds.

✔ **Taste:** Set up a snack area for a taste of treats ahead. Laying coasters and a central mat on the table will make it look as if you went to no trouble at all when you bring out drinks and nibbles for your guests later.

✔ **Touch:** Make the place look cosy. Position cushions at the base of chair backs, ready to give extra support.

Getting the Lighting Right

More than anything, getting the brightness right can disguise a less-than-clean home.

Turning lights on during the day makes your home appear fresher and sunnier. Estate agents use this trick because they know that bright homes sell faster. An exception is in the kitchen, where halogen or florescent lights seldom flatter. So simply turn on under-cupboard task lighting to direct the focus onto a clear worktop.

Candles are the ultimate in forgiving. Their soft glow hides dirt, yet throws warmth and soft colour around the room. Small groups of candles can effectively light a large lounge. From dusk, draw curtains, turn off any overhead lights, and use candles and table lamps instead.

Chapter 23

Ten Tips for Facing a Landlord Inspection

*I*f you rent, you may be subject to periodic inspections, as stated in your rental contract. Your rental contract lets you know how much notice the landlord has to give you before she, or an agent acting for her, carries out an inspection. So you can probably expect at least 24 hours.

When it's time to move out, you can expect a very thorough inspection. Be warned: If the place is found to be in disrepair, or simply plain dirty, you can expect to be fined, with the moneys taken out of your initial deposit. Use the tips in this chapter to ensure that it doesn't happen to you.

Getting Everyone to Help

Arrange a time of day for everyone who lives in the place to be in. Then commit the next hour – or better still, two hours – to working together on just this project. Tell anyone who can't, or won't, participate that they have to contribute in other ways. Buying cleaning supplies is fine. If the offer is drinks instead, get them to deliver in advance.

Checking Your Rental Agreement

You sign a contract when you first move in agreeing to keep the place in good order. But it's the detail you need right now. Read through your rental contract to see whether your responsibilities include keeping the garden neat, the paint fresh, or major appliances in good working order. You may find that you're not actually responsible for as much as you'd thought.

Your contract also reminds you of things you promised not to do, such as keeping a cat or running a home business. On inspection day, your conscience dictates whether you hide the kitten and professional power tools in a cupboard or come clean and hope you're not told to go.

Targeting Areas that Worry Landlords Most

To you, it's home. To your landlord, it's regular money now and perhaps a significant property sale at a later date. So to put yourself in your landlord's shoes, imagine you're a potential homebuyer, with one exception. There's no point spending time making the exterior sparkle. Your local-based landlord is likely to have driven by frequently.

Inside, focus on fixtures – the bathroom suite, fitted kitchen units, and carpets. These are the costliest items to replace and your landlord looks for visual reassurance that it will be ages until anything is needed. So clean the bathroom, kitchen, and floors with care.

Your landlord also expects to see any major items of furniture or appliances he provides. So if you sent the dining table and chairs to the garage to free up more room, now's the time to bring them back out.

Keeping the Numbers Down

Now is not the time for overnight visitors, especially any that have become semi-permanent. If you're a sole tenant, sweep into a suitcase or storage box all your girl or boyfriend's belongings littering the bedroom and bathroom. Also check clothing left out to dry and be certain that there are no letters in sight addressed to your partner at this address.

Repairing Minor Damage

Scratches and rips are part of everyday wear and tear, and your landlord will be able to include repairing them as a business expense. But an inspection is not the time for too many to come to light. Stains on the carpet also give the impression that this is a house of frequent partying. Use the Appendix on Stain Removal to get out those that you can. Conceal others by moving furniture; drape a throw over a chair. Your landlord or agent is likely to spend 30 minutes, top, in the place: there will be no time or inclination for checking under the sofa.

Hiring a Cleaner

Getting paid help can be money well spent. Look in your local paper for ads from domestic contract cleaners and get a quote. If your reaction is that you can't believe how much a spot of cleaning costs, let the thought of saving this sum of money spur you on to do the job yourself. Use Chapter 3 on techniques and timing as a starting point.

Creating Temporary Storage

You can clean up, vacuum, and sweep much faster if hoards of possessions aren't in your way slowing you down. Don't waste time finding cupboard space for items such as musical instruments, college course work, or piles of magazines that you know are going to go straight back onto the floor afterwards. Dump them into the car instead.

Shaping Up Outside

Cut the grass if needed. Put garden furniture into the shed if it is autumn or winter. Empty out any tubs or pots with long-dead plants still in them.

Asking for a Reprieve

When there's a genuine reason why you've fallen behind with everyday home care, tell your landlord. Leave out the bit about the brilliant birthday party, but you can talk about the increased pressure of a new job or a family member's illness. Your landlord simply wants to know that, when all's even again in your world, the house will return to order. Suggest a time within the next month to repeat the inspection.

Holding Out against Penalty Fines

After a final inspection, your landlord may decide to charge you a cleaning fee. Resist this and ask for specific areas where the place falls short. Get a list in precise detail, such as the oven is dirty or windows need cleaning. You can then choose to tackle these set tasks yourself or, for considerably less than the original blanket charge, pay someone to do the work at an agreed hourly rate.

Chapter 24

Being Clean in Other People's Homes

In This Chapter

▶ Making yourself into the ideal houseguest

▶ Knowing when and how to help clean up

*W*hether you're in someone else's home for 20 minutes or two weeks, you want to be sure your actions don't create a mess or tension between you and the host. These tips tell you how.

Letting Your Host Set the Standard

Take a quick look at your host's footwear whilst you're still on the porch, or on a mat. If she's wearing socks, but no shoes or slippers, this may be the dress code of the home. Most of the dirt that comes into a house does so through the shoes of people who walk around in it.

Your host might also have new, pale rugs or a just-cleaned carpet she is concerned about. So ask right away if she'd like you to slip off your shoes too (but for goodness sake, keep your socks on). Once you step into the lounge, it's too late.

Watching Where You Walk and Sit

Be alert for the unexpected when you walk around someone's home for the first time. A busy home with young children may have toys on the floor. Step on anything plastic, and you could break something irreplaceable. An immaculate, ordered lounge might have breakable ornaments perilously close to the edge of ledges and shelves. The people who live here are careful, so you need to slow down and take care, too. On chairs, be aware that if you've come out of the wet, dye from an untreated leather belt or bag could transfer to a pale fabric.

Taking Responsibility for Your Party

Children and pets you bring into someone else's home are under your instructions to behave cleanly. Sometimes, this gets complicated because your host doesn't know kids and hands around sticky chocolate or realises too late that claws and paws can ruin a leather sofa. If you bring messy people with you, bring your own clear-ups. Carry wet-wipes and small plastic sacks (nappy sacks are perfect) and a bag that you can dump them into.

Looking for Mats, Covers, and Coasters

Never assume that it's okay to put a drink straight down onto a hard surface. If you can't see a mat on the table, ask about one. If your host is out of the room hold onto your hot drink or create a makeshift safe place using a newspaper or magazine. A book may be okay, too, but only if you're sure that there are no drips on your mug. If you're trying to dump a drink you'd rather not have, a painted window shelf is about as safe as it gets. Again, check first for drips on the cup.

Helping Yourself from the Fridge and Home Bar

Check the location of the paper towels (or a clean sponge or cloth) before you prepare any snacks or drinks. Avoid using the last of anything. Should you get a spill, it won't become a problem if you can mop it away at once. Equipment you're not familiar with can make you clumsy. So use a corkscrew over the sink.

Behaving Beautifully in the Bathroom

There is an area where personal preferences are everything – your host's preferences, that is. Take just five seconds when you go into the room to notice the position of the seat lid and towels and whether the soap stands in a dish. Then leave everything exactly as it was before your visit.

If you can do so without too much snooping, re-freshen the toilet with cleaner if needed and pop on a new roll of tissue. Always report any sink or pan blockage.

If you're staying over, don't take over the bathroom shelf: Your flannels (washcloths), toothbrush, and make-up belong in the guest bedroom. Most domestic hot water tanks hold enough hot water for a maximum of two baths though electrically-heated showers can go on forever. So you can shower without worry (unless it is a power-shower, which can drain a hot-water tank rapidly if used excessively), but ask before taking a bath. Lay a towel on the floor where you'll step out, then put that towel into a wash basket. Vent the room afterwards, and then take it as your responsibility to close the window a short time later.

Knowing When to Stop in the Kitchen

Offering to do the dishes is great, especially if you've just enjoyed a meal prepared for you. But before you get going, and without making it into a huge event, ask a few questions about how your host likes things done, and which items go into the dishwasher.

It's fine to put cutlery back into the drawer afterwards, but leave out plates and pans, unless specifically instructed. Putting food back into the fridge and cupboards is also a no-no – you don't know the correct places. It's also an intrusion to start wiping down the table or worktops. Your host may feel you're criticising him for not being sufficiently clean.

Picking Up the Signal on Smoking

Never light up without asking first, even if you are in an outside room or the garden. Have a contingency plan, if you're a heavy smoker, for where to go. Don't neglect ash and stubs. No one wants to find a pile of evidence by their favourite spot in the garden! Indoors, putting still-warm stubs into a plastic waste bin can cause fires. So let your host take charge of ashtrays.

Keeping the Guest Room Sweet

Unlike at a hotel, you don't get maid service when you're staying with friends or family, so keep to good habits such as airing and making up the bed to increase your night-time comfort. As you leave, strip off the sheets and take the cover off the duvet if it was next to you. Leave the duvet and pillows neatly folded on the bed, with the used bedding piled alongside. Empty the rubbish bin into a plastic bag, and put this inside the main rubbish bin in the kitchen.

House-sitting When the Owners Are Away

Ask for a quick run through of what everyday cleaning is expected of you before your hosts leave you in charge of their home. Generally, all that's required is basic vacuuming and spot-cleaning in bathrooms and kitchens.

What may matter more to your hosts than a grubby mirror is finding everything in the wrong place. Familiarise yourself with how plates are stored in the kitchen and, if you move plants or ornaments that you find irksome, draw a sketch first, so you know where to return them.

Chapter 25

Extraordinary Uses for Ten Ordinary Items

*I*t's true that there's a piece of specialist cleaning equipment for every task that you may care to undertake. From stick-dusters to clean the thin gap between stacked video and DVD players to shovelling buckets that combine the flat edge of a dustpan with the volume of a rubbish bin, you can find hundreds of great tools.

However, limited storage space coupled with the fact that you have better things to spend spare money on, mean you may want to improvise. In this chapter, I show how things already in your home can become wickedly helpful cleaning tools, at no cost or effort.

Making a Friend of Cotton Buds

These small, yet perfectly formed make-up and hygiene aids can come to the rescue in dozens of intricate cleaning tasks. Use cotton buds (cotton swabs) to get dirt out of any tight corner – the telephone and computer keypads, the car dashboard, and that grimy bit where the tap (faucet) base meets the sink.

Their high absorbency makes them good stain-shifter tools, too. When you need to apply a solvent with precision, a cotton bud is the ideal implement.

Taking Aim with Sticks and Clubs

Using a hockey stick or even a golf club instead of a cleaning pole extension gives you an important advantage – you're holding a handle that you're already expert at gripping! Tie a microfibre or other quality soft cloth to the playing end of your stick to make a cracking tool to get down cobwebs and other ceiling dirt. Just don't take a swing at the light fitting.

Getting Stuck on Sticky Tape

My favourite tape is double-sided. It not only cleans by lifting off dry dirt and fur from fabrics and hard surfaces; it acts as an emergency repair kit. Use it to secretly hold up a trouser hem or keep everyday photos and artwork in place inside clip-on-frames.

When cleaning with sticky tape, the secret is in a firm pull-up. So lay the tape over the dirty or hair-covered area then lift off quickly as if you were pulling off a sticking plaster (bandage).

Cutting Down on Legwork with Tights

The gauze-like fabric of higher denier tights (pantyhose) makes them perfect filters. Use them whenever you suspect treasures like money or an earring may be hidden down the sofa or under the bed. Simply pop the foot of an old pair of tights over the suction hose of the vacuum, and get cleaning. Dust goes through to your cleaner but valuables stick to the tights.

Old tights are also handy in the washing-machine. To freshen fabric hair bunches (scrunchies) and accessories, pop a load inside a tight leg and tie a knot in the leg. Everything stays safely together in the machine, yet the mesh of the tights ensures things still get clean.

Tearing a Strip Off Old Sheets

Old rags are a cleaning must, but not just any old rags. You want to be sure that the items you are cleaning don't get covered with fluff or, worse, coloured by your cleaning cloth. Old bed sheets are perfect. The material is smooth, lint-free, and subject to minimal fraying. Use pinking-shears to cut the fabric into strips that measure roughly 30 centimetres (1 foot) by 60 centimetres (2 feet).

Whilst white is preferred, you can use coloured sheets, too. Soak them overnight in a weak solution of bleach – 10 millilitres (ml) (2 teaspoons) per 5 litres (1 gallon) of water – then wash them in the washing-machine on the hottest setting to get rid of the colour.

Laying It on the Line with Rulers

Take the short cut of measuring by height rather than volume when mixing up large quantities of cleaning solution. It's rare to find a bucket that has an inbuilt volume measure. So simply stand a plastic ruler in the bucket and use simple mathematics to get the correct ratio of water to cleaning solution.

The firm, flat edge of a ruler also makes a ruler good at getting solid or sticky spills up off the carpet. When there's too much for a spoon or a knife, hold the ruler at 45 degrees to the carpet at the edge of the accident. Push down to get under the spill, and then scoop as much as you can onto the ruler.

Rising to the Challenge with a Pastry Brush

The soft, uniform bristles on the type of brush you use for coating pies with milk or egg glazes are perfect for delicate cleaning tasks. Buy a second brush and use it to brush dirt from fabric lampshades and plastic blinds, as well as getting crumbs out from the sandwich toaster or food processor.

Lathering Up with a Natural Sponge

Never throw out those expensive face and body washers when they're no longer smart enough for the bath. Their high absorbency and capacity to resist staining mean they last far longer than synthetic sponges. Save them for big jobs such as washing down walls or kitchen units (cabinets).

Buffing with Old Carpet

This takes me back to the first item I ever cleaned – my Brownie trefoil badge, when I was eight years old. Not wanting the hassle and dirty fingers that go with using metal polish, I hit on the smart idea of rubbing the badge into the carpet. In seconds I worked up a brilliant shine and, because the carpet was dark and mottled, my mum was never any the wiser.

Nowadays, when I lay carpet, I keep small scraps in my polishing box. Shoes, leather bags – and of course badges – all get a great shine when briskly rubbed against carpet. Those with longer wool piles do the grandest job. The combination of grease- and dirt-absorbing fibres and the friction makes for a brilliant shine.

Brushing Up on the Many Uses of Toothbrushes

Scrubbing is what a toothbrush does best. If you're prepared to put in the extra effort that's needed when you use mini-tools, you can make hard surfaces that can withstand water look super by giving them the toothbrush treatment. Most popularly used for scrubbing at the grouting between tiles, you and your (old!) toothbrush can also take on blackened window ledges, the inside of scummy bud vases, fabric tennis shoes, and the wheels and bodywork of toy cars.

For super-charged results use old battery-powered ones.

The shine on leather shoes is particularly brilliant if you first apply shoe cream to the brush. However, you need to devote a toothbrush solely to this job: You won't be able to clean the bristles afterwards.

Appendix

Stain Removal Guide

● ●

*W*henever you have a stain to deal with, simply look up what to do in this guide. The advice in here gives the best way to shift a particular substance. However, where that substance landed may affect your success rate and may make you modify what steps you can take. For example, egg on a colourfast, washable fabric can be washed in hot water in the machine, whereas egg on a wool carpet cannot. So where useful, I give several alternatives.

Every spill is unique, and though there may be various methods for cleaning one or the other of the two items that come together to create a stain, only you have the stain in front of you, so it's your judgment that counts.

This Appendix assumes that clothes are washable and carpets up to home shampooing. Always wet an inconspicuous part of the stained item then blot with a clean, white cloth to check that the fabric is washable (it doesn't fade or pucker) and colourfast (colour doesn't come away on the cloth). Whilst this Appendix is put together in good faith and as a result of experience and research, it cannot guarantee success. You must always weigh up the risk that treating a stain can result in a mark that is more noticeable than the stain or may permanently damage the fabric or surface.

If the stained item is not washable, your options are limited and you may want to ask a professional dry-cleaner for advice.

Many cleaning products can be hazardous to your health if used improperly or without adequate ventilation. Always read and follow cautions on the package.

Following is an alphabetical list of stains and how to treat them.

Adhesive: Scrape off excess from fabric using a blunt knife; on carpet, pick bits out. Acetone (nail varnish remover) dissolves most general-purpose household glue but it can also dissolve acetate and other synthetic fabrics! For safety and precision, dab at the stain with a cotton bud (cotton swab) dipped in acetone. Wash afterwards. Some very strong glues may simply dissolve in soapy water if you get to them fast enough. If not, buy a glue remover from a DIY (hardware) store. See also *glue.*

Antiperspirant: Keep on top of the white marks by applying a spot stain remover to a fresh stain before machine-washing the item. If staining has built up, soften deposits with glycerine before applying the stain remover.

Ash: Keep it dry and ash is no problem. Use a brush to flick it off clothing. On carpets and curtains, suck it up with the crevice tool of the vacuum. To get rid of the residual smell of smoking, hang clothes to air and open windows to air rooms.

Avocado: Use a spoon to scrape off as much as you can. Very gently rub at the stain with a few drops of washing-up liquid or liquid detergent (wear gloves). Soak in cold water for 15 minutes, then machine-wash according to fabric.

Baby food: Rinse with warm water, then machine-wash. If you need to step up to a biological detergent, you may want to launder the item

again in non-bio detergent if your baby has delicate skin.

Banana: It looks worse than it is. Clothing: Scrape off solids, then machine-wash. Hard floors: Wipe with a cloth dipped in soapy water, then rinse and dry to prevent slippery residue.

Beer: Clothing: Rinse out in warm water and machine-wash. Carpet: Use a soda siphon or bottled water to lift all the beer up out of the carpet. Go over the area with a cloth dipped in a bowl of warm water and wrung out. To do a thorough job, keep rinsing out the cloth and repeating until no smell or stickiness remains. If the smell comes back later, rinse carpet with well-diluted white vinegar, then rinse again in clear water.

Beetroot (beets): Act fast, before this deep-colour dye dries. Force the stain back through the fabric by holding it inside out under the cold tap. Soak overnight in cold water. If necessary, soak again a pre-laundry stain treatment.

Berry juice: *See* Blackcurrant juice.

Bird droppings: Use a stiff brush to get them off when they're dry. Dip the bristles into a solution of bio –washing-powder o get at stubborn stains on garden chairs and stone driveways. On cars, use a sponge and neat washing-up liquid.

Biro: *See* Ink, biro and ballpoint.

Blackcurrant juice: Including damson, plum, and other bright berries and soft fruits. Clothing: Rinse under the cold tap, but expect to need something stronger. Most bio detergents and pre-wash stain treatments are very good indeed on fruit stains. If necessary, wash a second time. Remember to check that the stain is gone before putting the item into the drier or ironing it as heat can set the stain. Carpets: If shampooing fails, follow advice under *Jam.*

Bleach: Immediately dilute spills with cold water. If you've simply splashed your top whilst pouring out bleach, you may well be in time. Scrubbing at the mark with a paste of bicarbonate of soda may also help, particularly with bleach on the carpet. If the colour has already faded, your task is to restore it, rather than trying to get out the bleach. Options include: dyeing the entire garment to its original shade; disguising the faded area – on towels and carpet, you may try covering a mark with a suitable fabric pen.

Blood: Flush out the stain with cold water only. Never use warm or hot, as it may permanently set the stain. Clothing and sheets: Hold the unstained side under a full-on cold tap until all the colour has gone, then machine-wash. Mattresses: Cold water is unlikely to be enough for a dried stain. Instead, tip the mattress onto its side, sponge the stained area with cold water, then use a carpet shampoo. As you work, hold a towel in place under the stain so that unnecessary wet doesn't drip down the mattress. Carpet and upholstery: Sponge with

cold water then treat with carpet shampoo.

 Dried blood stains call for patience. Glycerine left on the blood for an hour may soften the stain sufficiently for you to treat it with carpet shampoo. A thick paste of bicarbonate of soda and water may help to lift the stain out of an absorbent fabric. Leave it to harden, then brush it off.

Burn marks: You can't remove scorching, but soaking fabric in a solution of 15 millilitres (ml) (1 tablespoon) of soda crystals in 500ml (1 pint) of water can fade the mark. You can try a dilute solution of chlorine bleach – 20ml (1½ table-spoons) per 5 litres (1 gallon) of hot water, but be careful to soak only the scorched area – you don't want fade on the rest of the garment. On carpets, trim away burnt pile.

Butter and margarine: Also other soft, spreading fats. Clothing: Spoon up as much as possible, then rub a little liquid detergent into the stain before machine-washing. Carpets and non-washables: Sprinkle the stain with baking soda to absorb the grease. This is a slow process, so sprinkle the stain before bed and brush or vacuum it the next day.

Chalk: Washes easily out of fabric. To remove coloured chalk on floors and outside paving, brush off loose chalk, then scrub with soapy water.

Chewing gum: Clothing: Put item in a sealed plastic bag and pop it directly into the freezer. Once frozen, simply crack and peel the gum off. Carpet, upholstery, and larger items: Apply ice cubes wrapped in plastic to the gum stain until the gum freezes.

Chocolate: Bio detergents are good on this at last, but not during the quick-wash programme (cycle). It can take time for detergent enzymes to break down chocolate, so rub liquid detergent into the stain then soak for up to an hour. Rinse and dry. If you're out and drop chocolate on yourself, allow the chocolate to set, then scrape off the dry deposits.

Coffee: Clothing: Rinse in warm water, then machine-wash with a bio detergent. Carpet and upholstery: Blot up with white paper towels or a white cloth, then sponge with warm water. Milky coffees may need a follow-up with carpet and upholstery shampoo to get rid of any grease residue. Dried coffee stains may need to be loosened first by soaking in glycerine.

Correction fluid: Pick it off fabrics after it sets. If it gets on the photocopier, dab it with methylated spirits (rubbing alcohol) using a cotton bud.

Cosmetics, powder: Including eye shadow, face powder, and so on. Clothing: Hold a flat tray directly under the stain and brush it using a clean, unused make-up brush. If powder has settled into the fabric, soak it in a pre-wash detergent then wash it in the machine. White spirit (turpentine) dabbed onto the

fabric with a cotton bud can also lift the stain, but do this with care because white spirit is flammable and a skin irritant. Do not resort to make-up remover. It creates its own stain. Carpet: Vacuum thoroughly over the spot, using the crevice tool.

Cough medicine: *See* syrup.

Crayon: Clothing: Machine-wash. Furniture, hard floors, work surfaces, and walls: Spray a lubricant, such as WD-40, on the stain, then wipe it away. Rinse to remove smell. Carpets: Cover thinly with non-gel toothpaste and leave to dry. Brush off.

Curry: This is the stain dry-cleaners dread! Curry combines colour dyes from spices, grease from cooking oils, and solids from vegetables or meat, so there's a lot to tackle. Try a proprietary stain remover if you have one. If not, rinse the stain in warm water, then rub in glycerine to soften it. Wait about an hour then rinse out the glycerine and machine-wash the item. Dilute hydrogen peroxide (1 part peroxide to 6 parts water) may shift old curry stains.

Deodorant: *See* antiperspirant.

Dye: Once it's dry, fabric dye, hair dye, and food dye do the job you bought them to do – permanently colour things. So treat dye stains promptly. Mop up spills with a dry cloth – a wet one merely spreads the dye. Blot well. On carpets follow up by dabbing on methylated spirits (rubbing alcohol).

Clothes: Buy a colour-removing product to use either as a pre-wash or in the washing-machine. On hard surfaces, such as bathroom fittings with splashes of hair dye, a paste made from cold cigarette ash and water can sometimes shift the stain.

Egg: Curiously, this is easy to get off clothes: Simply rinse in cold water, then wash using a bio detergent. But it's a tough stain to remove from china and cutlery, especially if it's baked on in the dishwasher. For ease, wipe egg off plates before using the dishwasher. To remove stubborn egg deposits, soak in a solution of laundry detergent. Rinse thoroughly.

Engine oil: Driveway: Blot fresh stains, then sprinkle on cat litter to absorb grease. Brush off. Treat remaining stain by scrubbing with hot, soapy water. On fabric, sprinkle salt to absorb grease. Then brush off and soak in hot detergent solution. See if you can now remove more oil from the fabric, using a blunt knife. Machine-wash in hot water with bio powder. If stain remains, try again. Instead of salt, try a paste of baking soda and water.

Faeces, animal: Scrape up pet deposits immediately with an old spoon. If there is no visible trace on the carpet, simply sponge the area with carpet shampoo. To remove liquid stains, use a carpet or general cleaner with oxygen to lift matter up out of the carpet pile. Blot this up with a thick pad of paper towelling. Repeat the spraying and blotting until the kitchen

paper blots up clear liquid. Add drops of disinfectant to a final blot with a dampened sheet of paper. If the smell persists, spray odour eliminator, but note that these clear only the smell – not the mess – so you must clean up first.

Faeces, human: As in infant (human). Dispose of solid matter down the toilet then soak soiled fabric nappies (diapers) in a solution of dilute bleach – 20 millilitres (ml) (1½ tablespoons) of bleach to 5 litres (1 gallon) of water. Machine-wash in hot water. When nappy contents land on furnishings and clothes, treat as **vomit**. *See also* Urine, human.

Glue: Quality paper glue is washable. Dab the area with washing-up liquid then rinse and dry. If the stain remains, it's probably because something else stuck to the glue. On kids, this is often **grass**; on adults, it may be **grease**.

Grass: Soak item overnight in solution of in 10 millilitres (ml) (2 teaspoons) of bleach to 5 litres (1 gallon) of water, then machine-wash in hot water. On coloured fabric, scrub at the stain using white toothpaste, then machine-wash. You can also buy a proprietary grass-stain remover. Specialist hand cleaners, sold in DIY (hardware) and car-parts shops, easily get grass stains off hands, and you can also use them on hard-to-shift stains on cotton fabrics.

Gravy: *See* Grease.

Grease: Clothing: The enzymes of bio detergents specifically aim to dissolve grease. So for fresh stains simply machine-wash. If you can't get promptly to the machine, use something absorbent – baking soda or talcum powder for example – to blot up the grease. Carpets: Use heat to liquefy and lift up the mark. Put heavy paper (brown paper or grocery bags [make sure the plain side touches the carpet] are good) over the stain, then run a warm iron over it until the grease is lifted up into the paper.

Hair gel: Lather up neat (undiluted) shampoo with a drop of water and apply to towels and clothes that have hair gel deposits. Launder as usual.

Ice cream: Act immediately with this one. You may be up against grease as well as colour if it's chocolate or strawberry. Soak the stain in cold water and rub to loosen the cream. Wash with bio detergent. Briefly soak difficult stains on upholstered chairs with dilute hydrogen peroxide (1 part peroxide to 6 parts water).

Ink, biro and ballpoint: Dip a cotton bud into a bottle of acetone (nail varnish remover) and gently dab at stains on fabric. Don't panic if things look worse initially – the ink may spread as you dab, but the colour should get lighter even as the stain spreads. Use the dry end of the bud to absorb the dissolved ink. Wash off the solvent using ordinary bathroom soap or washing-up liquid, whichever is closest to hand, and warm water. For large areas,

place the stain face down on an absorbent pad and work from the back. If acetone fails, rinse and try again using an alcohol-free hairspray. If that doesn't work, contact the manufacturer to see whether they sell a solvent.

Ink, felt-tip: With washable ones do just that: Lay the stained item on a thick tea towel, then dab at the ink with a damp cloth until the ink comes off. Repeat using a bar of soap. All types of ink come off more easily with hand soap than with laundry detergent.

Permanent ink needs a solvent to dissolve it. Try acetone (nail varnish remover) first, following the instructions under *Ink, biro and ballpoint.* If the stain is large, keep a dry cloth underneath to prevent dissolving ink from spreading to other parts of your item.

 Soaking the stain in a paste of milk and a bicarbonate of soda can sometimes succeed when acetone or machine-washing fail.

Insect remains: Chiefly a problem for windscreens and windows. Use a mild detergent solution. Rinse. Rinse again using dilute white vinegar, which acts as a mild insect repellent.

Jam: Not the big problem you might imagine. Most detergents are up to getting this out in one wash. Carpets: Treat with carpet shampoo, following the package directions. Get up any remaining residue with methylated spirits (rubbing alcohol). Before using the spirit, test it on a hidden area of carpet first.

With an old stain, soften it first by covering it lightly with glycerine. Rinse, then dab with a cotton cloth that has several drops of methylated spirits (rubbing alcohol) on it. Rinse thoroughly afterwards. This method also works for old berry juice stains.

Jelly: *See* Jam.

Ketchup: These tips work for other bottled sauces as well. Hold the fabric inside out under a running cold tap (faucet). Gently rub at the stain between your fingers if needed and keep going with the water for several minutes. If there's still a mark, rub washing-up liquid into the stain then rinse off. Next up, try lemon juice or hydrogen peroxide (1 part peroxide to 6 parts water) then machine-wash.

Lemon juice: Go at once to the cold tap (faucet) to stop this acid from taking the colour out of clothes and fabric. Rinse from the inside out to push the lemon juice back out of the fabric. Work at dry stains with a paste of bicarbonate of soda. Brush off when dry, then machine-wash the garment.

Lipstick: Tricky to remove, it is best to use a proprietary grease and stain remover. If you'd rather not, try coating the stain with soap and rubbing it between your fingers. Machine-wash.

Margarine: *See* Butter and margarine.

Mayonnaise: Sponge in warm water, then wash in bio detergent. To remove mayonnaise stains from silver cutlery, boil the cutlery in a pan with a scrunched ball of aluminium foil.

Mildew and mould: Fresh stains wash away easily, but old ones need bleach. Use 20 millilitres (ml) (1½ tablespoons) of bleach per 5 litres (1 gallon) of water. Soak white fabric for 30 minutes. If the fabric isn't bleach-safe, wash it with bio detergent. Increase room ventilation and treat any mould on the wall with proprietary mould killer to stop the problem from recurring.

Milk: The big issue is avoiding a lingering smell. It's easy to look at an item and think you've got out all the milk then have the smell kick in later. Clothes: Rinse promptly with just-warm water, then wash as usual, using a bio detergent. Carpets and upholstery: Play it safe by sponging the stain with warm water and following up with a spray stain remover.

Modelling clay: *See* Plasticine.

Mould: *See* Mildew and mould.

Mud: Relax and do nothing. Resist the temptation to dash about after dirty dog paws or teenage footballers. Let mud completely dry then brush it off fabric, shoes, carpets, and hard floors. Machine-wash clothes. Vacuuming can help suck up the last deposits on floors and furniture. You may need to sponge any remaining carpet or upholstery marks with appropriate shampoo to get rid of them completely.

Nail polish: Use acetone, a solvent also sold as non-oily nail polish remover. Be prepared to be patient as you need to repeatedly dab the stain with acetone then blot it with a dry pad before it lifts. You may decide to cut out a small mark on carpet instead of going to all the trouble as well as avoiding the risk that acetone can take the colour out of your non-colourfast carpet.

Nappies: *See* Faeces, human.

Nicotine: To get nicotine stains off fingernails, add smokers' toothpaste to a nail scrubbing brush and scrub.

Paint, children's: Poster and powder paints are water-based. Clothing: Simply machine-wash the affected item. Tables and floors: Do not use a wet cloth to clear spilt powder. Simply brush it off or sweep it up. Use a soapy solution of washing-up liquid to clean dried paint.

Paint, emulsion (latex): Washes easily from carpet, hard surfaces, and fabric whilst it's still wet. Rinse clothes inside out under the cold tap (faucet). Blot up excess on carpets, then sponge splashes with water. Dried stains need methylated spirits (rubbing alcohol).

Paint, gloss (oil): Use white spirit (turpentine), which is sold as paint thinner. Dab the spirit on using a white cloth; rinse thoroughly afterwards.

Pencil: Rubs out of all surfaces, not just paper, with an ordinary pencil eraser. Be sure the eraser is totally clean before rubbing on fabric or walls. It is easy to create a secondary stain with a dirty eraser.

Perspiration: *See* Sweat.

Plasticine (modelling clay): Scrape excess with blunt knife; use ice cubes to freeze the remaining clay to make it easy to pick off.

Pollen: Use quality sticky tape to directly lift pollen off fabric and carpet. Do not risk spreading the pollen by giving the item a good shake. Do *not* soak in water. Use a proprietary grass stain remover or a bio detergent on a hot setting. On walls, use a rubber eraser.

Rust: Cover with lemon juice for an hour. Rinse, then machine-wash.

Salt: Including sea and rain water rings. Clothing: Rewetting the entire garment is often enough. Shoes: Brush out marks on suede. Re-wet leather with a damp cloth then rub the shoe dry with a second soft cloth. If it's still marked, buy a proprietary shoe cleaner.

Shoe polish: Scrape deposits with a blunt knife. Dab a cloth with several drops of white spirit (turpentine) onto carpet stains. Rinse, then if stain persists, dab with a cloth dampened with methylated spirits (rubbing alcohol). Shampoo and rinse.

Sun protection lotion: Clothing: Machine-wash on hot to dissolve away grease. If you're away from a washing-machine, scrape off liquid with a blunt knife then sprinkle with talcum powder to absorb grease. Carpets: If you have no carpet shampooer to hand, spray shaving foam on the stain. Work it into the carpet with a cloth, then rinse and blot up the liquid.

Sunscreen: *See* Sun protection lotion.

Sweat: A pre-wash stain treatment shifts most fresh stains. For built-up stains, soak the item in cold water overnight, then use a scrubbing brush on the stain before machine-washing. You can soak fabrics that are bleach-safe in 10 millilitres (ml) (2 teaspoons) of bleach to 5 litres (1 gallon) of water. White vinegar removes the smell and some of the marking from non-washables. Use a cloth dipped in a very diluted solution – 1 teaspoon to 100ml (½ cup) of warm water.

Syrup: Rinse first in cold water then warm water. If that fails, use more force to push the stickiness from the fabric. Hold the stained area face down and taut – use an embroidery hoop if you have one – and pour hot water through the stain.

Tar: Clothing and canvas shoes: Apply eucalyptus oil from underneath the stain to push out tar deposits. Carpets: Soften the stain

with glycerine then use a spot stain remover.

Tea: Clothing: Biological detergents have no problems getting tea out. Just rinse the item promptly with warm water and machine-wash. Mugs and teapots: Get stubborn tea stains out by soaking them in dilute laundry detergent. Wash thoroughly afterwards.

Toothpaste: Hold the garment inside-out under the cold tap (faucet) to push the stain out. If that doesn't work, add a drop of washing-up liquid (not bar soap) and rub the fabric together. Rinse and dry (you can use a hairdryer if it's that day's work clothes).

Urine, animal: Carpet: Blot up what you can with paper towels – stand on the paper to help it soak up the urine. Then bring two bowls to the spot – one empty, one with cold water – along with a sponge. Dab the stain with cold water, wring out the sponge in the empty bowl, dip it in the cold water and dab the stain again. Don't get the area too wet, though. It is essential to avoid letting even diluted urine penetrate the carpet backing and underlay. To finish, add a few drops of disinfectant to a final sponge-rinse.

Urine, human: Clothing and bedding: Rinse then soak clothes and bedding overnight in bio detergent. Wash in the machine on the hottest programme (cycle) safe for the item. Shoes: Wipe leather shoes with a cloth wrung out from warm water. Mattresses: Treat as for *blood*. However, because the stained area is likely to be far greater, use a hairdryer to speed up drying after treatment. Carpet: Blot up stains, then sponge with carpet shampoo.

Vomit: If clearing this up makes you feel like heaving, put on a mask to cover your nose and mouth. The key to success lies in getting up all the surface deposits. So wear gloves and scrape up using a spoon then go over the fabric of the carpet, clothing, or bedding again with a blunt knife to get up final traces. Drop these down the toilet. Clothing: Flush by holding the material stain-side-down under a running tap (faucet). Machine-wash with bio detergent and air-dry, preferably outside, to remove the smell. If the smell remains, bio-wash again. It is not unusual to need to do this three times. Sadly, dry-cleaning isn't an alternative. Typically wet-cleaning gives a better final result. Carpet: Use a soda siphon or fizzy bottled water (club soda) to push the stain out of the fabric. Rub in carpet shampoo, rinse then add drops of a liquid antiseptic to a final rinse. Car interior: Treat as carpet. Leave the doors open to air the car if you can safely do so. Remember to deactivate the interior light first.

Wax: Wait until it sets hard then scrape away what you can. Use a blunt knife to scrape wax on clothing, serviettes (napkins), and tablecloths. On scratchable tables and work surfaces, use your fingernail or a non-scratching spatula. Next, use an iron on the lowest possible setting to melt the remaining wax. On carpets and upholstered furniture, put brown paper or absorbent kitchen roll (paper towels) over the stain. On clothes and tablecloths, put paper on both sides of the fabric. Using a warm iron, press the paper until the wax melts and is absorbed into the paper. Take great care to keep the iron moving to avoid scorching.

Wine, red: Blot the spill at once, then rinse clothes in warm water and machine wash promptly. Soak tablecloths in bio detergent, until you're able to machine-wash. On the carpet or sofa: blot at once. Use a soda siphon or fizzy bottled water (club soda) – not white wine, as is so often suggested unless you're ready to waste a good glassful – to lift up the stain. If any mark remains, treat it with carpet shampoo. Dried stains may need proprietary stain remover. First though, try using glycerine to soften the stain before applying carpet shampoo.

Wine, white: Causes few problems. Blot up, then rinse in warm water. Machine-wash.

Index

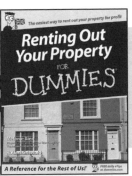
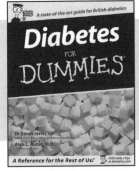
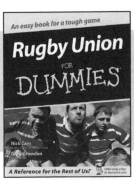
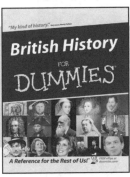
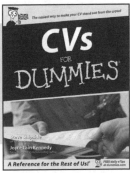
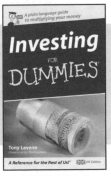
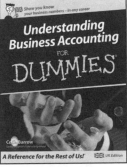
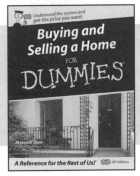

FOR DUMMIES

The easy way to get more done and have more fun

GENERAL INTEREST & HOBBIES

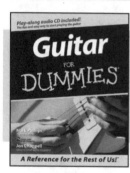

0-7645-5106-X

0-7645-5194-9

0-7645-5193-0

0-7645-5196-5

0-7645-5434-4

0-7645-1771-6

Also available:

Japanese For Dummies®
0-7645-5429-8

Architecture For
Dummies®
0-7645-5396-8

Rock Guitar For
Dummies®
0-7645-5356-9

Anatomy and
Physiology For
Dummies®
0-7645-5422-0

German For Dummies®
0-7645-5195-7

Weight Training For
Dummies®, 2nd Edition
0-7645-5168-X

Project Management
For Dummies®
0-7645-5283-X

Piano For Dummies®
0-7645-5105-1

Latin For Dummies®
0-7645-5431-X

Songwriting For
Dummies®
0-7645-5404-2

Marketing For
Dummies®
2nd Edition
0-7645-5600-2

Parenting For
Dummies®
2nd Edition
0-7645-5418-2

Fitness For Dummies®
2nd Edition
0-7645-5167-1

Religion For Dummies®
0-7645-5264-3

Selling For Dummies®
2nd Edition
0-7645-5363-1

Improving Your Memory
For Dummies®
0-7645-5435-2

Islam For Dummies®
0-7645-5503-0

Golf For Dummies®
2nd Edition
0-7645-5146-9

The Complete MBA For
Dummies®
0-7645-5204-X

Astronomy For
Dummies®
0-7645-5155-8

Customer Service For
Dummies®, 2nd Edition
0-7645-5209-0

Mythology For
Dummies®
0-7645-5432-8

Pilates For Dummies®
0-7645-5397-6

Managing Teams For
Dummies®
0-7645-5408-5

Screenwriting For
Dummies®
0-7645-5486-7

Drawing For Dummies
0-7645-5476-X

Controlling Cholesterol
For Dummies®
0-7645-5440-9

Martial Arts For
Dummies®
0-7645-5358-5

Meditation For
Dummies®
0-7645-5166-7

Wine For Dummies®
3rd Edition
0-7645-2544-1

Yoga For Dummies®
0-7645-5117-5

Drums For Dummies®
0-7645-5357-7

Singing For Dummies®
0-7645-2475-5

**Available in the UK at bookstores nationwide and online at
www.wileyeurope.com or call 0800 243407 to order direct**

Also available in the United States at www.dummies.com

FOR DUMMIES®

The easy way to get more done and have more fun

COMPUTING & TECHNOLOGY

Windows® XP FOR DUMMIES®

0-7645-0893-8

Photoshop® CS FOR DUMMIES®

0-7645-4356-3

Digital Photography FOR DUMMIES®

0-7645-1664-7

PCs FOR DUMMIES®

0-7645-4074-2

WINDOWS® 98 FOR DUMMIES®

0-7645-0261-1

The Internet FOR DUMMIES®

0-7645-4173-0

FOR
DUMMIES®

The easy way to get more done and have more fun

TRAVEL

Walt Disney World & Orlando FOR DUMMIES

A Travel Guide for the Rest of Us!

0-7645-3875-6

Germany FOR DUMMIES

A Travel Guide for the Rest of Us!

0-7645-5478-6

Ireland FOR DUMMIES

A Travel Guide for the Rest of Us!

0-7645-5455-7

Spain FOR DUMMIES

A Travel Guide for the Rest of Us!

0-7645-5495-6

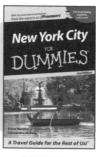

New York City FOR DUMMIES

A Travel Guide for the Rest of Us!

0-7645-5451-4

Scotland FOR DUMMIES

A Travel Guide for the Rest of Us!

0-7645-5477-8

Paris FOR DUMMIES

A Travel Guide for the Rest of Us!

0-7645-5494-8

Italy FOR DUMMIES

A Travel Guide for the Rest of Us!

0-7645-5453-0

Florida FOR DUMMIES

A Travel Guide for the Rest of Us!

0-7645-1979-4